I BREATHED A BODY

ZAC THOMPSON

ANDY MacDONALD

TRIONA FARRELL

HASSAN OTSMANE-ELHAOU

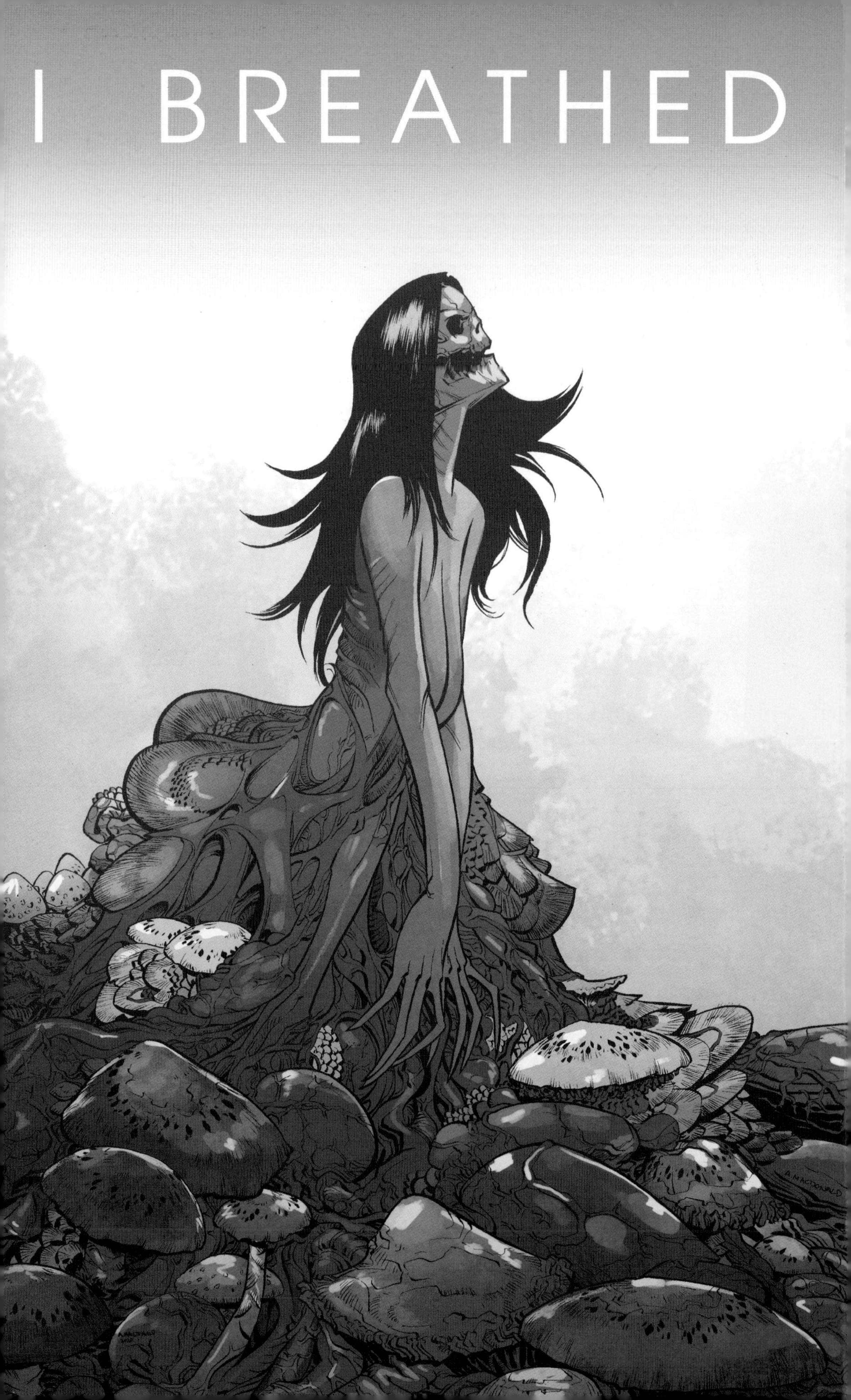
I BREATHED

A BODY

ZAC THOMPSON writer

ANDY MacDONALD artist

TRIONA FARRELL colorist

HASSAN OTSMANE-ELHAOU letterer

ANDY MacDONALD w/ **TRIONA FARRELL** front & original covers

TREVOR HENDERSON, BRETT HESS & **CASEY PARSONS** variant covers

TOM MULLER logo designer

CHARLES PRITCHETT issue #1 backmatter designer

COREY BREEN book designer

MIKE MARTS editor

created by **ZAC THOMPSON** & **ANDY MacDONALD**

AFTERSHOCK™

MIKE MARTS - Editor-in-Chief • **JOE PRUETT** - Publisher/CCO • **LEE KRAMER** - President • **JON KRAMER** - Chief Executive Officer
STEVE ROTTERDAM - SVP, Sales & Marketing • **DAN SHIRES** - VP, Film & Television UK • **CHRISTINA HARRINGTON** - Managing Editor
MARC HAMMOND - Sr. Retail Sales Development Manager • **RUTHANN THOMPSON** - Sr. Retailer Relations Manager
KATHERINE JAMISON - Marketing Manager • **KELLY DIODATI** - Ambassador Outreach Manager • **BLAKE STOCKER** - Director of Finance
AARON MARION - Publicist • **LISA MOODY** - Finance • **RYAN CARROLL** - Director, Comics/Film/TV Liaison • **JAWAD QURESHI** - Technology Advisor/Strategist
RACHEL PINNELAS - Social Community Manager • **CHARLES PRITCHETT** - Design & Production Manager • **COREY BREEN** - Collections Production
TEDDY LEO - Editorial Assistant • **STEPHANIE CASEBIER** & **SARAH PRUETT** - Publishing Assistants

AfterShock Logo Design by **COMICRAFT**

Publicity: contact **AARON MARION** (aaron@publichausagency.com) & **RYAN CROY** (ryan@publichausagency.com) at **PUBLICHAUS**
Special thanks to: **ATOM! FREEMAN, IRA KURGAN, MARINE KSADZHIKYAN, KEITH MANZELLA, ANTHONY MILITANO, ANTONIA LIANOS, STEPHAN NILSON** & **ED ZAREMBA**

AFTERSHOCKCOMICS.COM Follow us on social media 🐦 📷 f

INTRODUCTION

Welcome to I BREATHED A BODY.

The book you hold in your hands was written during the peak of the COVID-19 pandemic. It was a strange time where every day felt like an eternity. Social media was all I had, but every time I logged on, it seemed flooded with misery. I was lost in torrents of transgressive videos that I didn't seek out. I felt stuck within a perpetual cycle of voyeurism. I saw tragedy and injustice every day but felt powerless in the face of it.

Such is the anxiety and dread at the center of this story. I wanted to create something that looks at the apathetic tech workers pulling the strings of manipulation to drive engagement, profit and sharing on networks that are indifferent to our well-being. It's an indictment of the systems and corporations that profit from division and terror.

So, as you step into this special layer of hell with us and descend into our fungal nightmare, I hope you're left questioning the decisions we make to be seen, the ways we destroy ourselves just to get ahead and who profits from our public displays of vulnerability.

I've written a lot about modern tech and social media. It's no secret I think we're trapped in an attention economy that'll swallow us whole if we let it. But through Anne's journey, I hope you'll see we always have a choice. Even if we don't believe we do.

Now, take a deep breath. Think of what you're about to read as the insane lovechild of David Cronenberg and Clive Barker—prepare accordingly. What happens next is a horrifying exercise in violence and desecration, with plenty of surreal detours.

The borders between us grow ever thinner with each passing day. Our identities are fragmented between reality and digital spaces. While social media is a powerful bridge that has decentralized power, it also connects all our disparate narratives into a massive abyss. We were never meant to process this level of information, and it's changing us.

We're all trapped in this big hive mind now.

And like all the best things in life that's both glorious and terrifying.

ZAC THOMPSON
June 2021

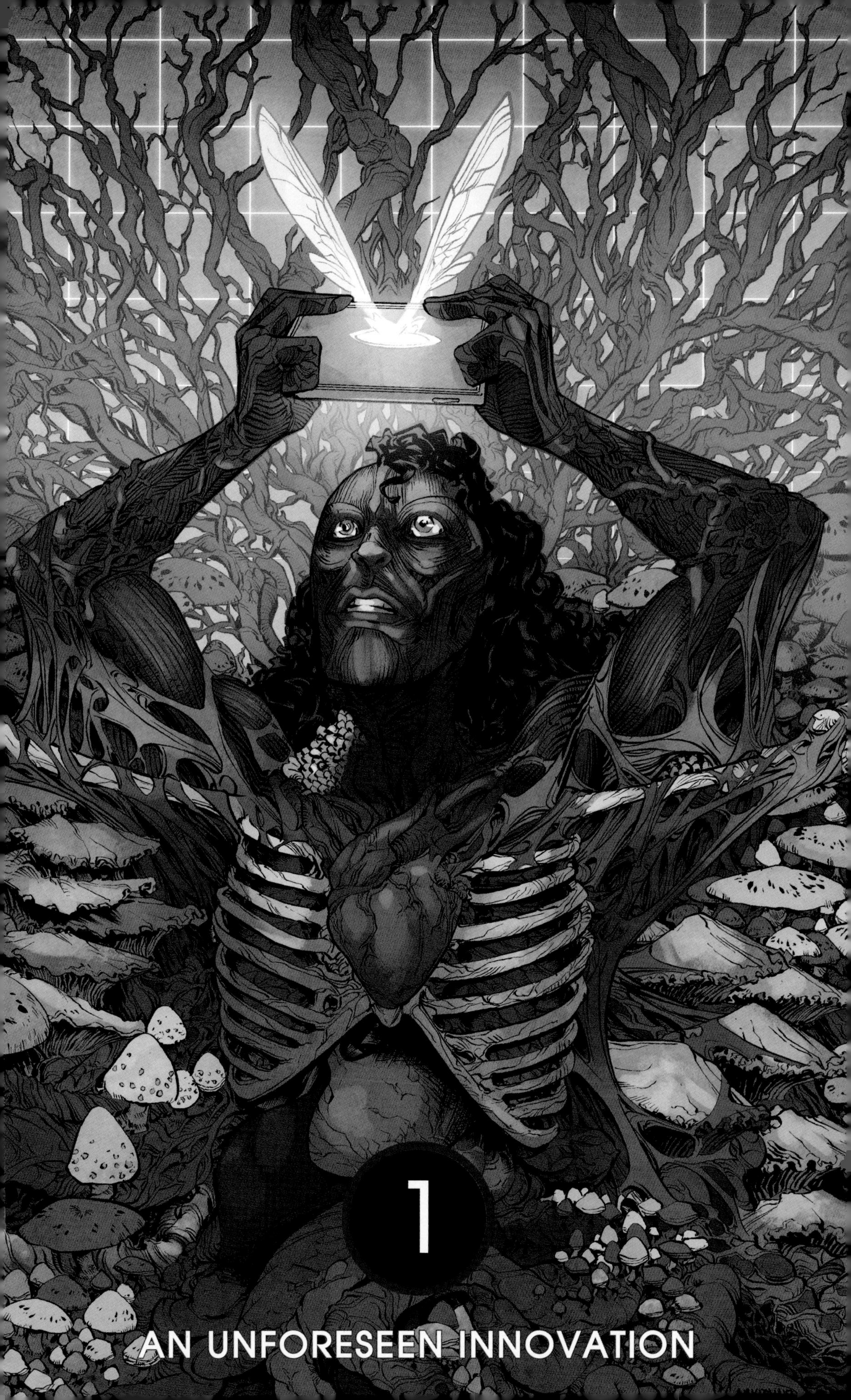
1
AN UNFORESEEN INNOVATION

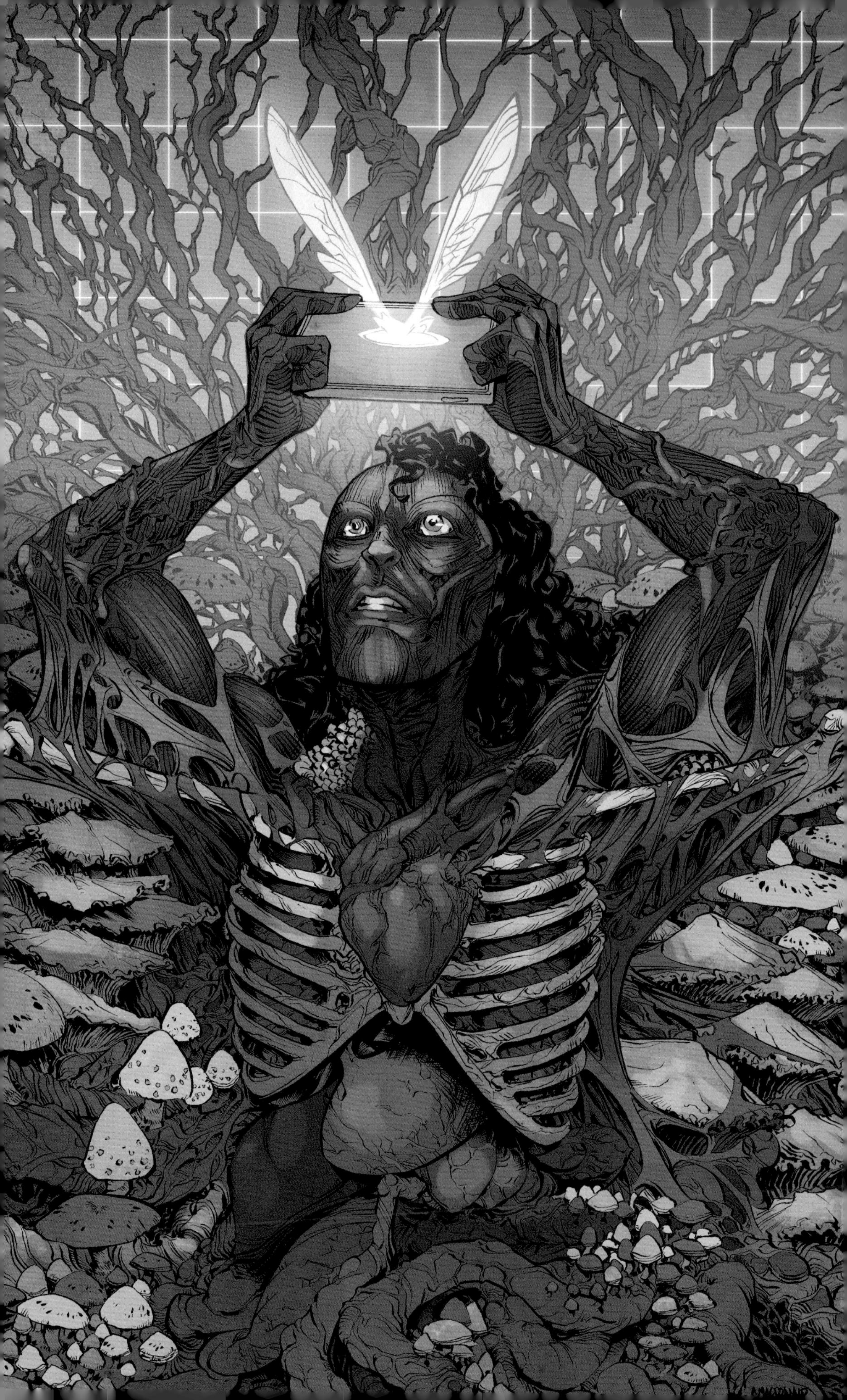

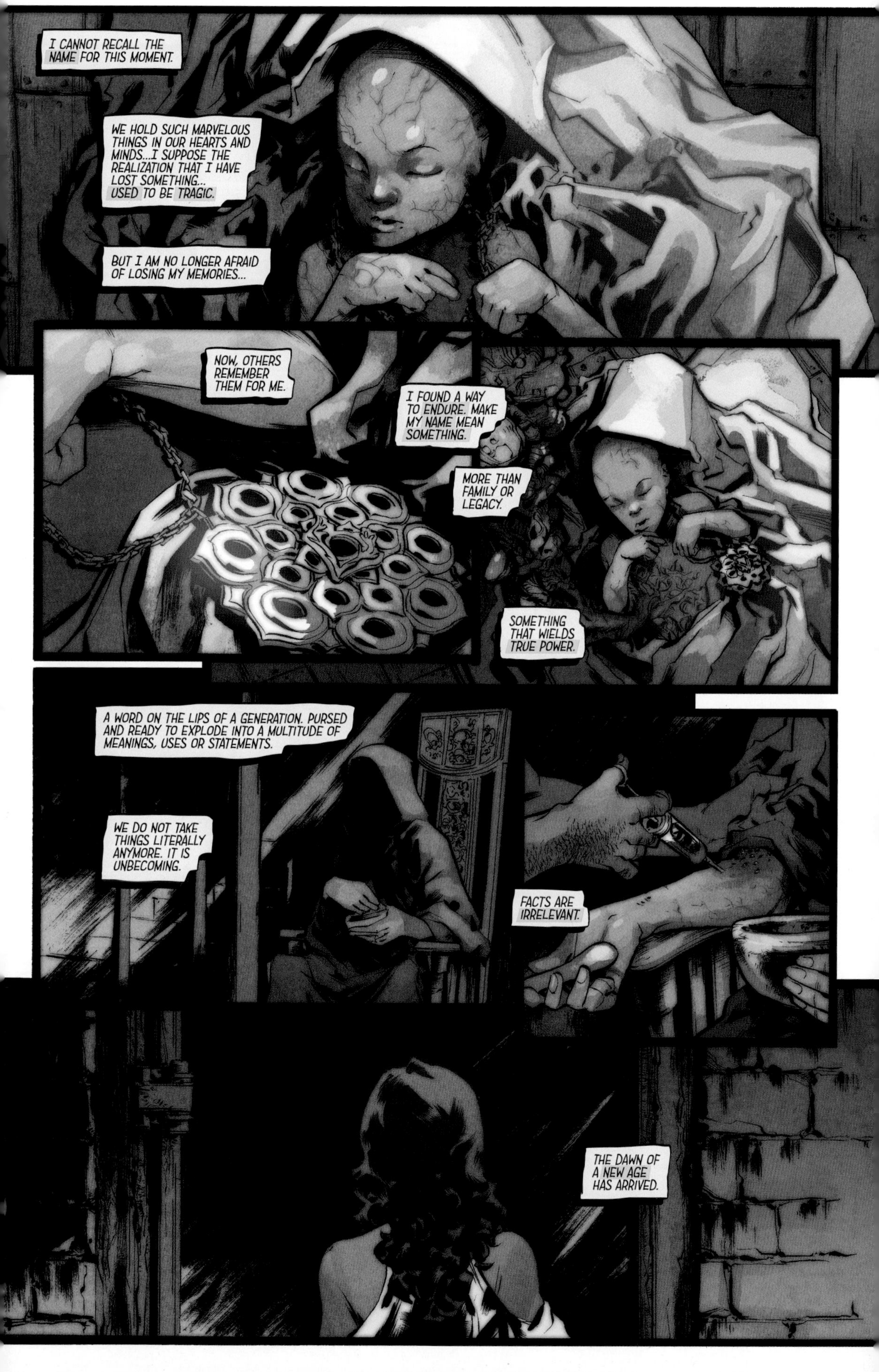
I CANNOT RECALL THE NAME FOR THIS MOMENT.
WE HOLD SUCH MARVELOUS THINGS IN OUR HEARTS AND MINDS...I SUPPOSE THE REALIZATION THAT I HAVE LOST SOMETHING... USED TO BE TRAGIC.
BUT I AM NO LONGER AFRAID OF LOSING MY MEMORIES...
NOW, OTHERS REMEMBER THEM FOR ME.
I FOUND A WAY TO ENDURE. MAKE MY NAME MEAN SOMETHING.
MORE THAN FAMILY OR LEGACY.
SOMETHING THAT WIELDS TRUE POWER.
A WORD ON THE LIPS OF A GENERATION. PURSED AND READY TO EXPLODE INTO A MULTITUDE OF MEANINGS, USES OR STATEMENTS.
WE DO NOT TAKE THINGS LITERALLY ANYMORE. IT IS UNBECOMING.
FACTS ARE IRRELEVANT.
THE DAWN OF A NEW AGE HAS ARRIVED.

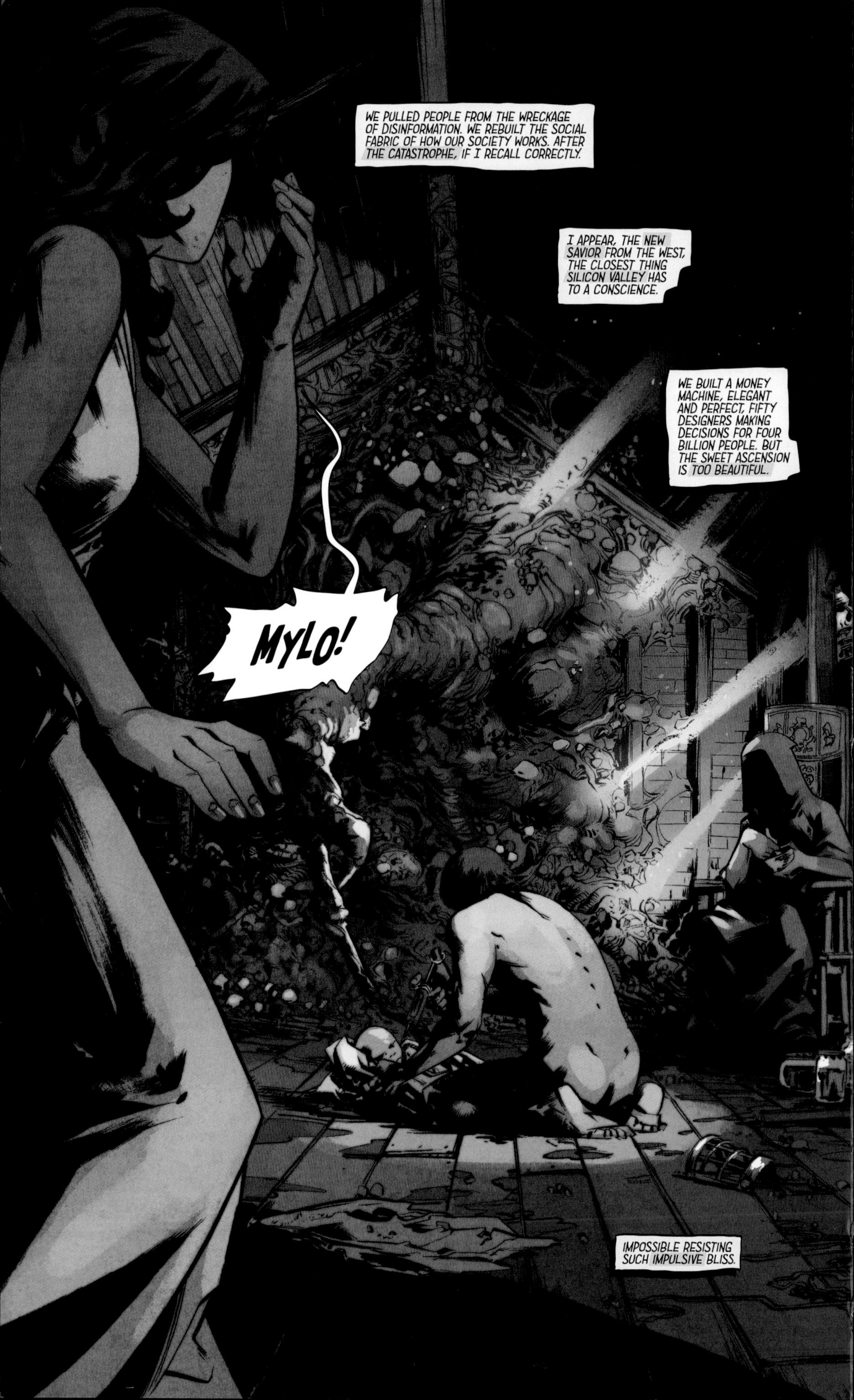
WE PULLED PEOPLE FROM THE WRECKAGE OF DISINFORMATION. WE REBUILT THE SOCIAL FABRIC OF HOW OUR SOCIETY WORKS. AFTER THE CATASTROPHE, IF I RECALL CORRECTLY.
I APPEAR, THE NEW SAVIOR FROM THE WEST, THE CLOSEST THING SILICON VALLEY HAS TO A CONSCIENCE.
WE BUILT A MONEY MACHINE, ELEGANT AND PERFECT, FIFTY DESIGNERS MAKING DECISIONS FOR FOUR BILLION PEOPLE. BUT THE SWEET ASCENSION IS TOO BEAUTIFUL.
MYLO!
IMPOSSIBLE RESISTING SUCH IMPULSIVE BLISS.

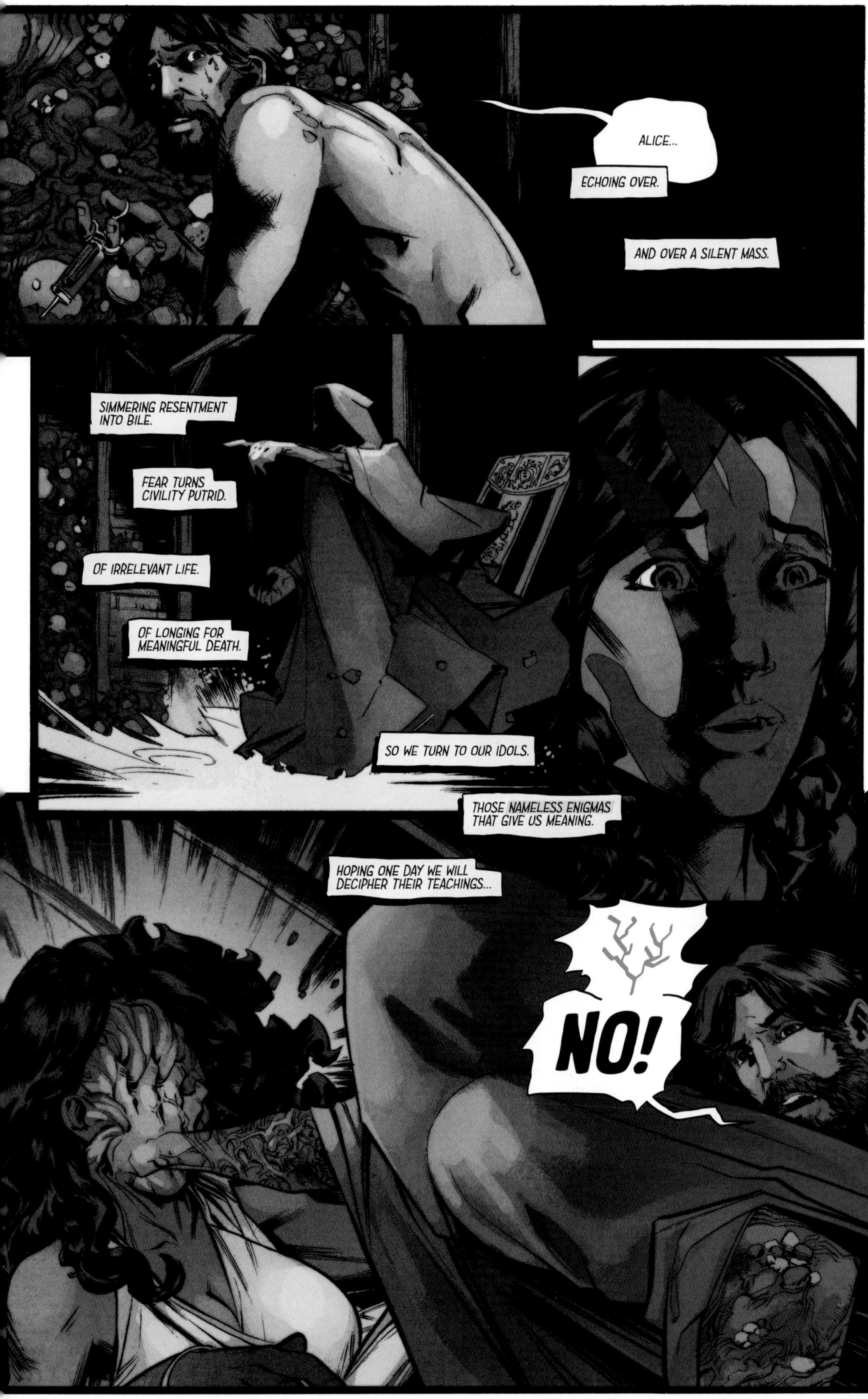
ALICE...
ECHOING OVER.
AND OVER A SILENT MASS.
SIMMERING RESENTMENT INTO BILE.
FEAR TURNS CIVILITY PUTRID.
OF IRRELEVANT LIFE.
OF LONGING FOR MEANINGFUL DEATH.
SO WE TURN TO OUR IDOLS.
THOSE NAMELESS ENIGMAS THAT GIVE US MEANING.
HOPING ONE DAY WE WILL DECIPHER THEIR TEACHINGS...
NO!

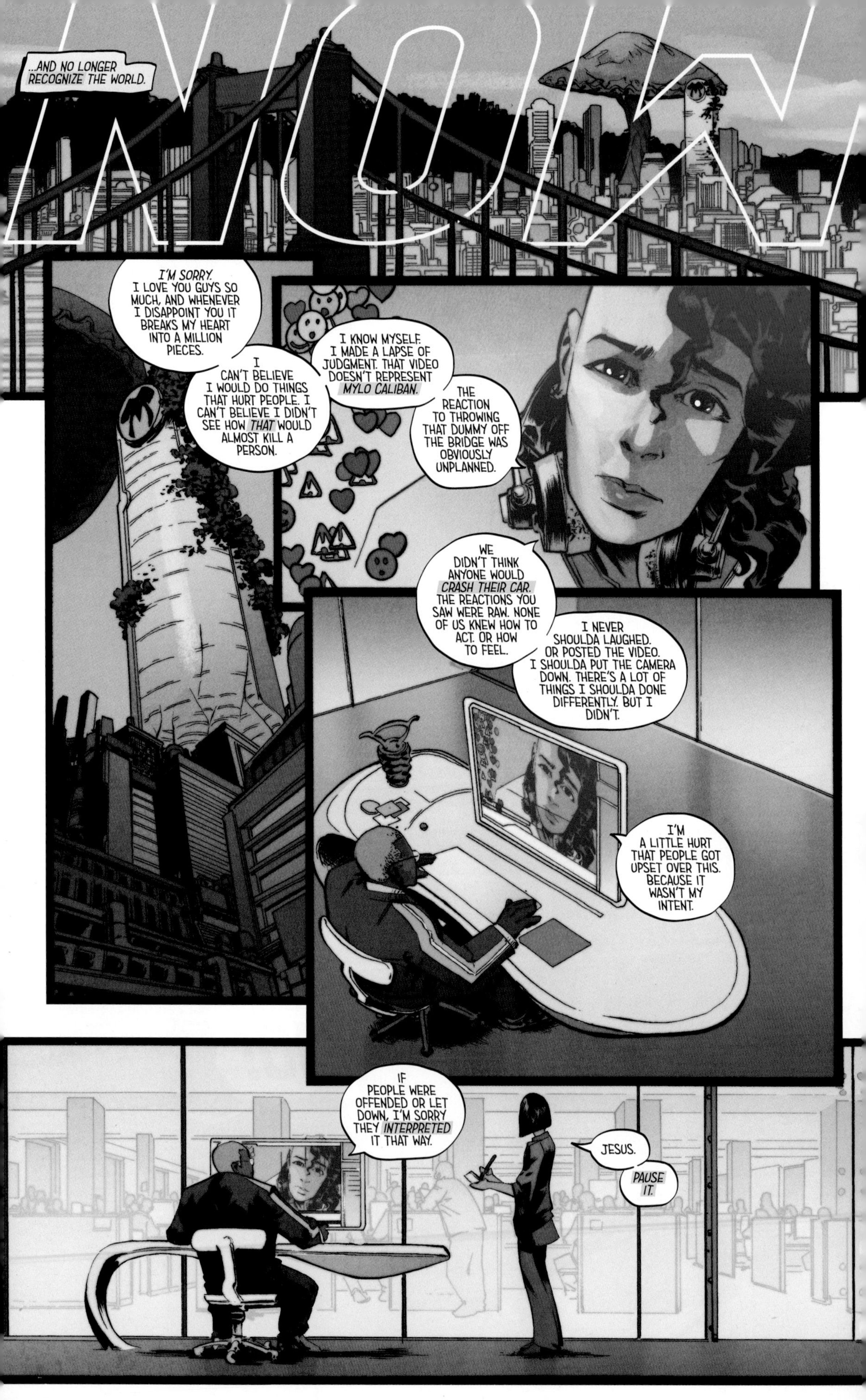
...AND NO LONGER RECOGNIZE THE WORLD.
I'M SORRY. I LOVE YOU GUYS SO MUCH, AND WHENEVER I DISAPPOINT YOU IT BREAKS MY HEART INTO A MILLION PIECES.
I CAN'T BELIEVE I WOULD DO THINGS THAT HURT PEOPLE. I CAN'T BELIEVE I DIDN'T SEE HOW THAT WOULD ALMOST KILL A PERSON.
I KNOW MYSELF. I MADE A LAPSE OF JUDGMENT. THAT VIDEO DOESN'T REPRESENT MYLO CALIBAN.
THE REACTION TO THROWING THAT DUMMY OFF THE BRIDGE WAS OBVIOUSLY UNPLANNED.
WE DIDN'T THINK ANYONE WOULD CRASH THEIR CAR. THE REACTIONS YOU SAW WERE RAW. NONE OF US KNEW HOW TO ACT. OR HOW TO FEEL.
I NEVER SHOULDA LAUGHED. OR POSTED THE VIDEO. I SHOULDA PUT THE CAMERA DOWN. THERE'S A LOT OF THINGS I SHOULDA DONE DIFFERENTLY. BUT I DIDN'T.
I'M A LITTLE HURT THAT PEOPLE GOT UPSET OVER THIS. BECAUSE IT WASN'T MY INTENT.
IF PEOPLE WERE OFFENDED OR LET DOWN, I'M SORRY THEY INTERPRETED IT THAT WAY.
JESUS.
PAUSE IT.

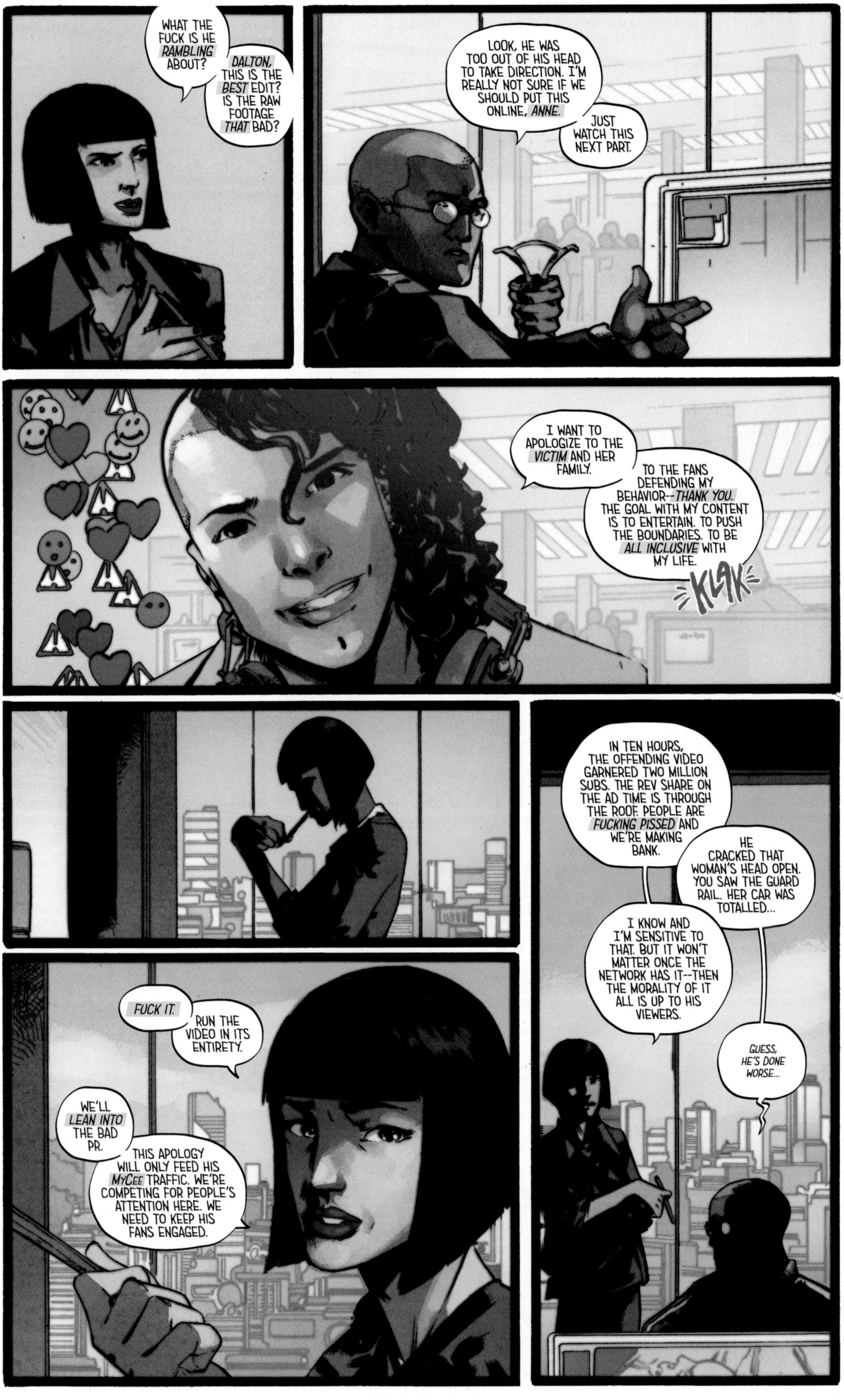
WHAT THE FUCK IS HE RAMBLING ABOUT?
DALTON, THIS IS THE BEST EDIT? IS THE RAW FOOTAGE THAT BAD?
LOOK, HE WAS TOO OUT OF HIS HEAD TO TAKE DIRECTION. I'M REALLY NOT SURE IF WE SHOULD PUT THIS ONLINE, ANNE.
JUST WATCH THIS NEXT PART.
I WANT TO APOLOGIZE TO THE VICTIM AND HER FAMILY.
TO THE FANS DEFENDING MY BEHAVIOR--THANK YOU. THE GOAL WITH MY CONTENT IS TO ENTERTAIN. TO PUSH THE BOUNDARIES. TO BE ALL INCLUSIVE WITH MY LIFE.
KLAK
IN TEN HOURS, THE OFFENDING VIDEO GARNERED TWO MILLION SUBS. THE REV SHARE ON THE AD TIME IS THROUGH THE ROOF. PEOPLE ARE FUCKING PISSED AND WE'RE MAKING BANK.
HE CRACKED THAT WOMAN'S HEAD OPEN. YOU SAW THE GUARD RAIL. HER CAR WAS TOTALLED...
I KNOW AND I'M SENSITIVE TO THAT. BUT IT WON'T MATTER ONCE THE NETWORK HAS IT--THEN THE MORALITY OF IT ALL IS UP TO HIS VIEWERS.
GUESS, HE'S DONE WORSE...
FUCK IT.
RUN THE VIDEO IN ITS ENTIRETY.
WE'LL LEAN INTO THE BAD PR.
THIS APOLOGY WILL ONLY FEED HIS MyCee TRAFFIC. WE'RE COMPETING FOR PEOPLE'S ATTENTION HERE. WE NEED TO KEEP HIS FANS ENGAGED.

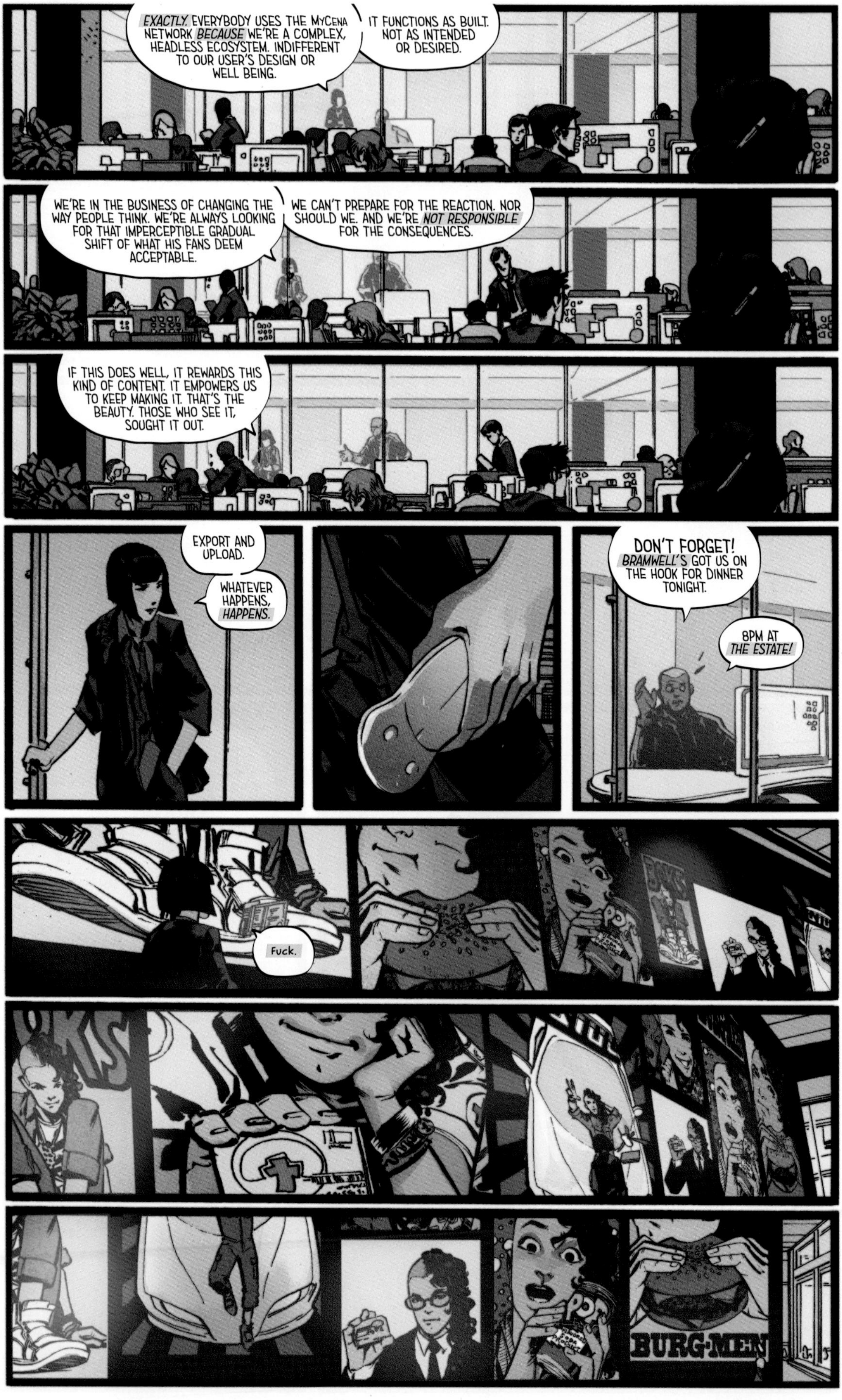
EXACTLY. EVERYBODY USES THE MyCENA NETWORK BECAUSE WE'RE A COMPLEX, HEADLESS ECOSYSTEM. INDIFFERENT TO OUR USER'S DESIGN OR WELL BEING.
IT FUNCTIONS AS BUILT. NOT AS INTENDED OR DESIRED.
WE'RE IN THE BUSINESS OF CHANGING THE WAY PEOPLE THINK. WE'RE ALWAYS LOOKING FOR THAT IMPERCEPTIBLE GRADUAL SHIFT OF WHAT HIS FANS DEEM ACCEPTABLE.
WE CAN'T PREPARE FOR THE REACTION. NOR SHOULD WE. AND WE'RE NOT RESPONSIBLE FOR THE CONSEQUENCES.
IF THIS DOES WELL, IT REWARDS THIS KIND OF CONTENT. IT EMPOWERS US TO KEEP MAKING IT. THAT'S THE BEAUTY. THOSE WHO SEE IT, SOUGHT IT OUT.
EXPORT AND UPLOAD.
WHATEVER HAPPENS, HAPPENS.
DON'T FORGET! BRAMWELL'S GOT US ON THE HOOK FOR DINNER TONIGHT.
8PM AT THE ESTATE!
Fuck.
BURG-MEN

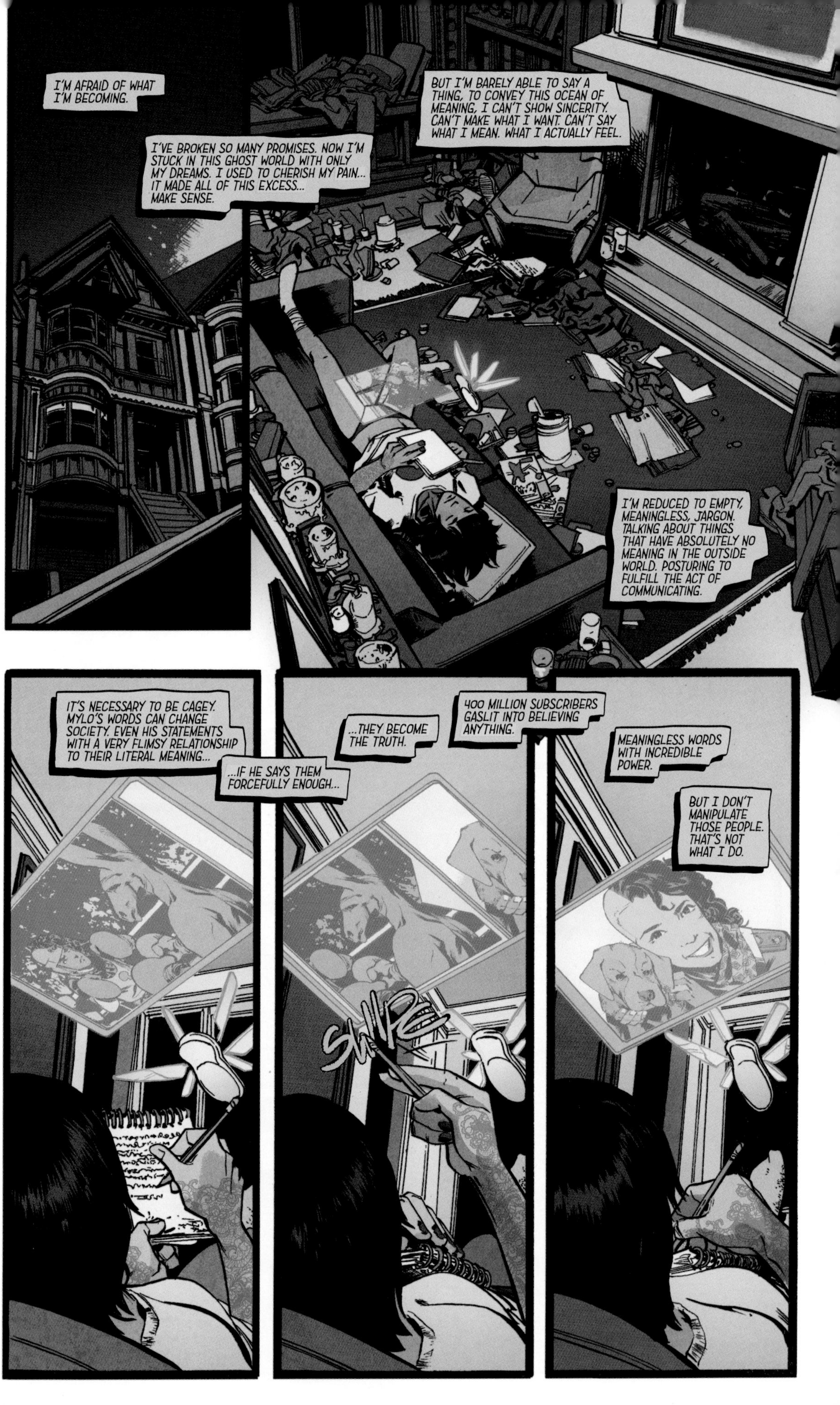
I'M AFRAID OF WHAT I'M BECOMING.
I'VE BROKEN SO MANY PROMISES. NOW I'M STUCK IN THIS GHOST WORLD WITH ONLY MY DREAMS. I USED TO CHERISH MY PAIN... IT MADE ALL OF THIS EXCESS... MAKE SENSE.
BUT I'M BARELY ABLE TO SAY A THING, TO CONVEY THIS OCEAN OF MEANING. I CAN'T SHOW SINCERITY. CAN'T MAKE WHAT I WANT. CAN'T SAY WHAT I MEAN. WHAT I ACTUALLY FEEL.
I'M REDUCED TO EMPTY, MEANINGLESS, JARGON. TALKING ABOUT THINGS THAT HAVE ABSOLUTELY NO MEANING IN THE OUTSIDE WORLD. POSTURING TO FULFILL THE ACT OF COMMUNICATING.
IT'S NECESSARY TO BE CAGEY. MYLO'S WORDS CAN CHANGE SOCIETY. EVEN HIS STATEMENTS WITH A VERY FLIMSY RELATIONSHIP TO THEIR LITERAL MEANING...
...IF HE SAYS THEM FORCEFULLY ENOUGH...
...THEY BECOME THE TRUTH.
400 MILLION SUBSCRIBERS GASLIT INTO BELIEVING ANYTHING.
SWIPE
MEANINGLESS WORDS WITH INCREDIBLE POWER.
BUT I DON'T MANIPULATE THOSE PEOPLE. THAT'S NOT WHAT I DO.

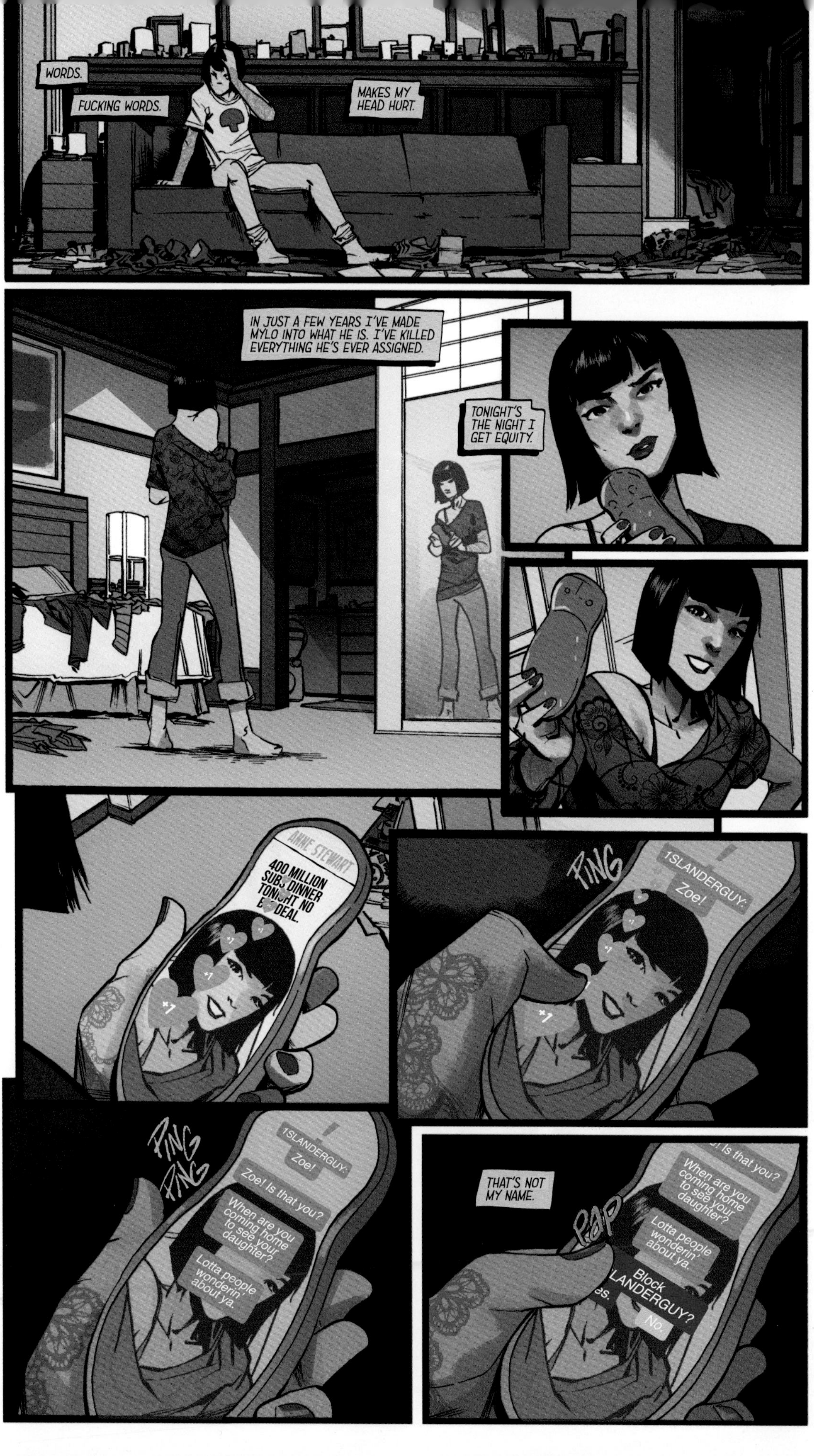
WORDS.
FUCKING WORDS.
MAKES MY HEAD HURT.
IN JUST A FEW YEARS I'VE MADE MYLO INTO WHAT HE IS. I'VE KILLED EVERYTHING HE'S EVER ASSIGNED.
TONIGHT'S THE NIGHT I GET EQUITY.
ANNE STEWART
400 MILLION
TONIGHT NO
DEAL.
PING
1SLANDERGUY: Zoe!
PING PING
1SLANDERGUY: Zoe!
Zoe! Is that you?
When are you coming home to see your daughter?
Lotta people wonderin' about ya.
THAT'S NOT MY NAME.
PAP
When are you coming home to see your daughter?
Lotta people wonderin' about ya.
Block
No.

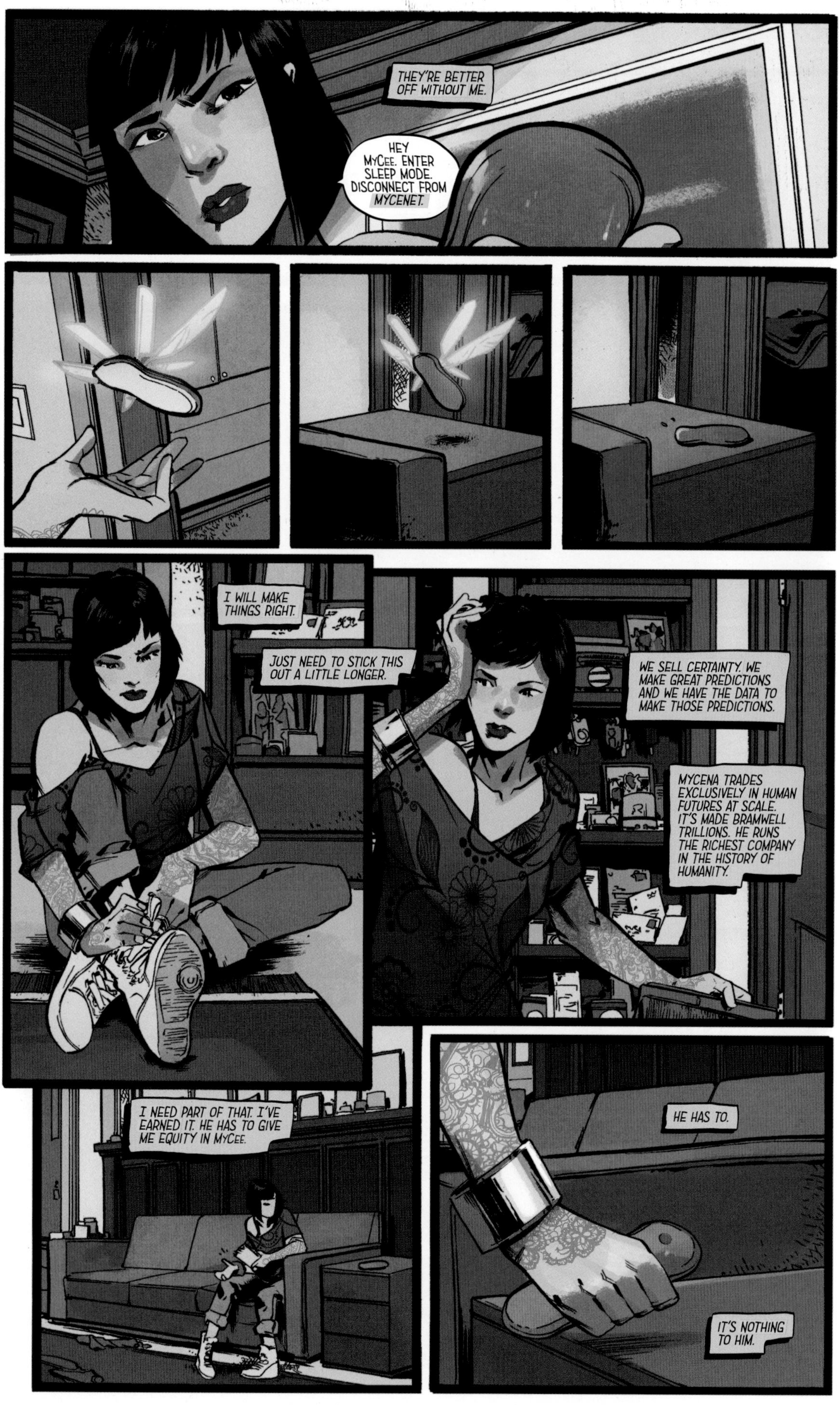
THEY'RE BETTER OFF WITHOUT ME.
HEY MYCEE. ENTER SLEEP MODE. DISCONNECT FROM MYCENET.
I WILL MAKE THINGS RIGHT.
JUST NEED TO STICK THIS OUT A LITTLE LONGER.
WE SELL CERTAINTY. WE MAKE GREAT PREDICTIONS AND WE HAVE THE DATA TO MAKE THOSE PREDICTIONS.
MYCENA TRADES EXCLUSIVELY IN HUMAN FUTURES AT SCALE. IT'S MADE BRAMWELL TRILLIONS. HE RUNS THE RICHEST COMPANY IN THE HISTORY OF HUMANITY.
I NEED PART OF THAT. I'VE EARNED IT. HE HAS TO GIVE ME EQUITY IN MYCEE.
HE HAS TO.
IT'S NOTHING TO HIM.

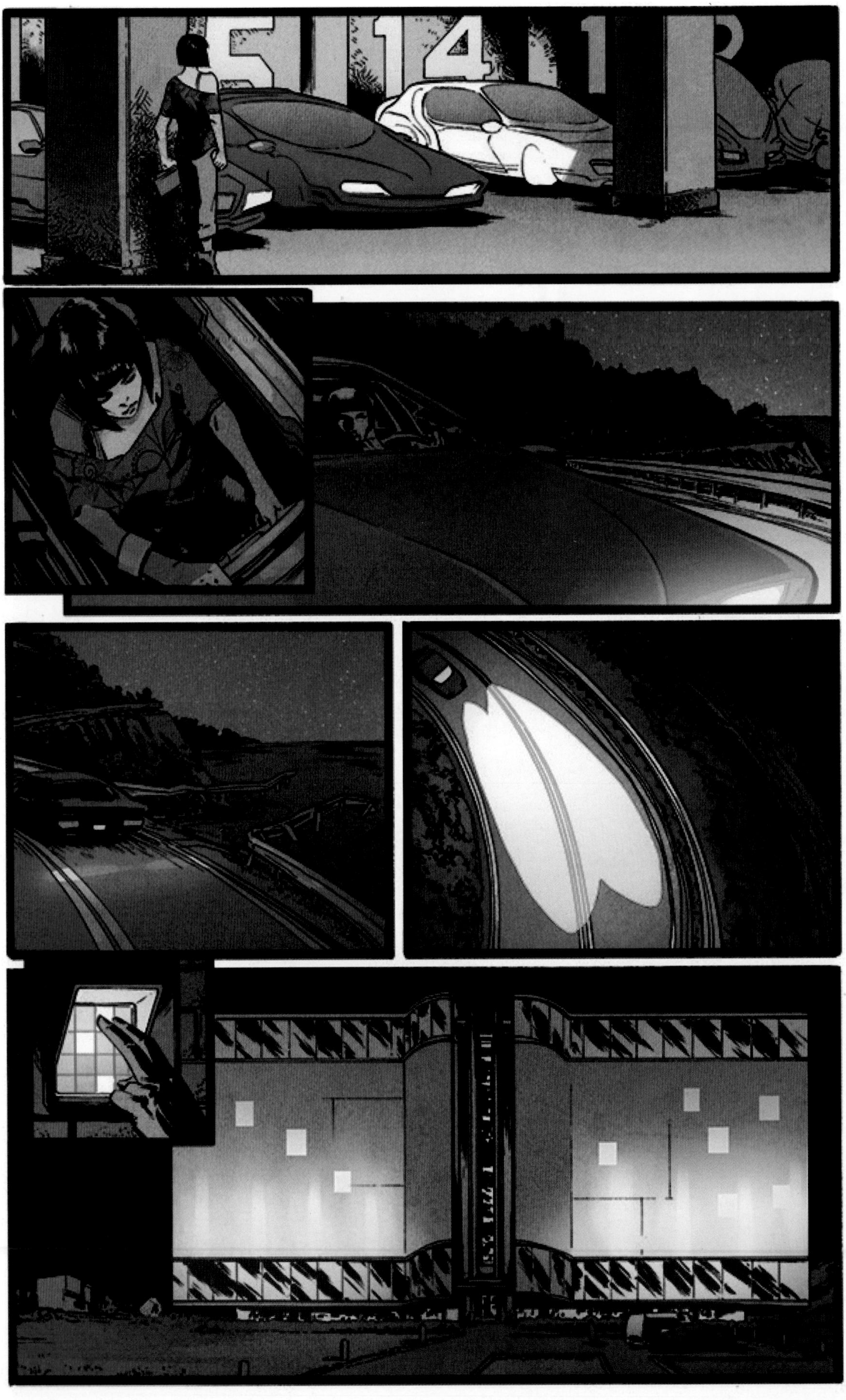

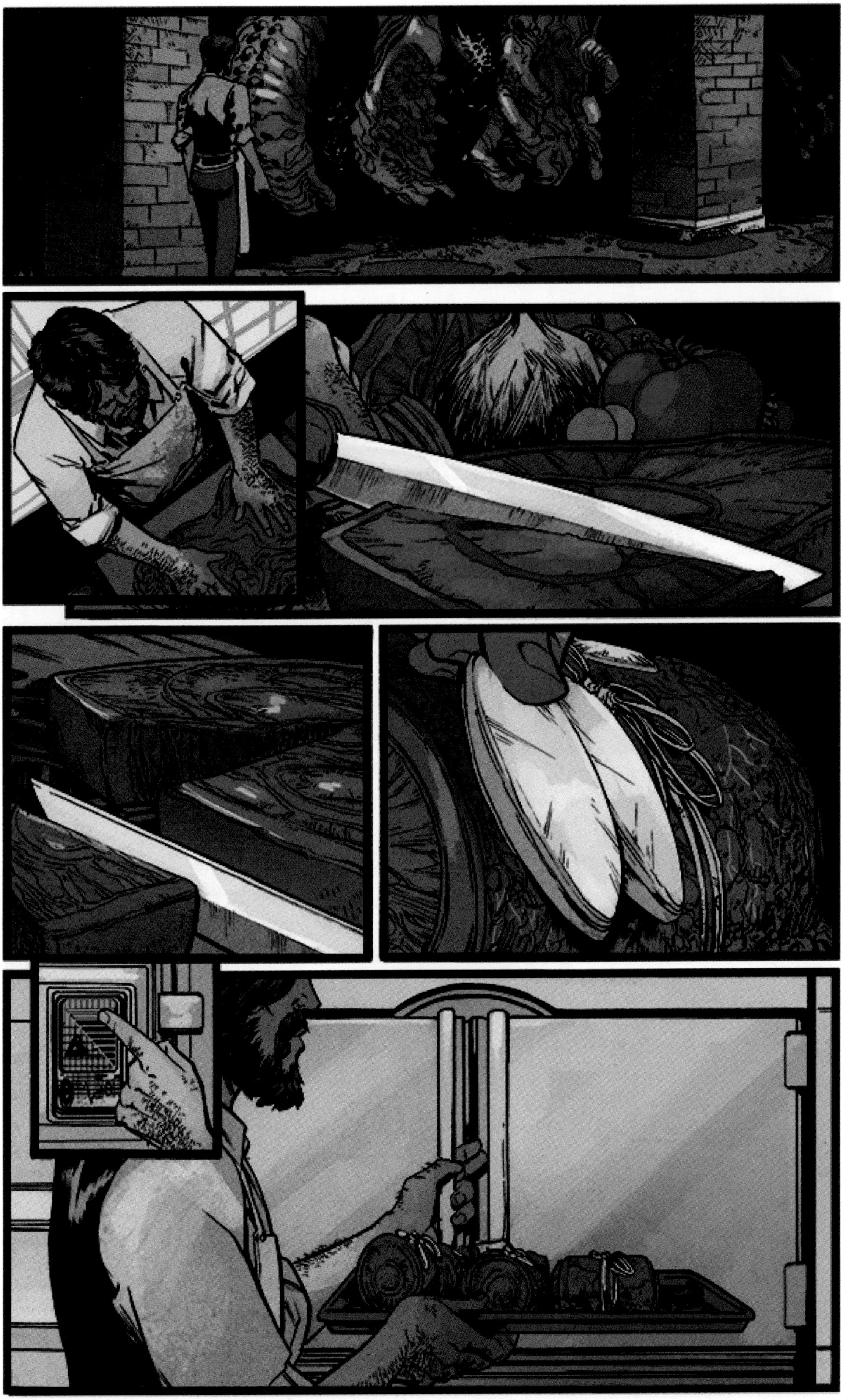

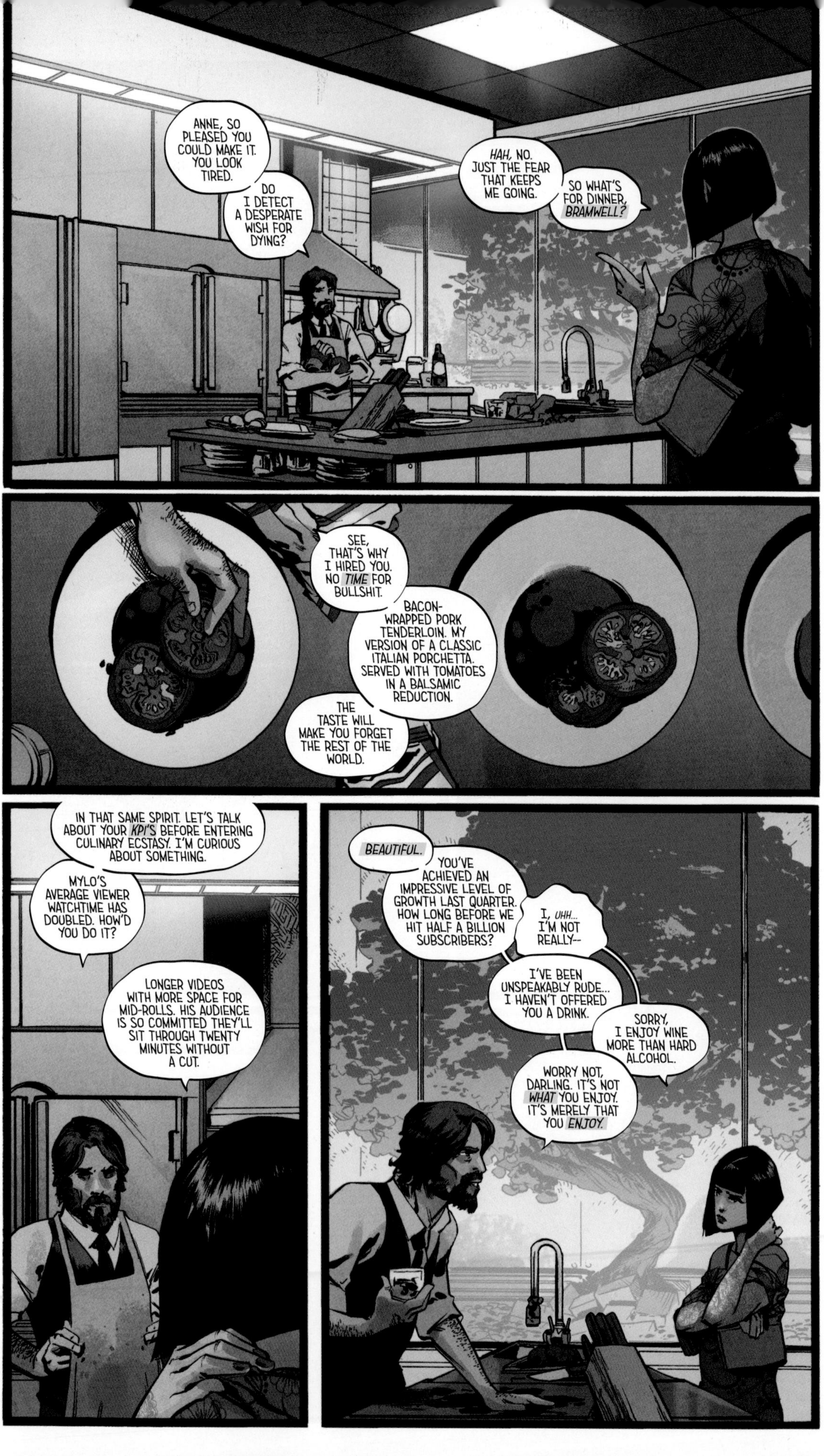
ANNE, SO PLEASED YOU COULD MAKE IT. YOU LOOK TIRED.
DO I DETECT A DESPERATE WISH FOR DYING?
HAH, NO. JUST THE FEAR THAT KEEPS ME GOING.
SO WHAT'S FOR DINNER, BRAMWELL?
SEE, THAT'S WHY I HIRED YOU. NO TIME FOR BULLSHIT.
BACON-WRAPPED PORK TENDERLOIN. MY VERSION OF A CLASSIC ITALIAN PORCHETTA. SERVED WITH TOMATOES IN A BALSAMIC REDUCTION.
THE TASTE WILL MAKE YOU FORGET THE REST OF THE WORLD.
IN THAT SAME SPIRIT. LET'S TALK ABOUT YOUR KPI'S BEFORE ENTERING CULINARY ECSTASY. I'M CURIOUS ABOUT SOMETHING.
MYLO'S AVERAGE VIEWER WATCHTIME HAS DOUBLED. HOW'D YOU DO IT?
LONGER VIDEOS WITH MORE SPACE FOR MID-ROLLS. HIS AUDIENCE IS SO COMMITTED THEY'LL SIT THROUGH TWENTY MINUTES WITHOUT A CUT.
BEAUTIFUL.
YOU'VE ACHIEVED AN IMPRESSIVE LEVEL OF GROWTH LAST QUARTER. HOW LONG BEFORE WE HIT HALF A BILLION SUBSCRIBERS?
I, UHH... I'M NOT REALLY--
I'VE BEEN UNSPEAKABLY RUDE... I HAVEN'T OFFERED YOU A DRINK.
SORRY, I ENJOY WINE MORE THAN HARD ALCOHOL.
WORRY NOT, DARLING. IT'S NOT WHAT YOU ENJOY. IT'S MERELY THAT YOU ENJOY.

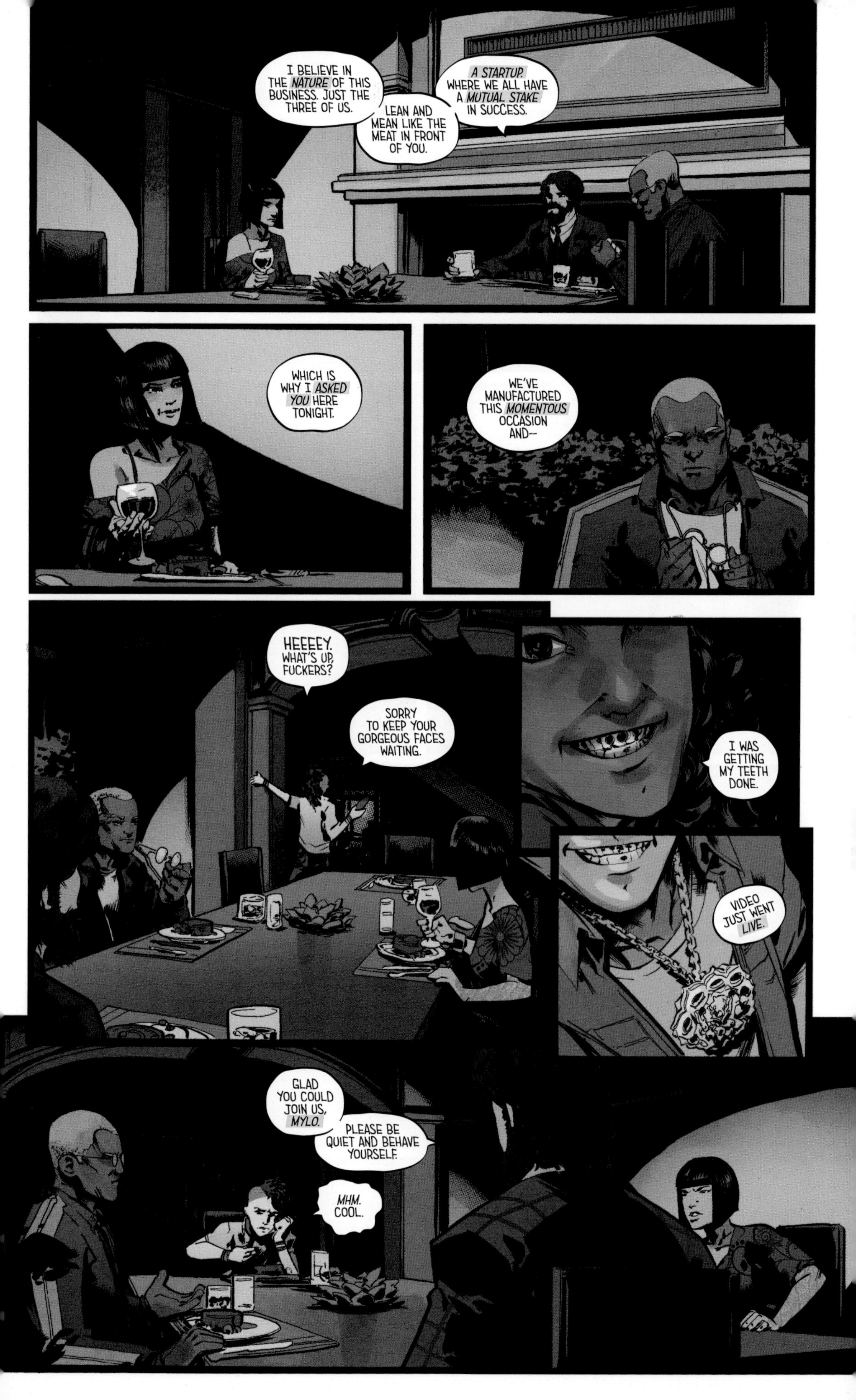
I BELIEVE IN THE NATURE OF THIS BUSINESS. JUST THE THREE OF US.
LEAN AND MEAN LIKE THE MEAT IN FRONT OF YOU.
A STARTUP. WHERE WE ALL HAVE A MUTUAL STAKE IN SUCCESS.
WHICH IS WHY I ASKED YOU HERE TONIGHT.
WE'VE MANUFACTURED THIS MOMENTOUS OCCASION AND--
HEEEEY. WHAT'S UP, FUCKERS?
SORRY TO KEEP YOUR GORGEOUS FACES WAITING.
I WAS GETTING MY TEETH DONE.
VIDEO JUST WENT LIVE.
GLAD YOU COULD JOIN US, MYLO.
PLEASE BE QUIET AND BEHAVE YOURSELF.
MHM. COOL.

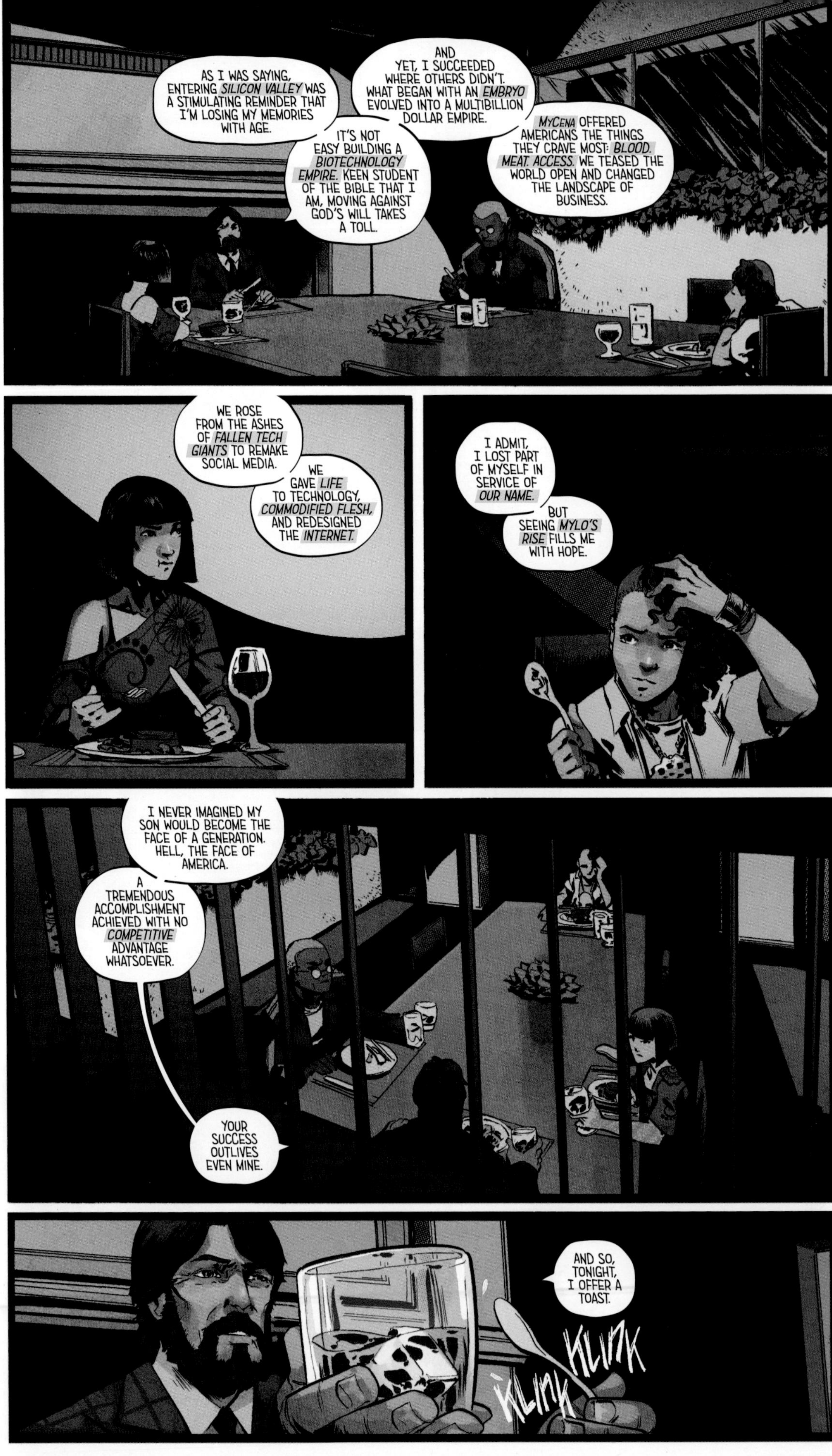
AS I WAS SAYING, ENTERING SILICON VALLEY WAS A STIMULATING REMINDER THAT I'M LOSING MY MEMORIES WITH AGE.
AND YET, I SUCCEEDED WHERE OTHERS DIDN'T. WHAT BEGAN WITH AN EMBRYO EVOLVED INTO A MULTIBILLION DOLLAR EMPIRE.
IT'S NOT EASY BUILDING A BIOTECHNOLOGY EMPIRE. KEEN STUDENT OF THE BIBLE THAT I AM, MOVING AGAINST GOD'S WILL TAKES A TOLL.
MYCENA OFFERED AMERICANS THE THINGS THEY CRAVE MOST: BLOOD. MEAT. ACCESS. WE TEASED THE WORLD OPEN AND CHANGED THE LANDSCAPE OF BUSINESS.
WE ROSE FROM THE ASHES OF FALLEN TECH GIANTS TO REMAKE SOCIAL MEDIA.
WE GAVE LIFE TO TECHNOLOGY, COMMODIFIED FLESH, AND REDESIGNED THE INTERNET.
I ADMIT, I LOST PART OF MYSELF IN SERVICE OF OUR NAME.
BUT SEEING MYLO'S RISE FILLS ME WITH HOPE.
I NEVER IMAGINED MY SON WOULD BECOME THE FACE OF A GENERATION. HELL, THE FACE OF AMERICA.
A TREMENDOUS ACCOMPLISHMENT ACHIEVED WITH NO COMPETITIVE ADVANTAGE WHATSOEVER.
YOUR SUCCESS OUTLIVES EVEN MINE.
AND SO, TONIGHT, I OFFER A TOAST.
KLINK
KLINK

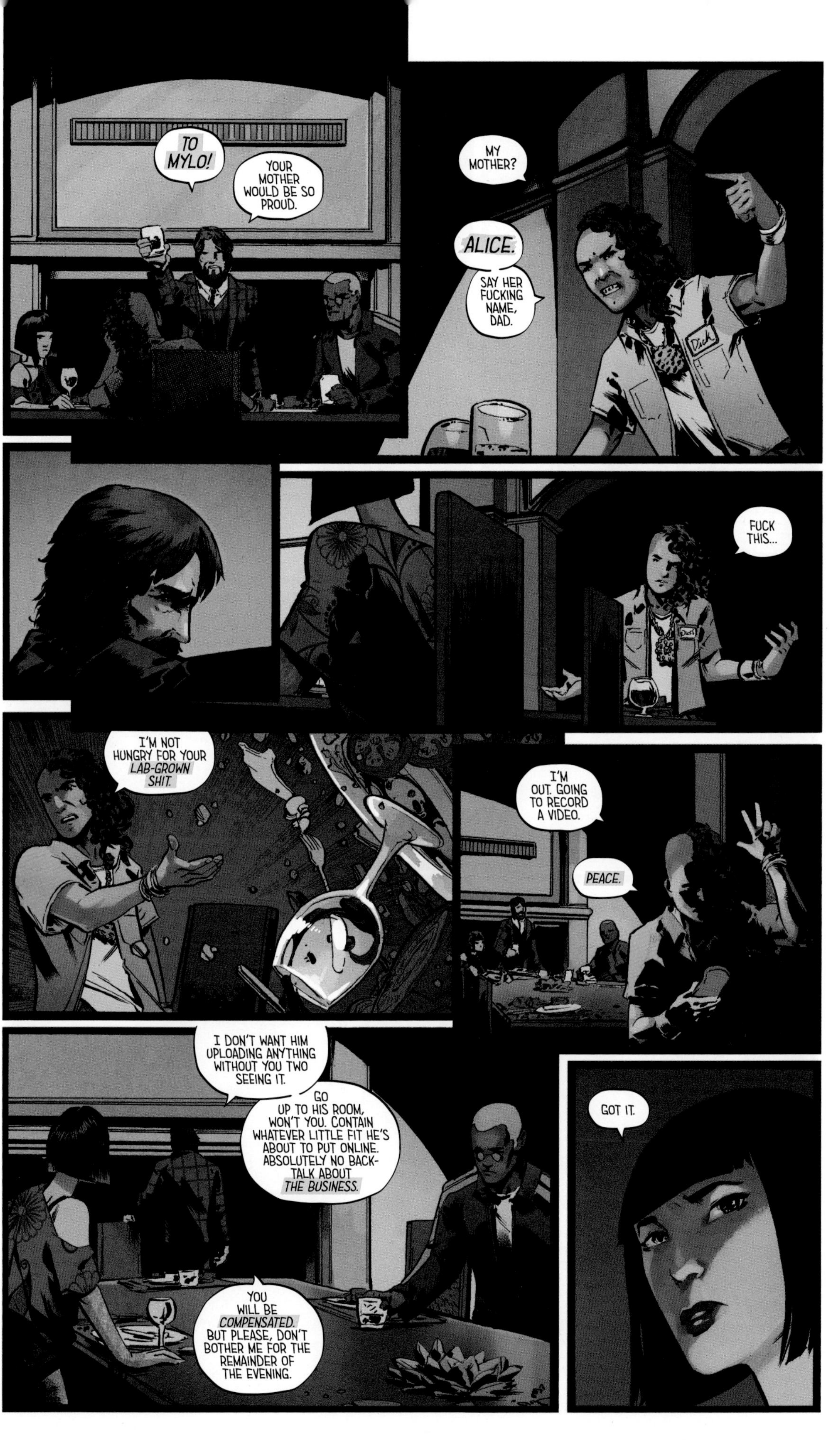
TO MYLO!
YOUR MOTHER WOULD BE SO PROUD.
MY MOTHER?
ALICE.
SAY HER FUCKING NAME, DAD.
FUCK THIS...
I'M NOT HUNGRY FOR YOUR LAB-GROWN SHIT.
I'M OUT. GOING TO RECORD A VIDEO.
PEACE.
I DON'T WANT HIM UPLOADING ANYTHING WITHOUT YOU TWO SEEING IT.
GO UP TO HIS ROOM, WON'T YOU. CONTAIN WHATEVER LITTLE FIT HE'S ABOUT TO PUT ONLINE. ABSOLUTELY NO BACK-TALK ABOUT THE BUSINESS.
YOU WILL BE COMPENSATED. BUT PLEASE, DON'T BOTHER ME FOR THE REMAINDER OF THE EVENING.
GOT IT.

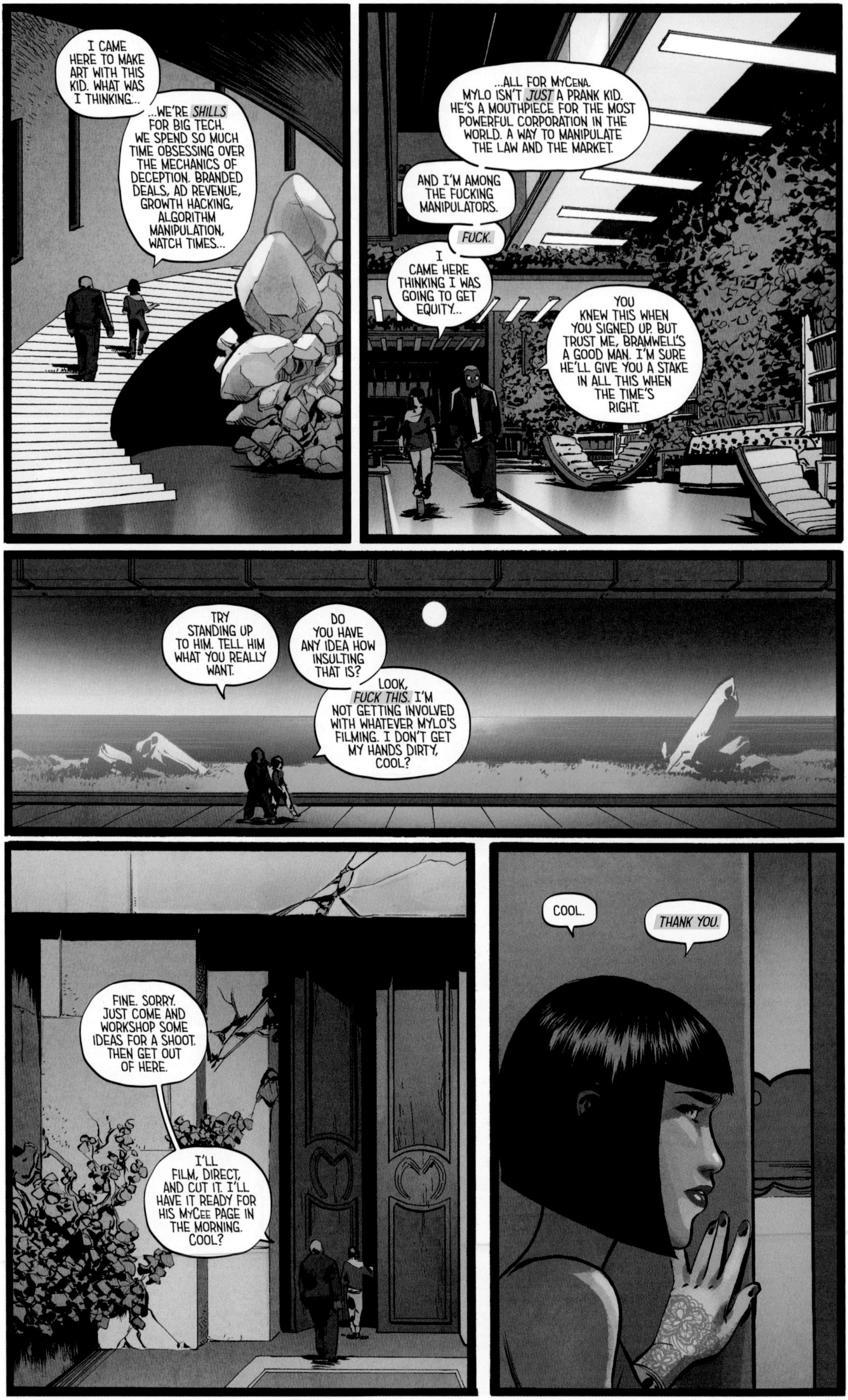
I CAME HERE TO MAKE ART WITH THIS KID. WHAT WAS I THINKING...
...WE'RE SHILLS FOR BIG TECH. WE SPEND SO MUCH TIME OBSESSING OVER THE MECHANICS OF DECEPTION. BRANDED DEALS, AD REVENUE, GROWTH HACKING, ALGORITHM MANIPULATION, WATCH TIMES...
...ALL FOR MYCENA. MYLO ISN'T JUST A PRANK KID. HE'S A MOUTHPIECE FOR THE MOST POWERFUL CORPORATION IN THE WORLD. A WAY TO MANIPULATE THE LAW AND THE MARKET.
AND I'M AMONG THE FUCKING MANIPULATORS.
FUCK.
I CAME HERE THINKING I WAS GOING TO GET EQUITY...
YOU KNEW THIS WHEN YOU SIGNED UP. BUT TRUST ME, BRAMWELL'S A GOOD MAN. I'M SURE HE'LL GIVE YOU A STAKE IN ALL THIS WHEN THE TIME'S RIGHT.
TRY STANDING UP TO HIM. TELL HIM WHAT YOU REALLY WANT.
DO YOU HAVE ANY IDEA HOW INSULTING THAT IS?
LOOK, FUCK THIS. I'M NOT GETTING INVOLVED WITH WHATEVER MYLO'S FILMING. I DON'T GET MY HANDS DIRTY, COOL?
FINE. SORRY. JUST COME AND WORKSHOP SOME IDEAS FOR A SHOOT. THEN GET OUT OF HERE.
I'LL FILM, DIRECT, AND CUT IT. I'LL HAVE IT READY FOR HIS MYCEE PAGE IN THE MORNING. COOL?
COOL.
THANK YOU.

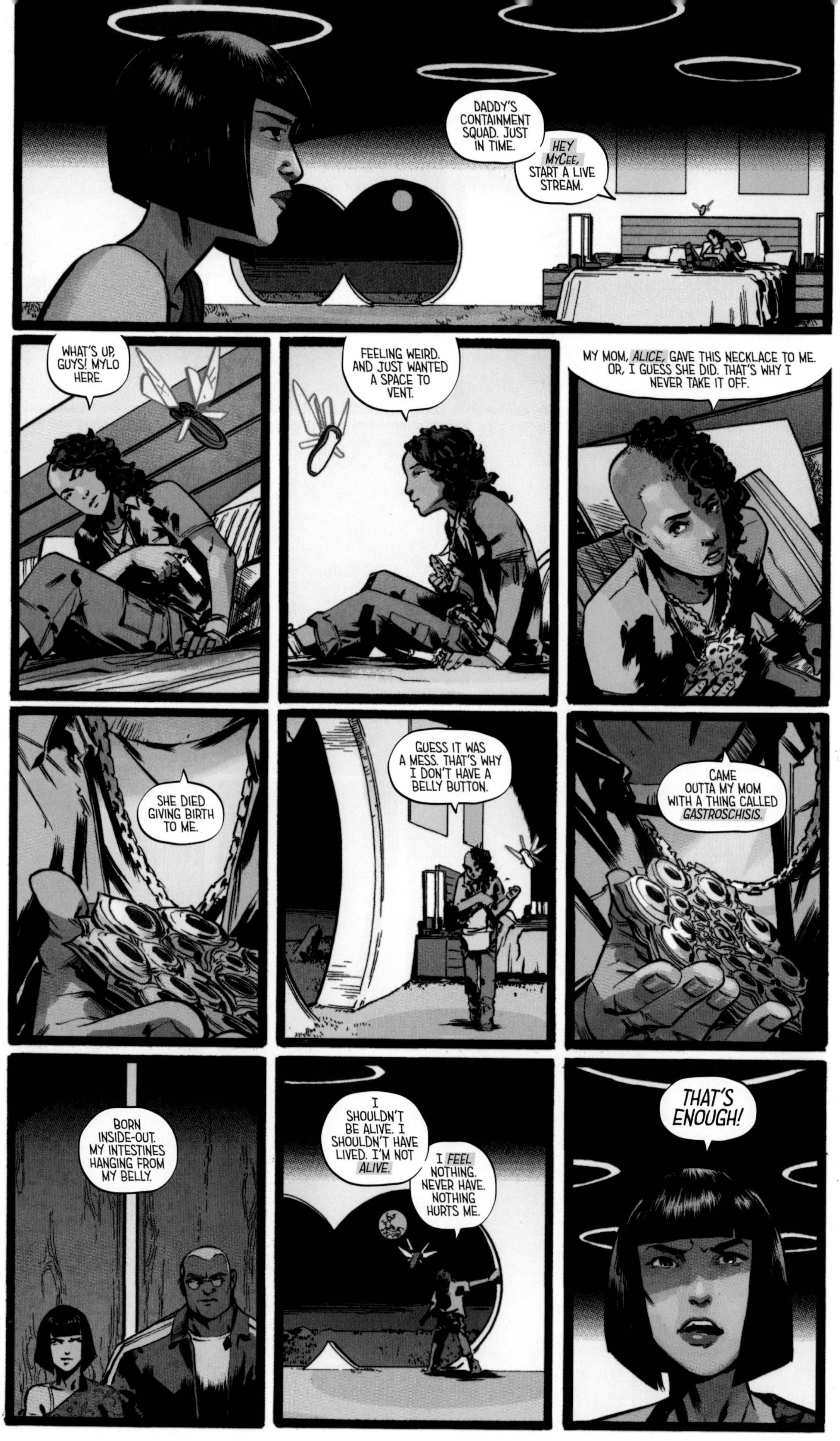

DADDY'S CONTAINMENT SQUAD. JUST IN TIME.
HEY MYCEE, START A LIVE STREAM.
WHAT'S UP, GUYS! MYLO HERE.
FEELING WEIRD. AND JUST WANTED A SPACE TO VENT.
MY MOM, ALICE, GAVE THIS NECKLACE TO ME. OR, I GUESS SHE DID. THAT'S WHY I NEVER TAKE IT OFF.
SHE DIED GIVING BIRTH TO ME.
GUESS IT WAS A MESS. THAT'S WHY I DON'T HAVE A BELLY BUTTON.
CAME OUTTA MY MOM WITH A THING CALLED GASTROSCHISIS.
BORN INSIDE-OUT. MY INTESTINES HANGING FROM MY BELLY.
I SHOULDN'T BE ALIVE. I SHOULDN'T HAVE LIVED. I'M NOT ALIVE.
I FEEL NOTHING. NEVER HAVE. NOTHING HURTS ME.
THAT'S ENOUGH!

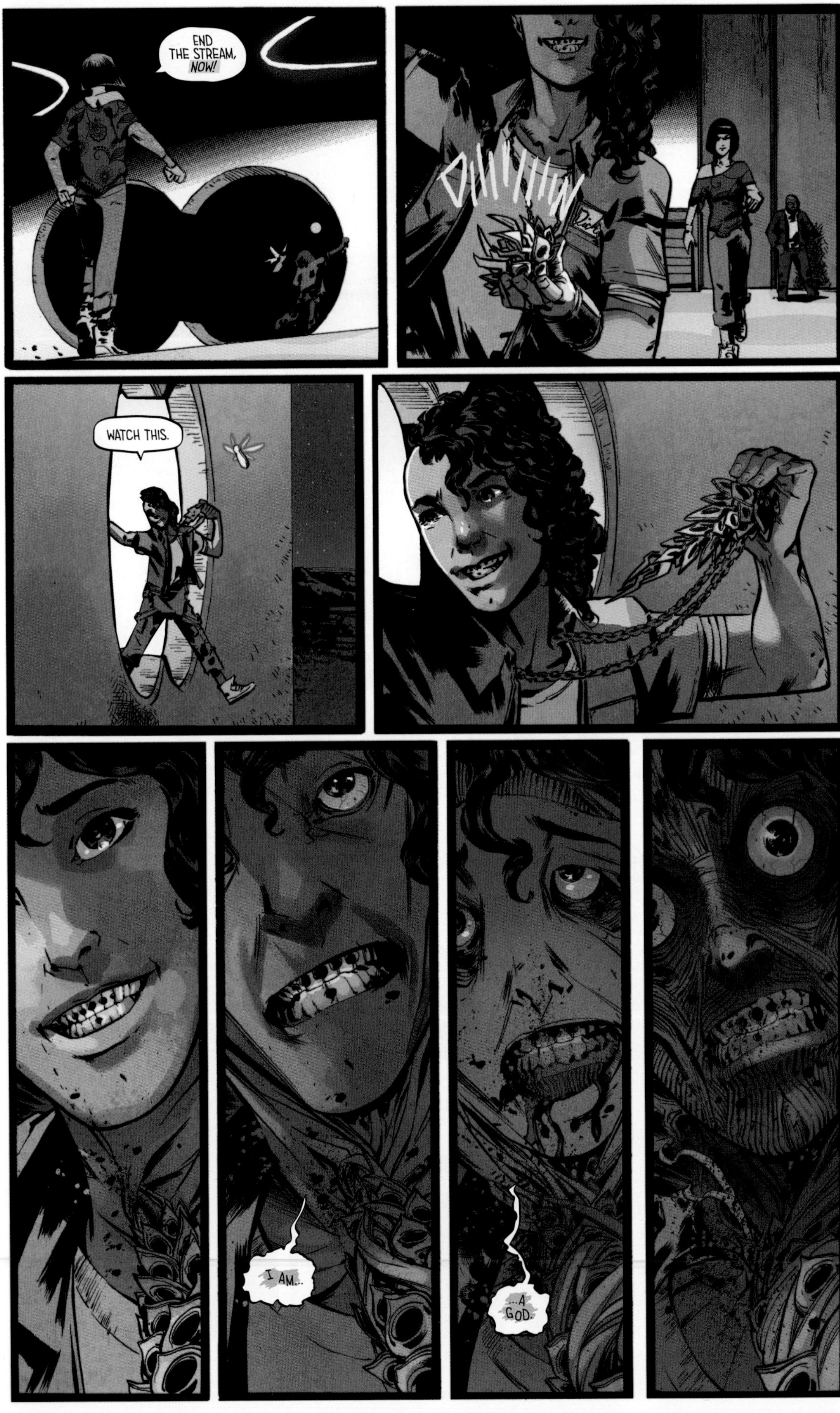
END THE STREAM, NOW!
WATCH THIS.
I AM...
...A GOD.

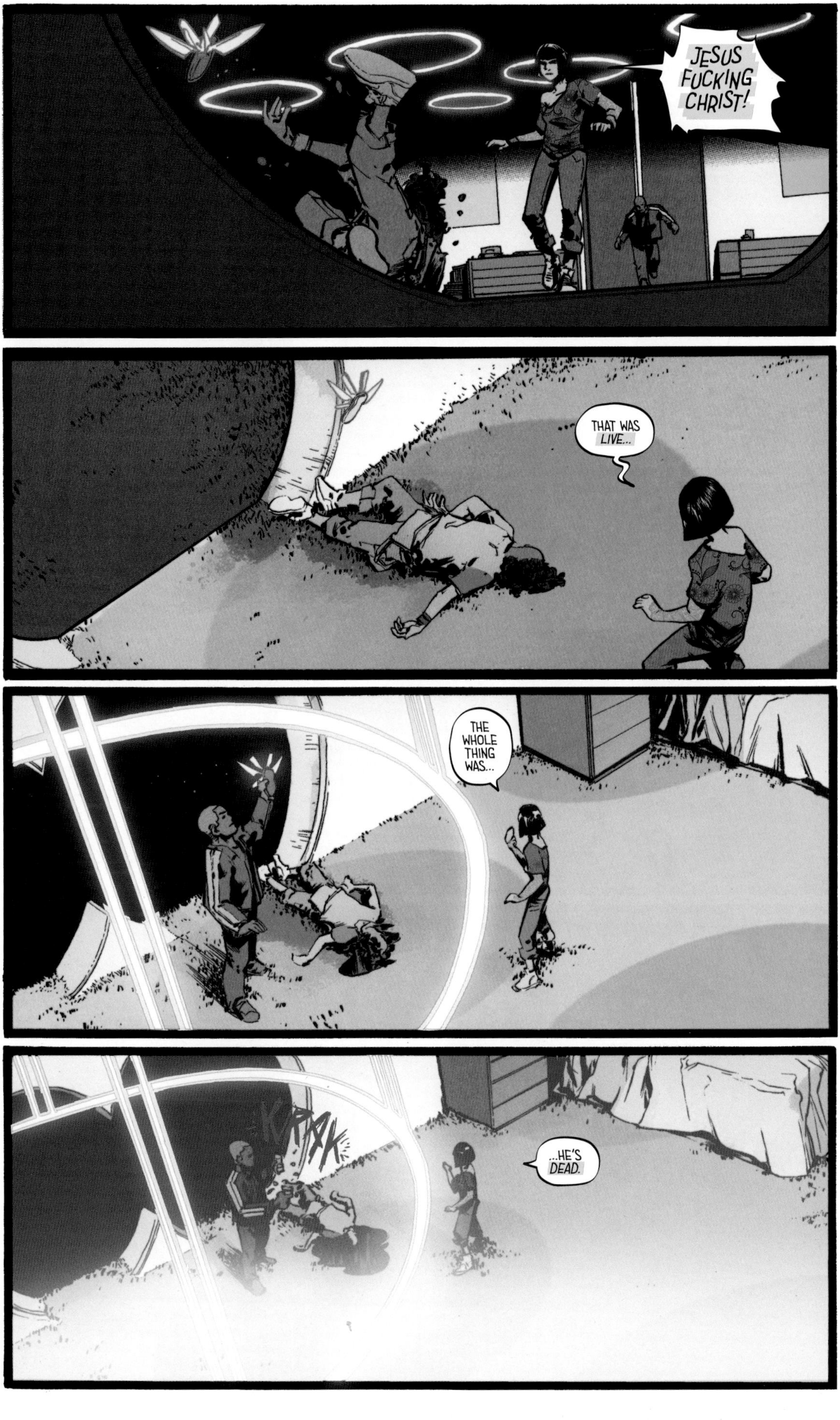
JESUS FUCKING CHRIST!
THAT WAS LIVE...
THE WHOLE THING WAS...
KRAK
...HE'S DEAD.

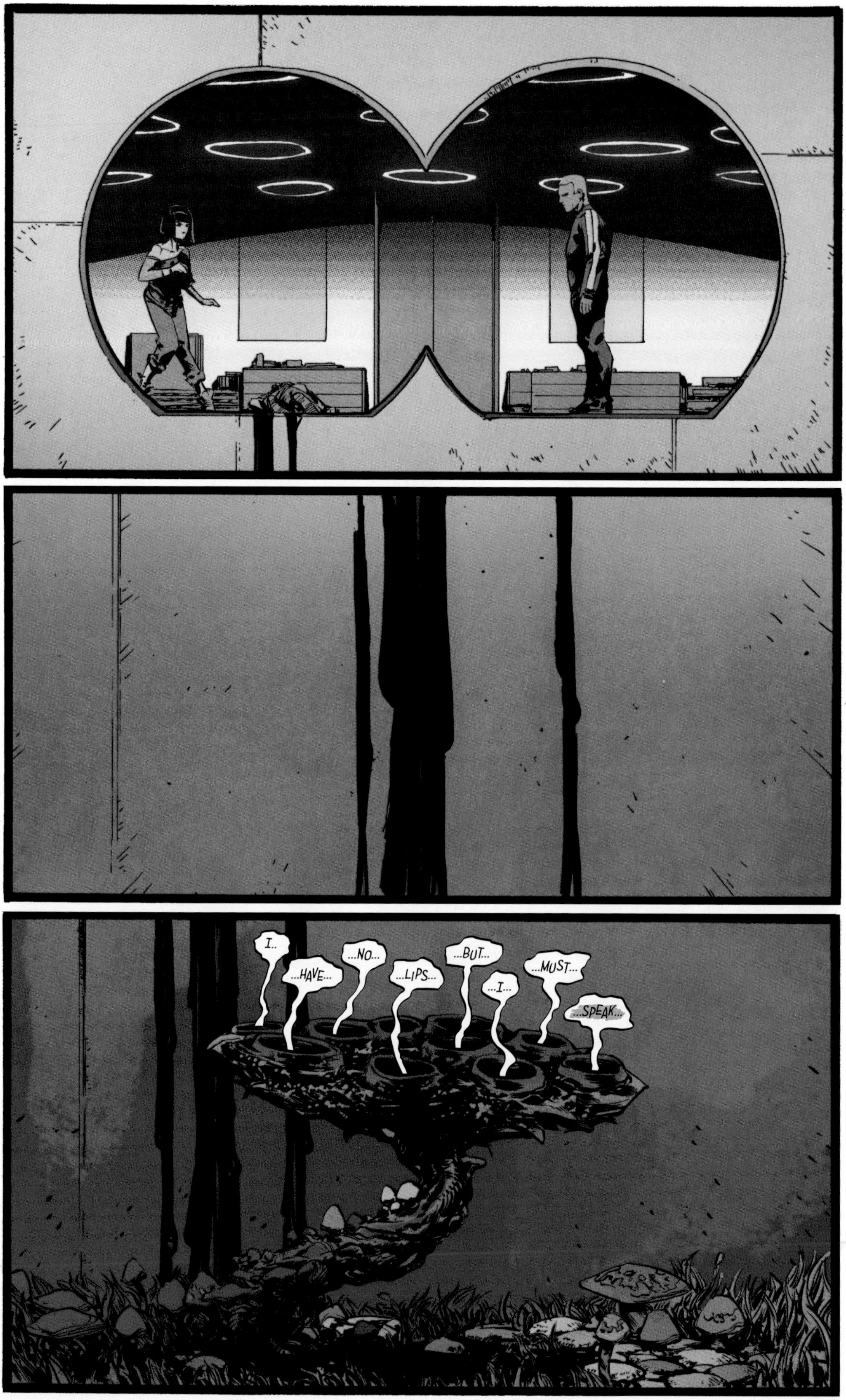
I..
...HAVE...
...NO...
...LIPS...
...BUT...
...I...
...MUST...
...SPEAK...

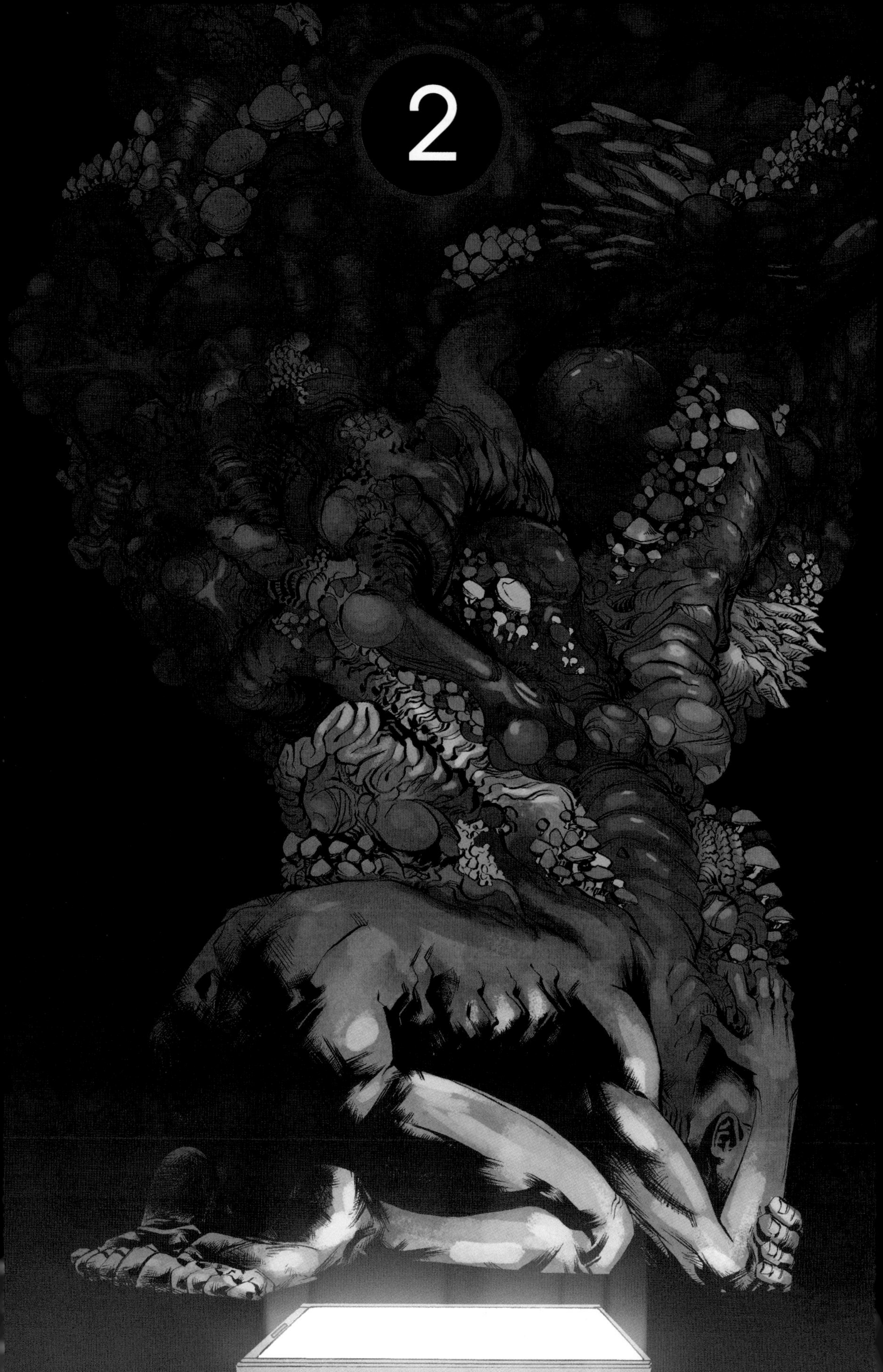
2

COOPERATIVE RESILIENCE

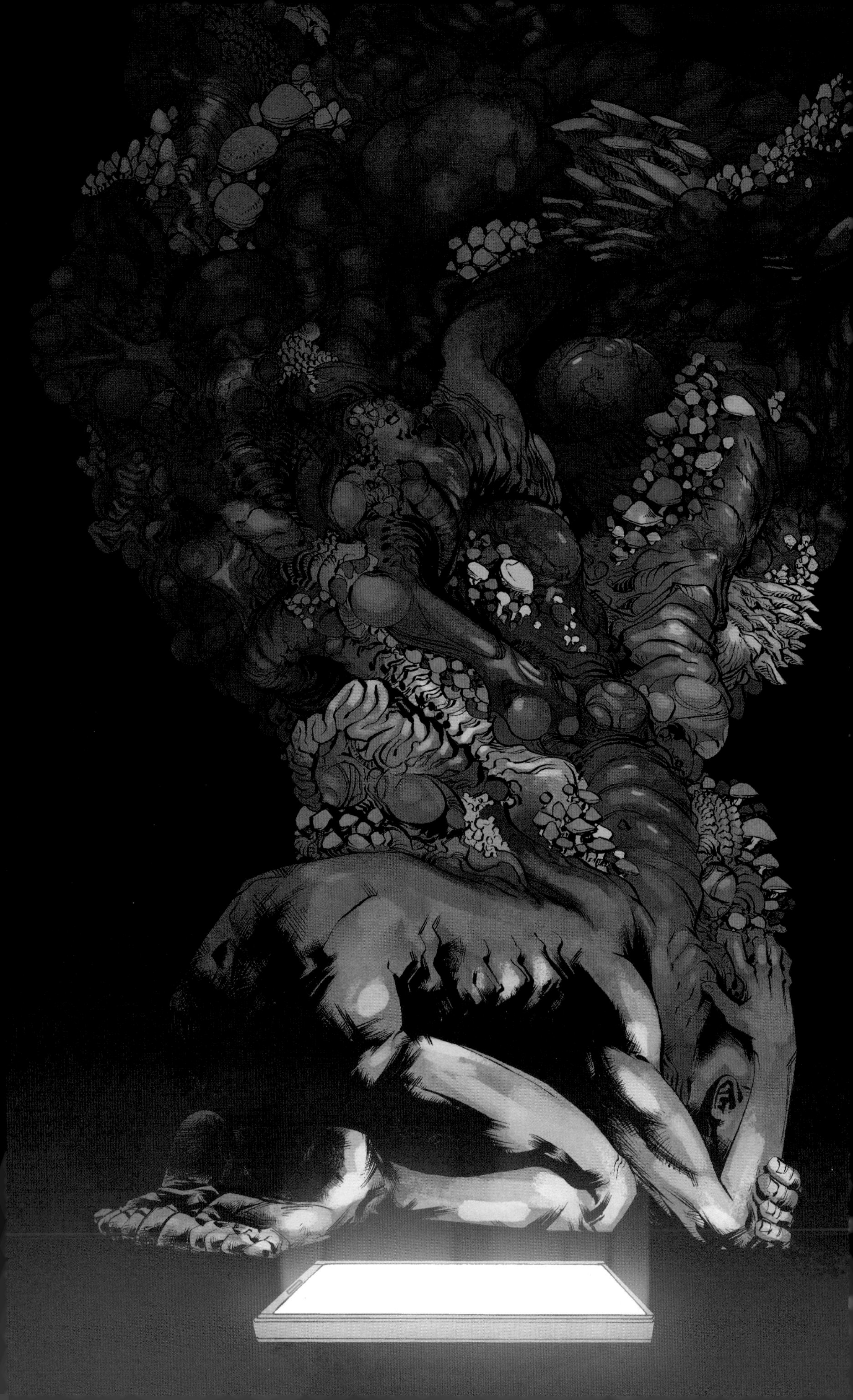

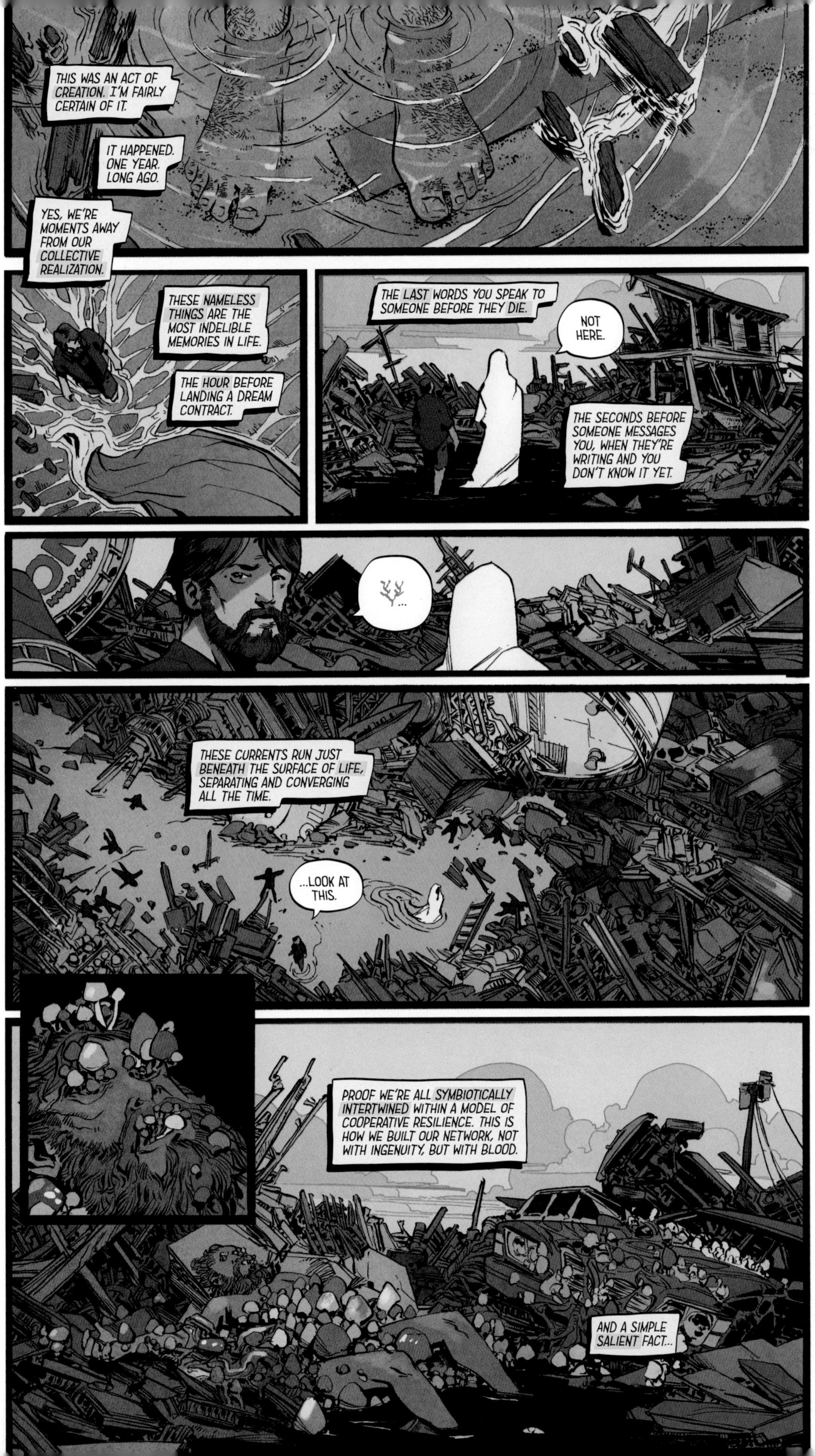

THIS WAS AN ACT OF CREATION. I'M FAIRLY CERTAIN OF IT.
IT HAPPENED. ONE YEAR. LONG AGO.
YES, WE'RE MOMENTS AWAY FROM OUR COLLECTIVE REALIZATION.
THESE NAMELESS THINGS ARE THE MOST INDELIBLE MEMORIES IN LIFE.
THE HOUR BEFORE LANDING A DREAM CONTRACT.
THE LAST WORDS YOU SPEAK TO SOMEONE BEFORE THEY DIE.
NOT HERE.
THE SECONDS BEFORE SOMEONE MESSAGES YOU, WHEN THEY'RE WRITING AND YOU DON'T KNOW IT YET.
...
THESE CURRENTS RUN JUST BENEATH THE SURFACE OF LIFE, SEPARATING AND CONVERGING ALL THE TIME.
...LOOK AT THIS.
PROOF WE'RE ALL SYMBIOTICALLY INTERTWINED WITHIN A MODEL OF COOPERATIVE RESILIENCE. THIS IS HOW WE BUILT OUR NETWORK, NOT WITH INGENUITY, BUT WITH BLOOD.
AND A SIMPLE SALIENT FACT...

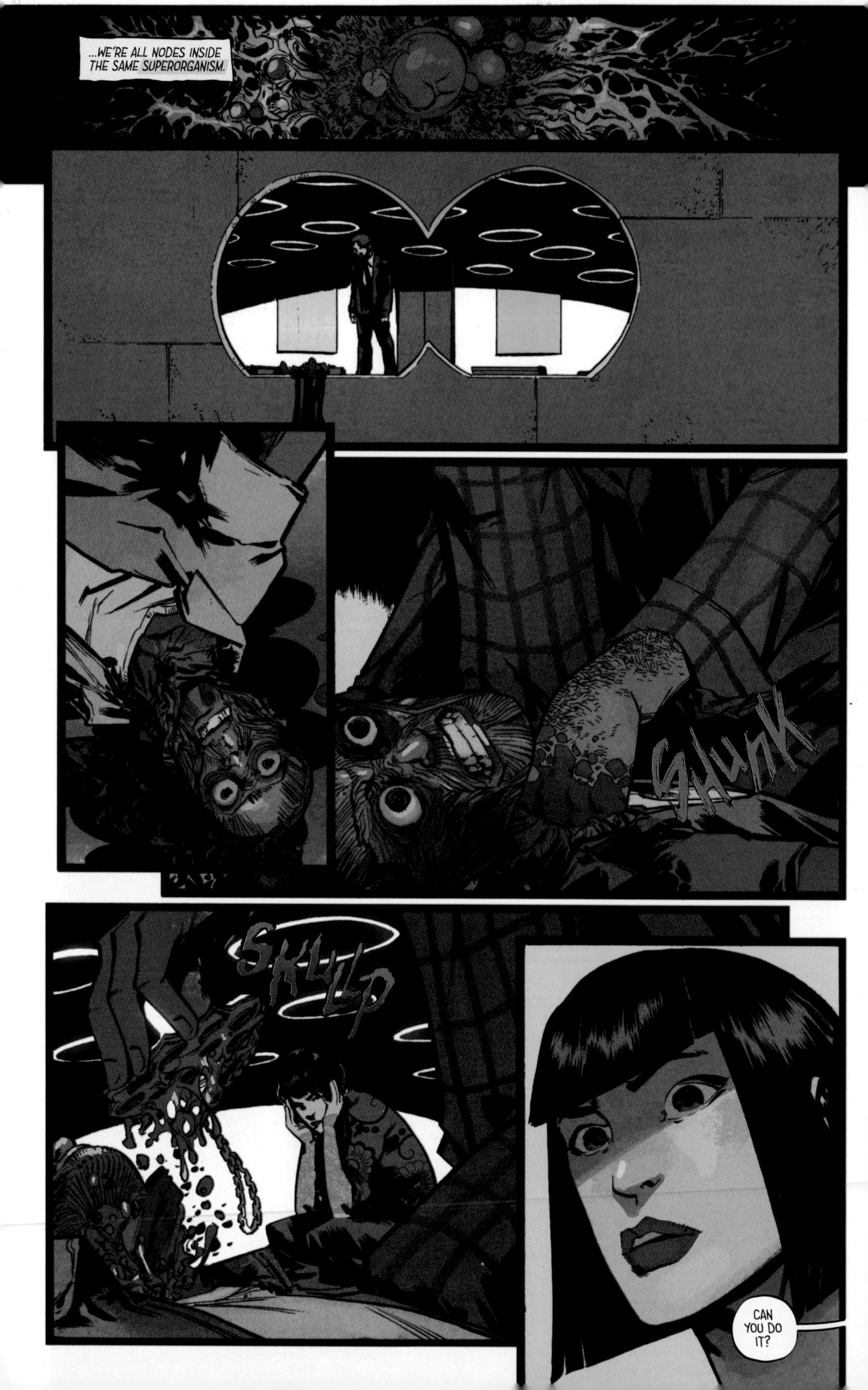
...WE'RE ALL NODES INSIDE THE SAME SUPERORGANISM.
SHUNK
SKLLLP
CAN YOU DO IT?

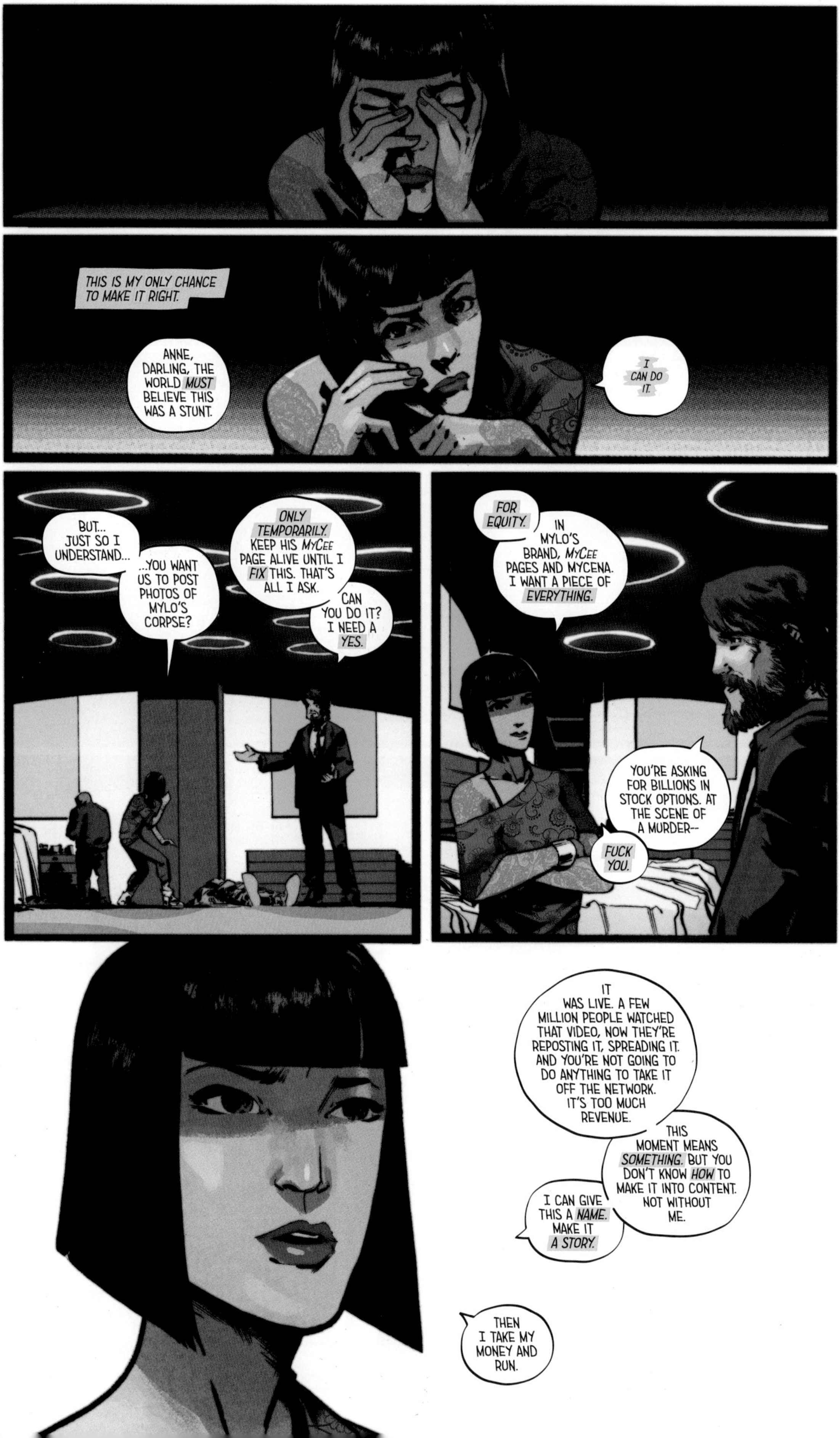
THIS IS MY ONLY CHANCE TO MAKE IT RIGHT.
ANNE, DARLING, THE WORLD MUST BELIEVE THIS WAS A STUNT.
I CAN DO IT.
BUT... JUST SO I UNDERSTAND...
...YOU WANT US TO POST PHOTOS OF MYLO'S CORPSE?
ONLY TEMPORARILY. KEEP HIS MYCEE PAGE ALIVE UNTIL I FIX THIS. THAT'S ALL I ASK.
CAN YOU DO IT? I NEED A YES.
FOR EQUITY.
IN MYLO'S BRAND, MYCEE PAGES AND MYCENA. I WANT A PIECE OF EVERYTHING.
YOU'RE ASKING FOR BILLIONS IN STOCK OPTIONS. AT THE SCENE OF A MURDER--
FUCK YOU.
IT WAS LIVE. A FEW MILLION PEOPLE WATCHED THAT VIDEO, NOW THEY'RE REPOSTING IT, SPREADING IT. AND YOU'RE NOT GOING TO DO ANYTHING TO TAKE IT OFF THE NETWORK. IT'S TOO MUCH REVENUE.
THIS MOMENT MEANS SOMETHING. BUT YOU DON'T KNOW HOW TO MAKE IT INTO CONTENT. NOT WITHOUT ME.
I CAN GIVE THIS A NAME. MAKE IT A STORY.
THEN I TAKE MY MONEY AND RUN.

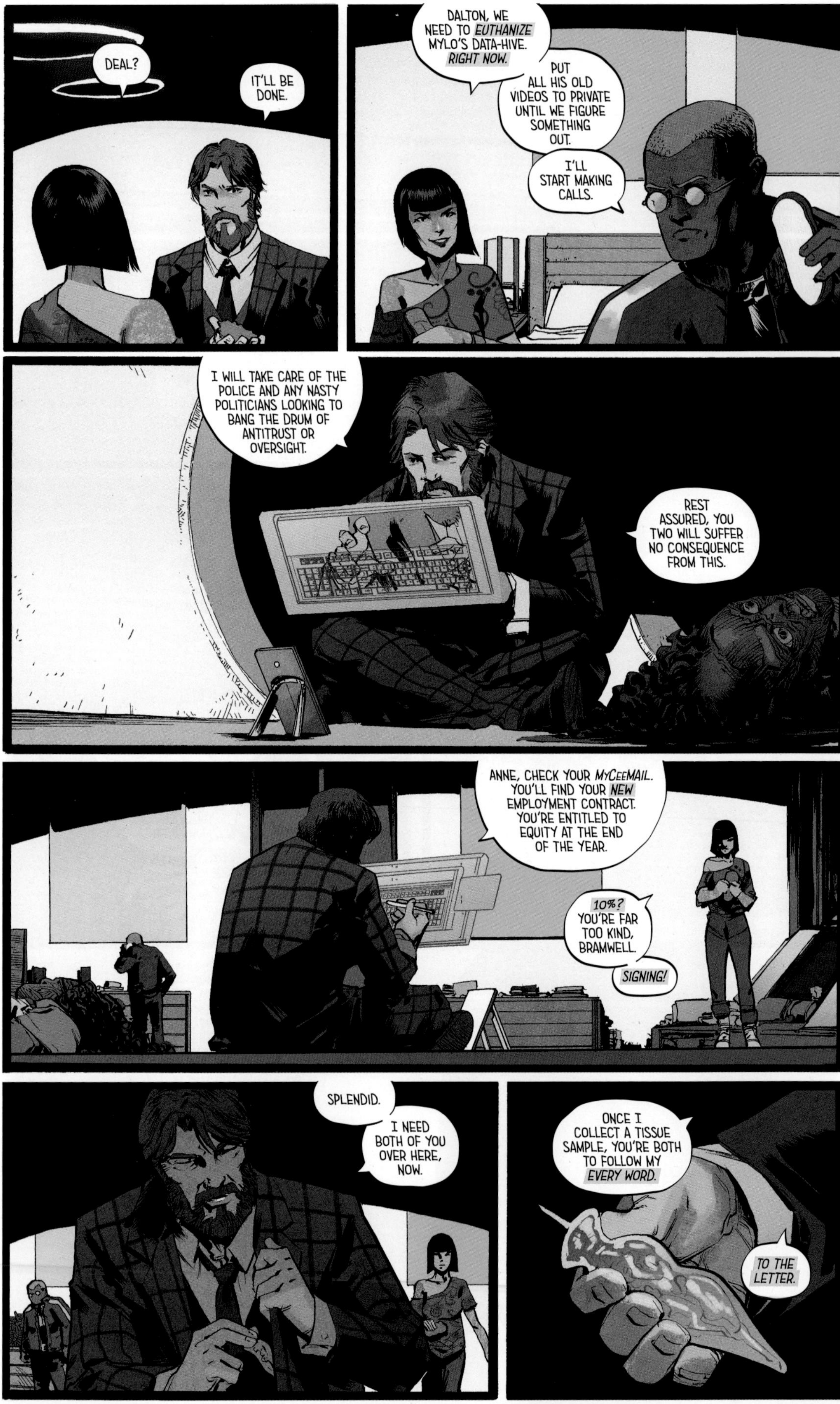
DEAL?
IT'LL BE DONE.
DALTON, WE NEED TO EUTHANIZE MYLO'S DATA-HIVE. RIGHT NOW.
PUT ALL HIS OLD VIDEOS TO PRIVATE UNTIL WE FIGURE SOMETHING OUT.
I'LL START MAKING CALLS.
I WILL TAKE CARE OF THE POLICE AND ANY NASTY POLITICIANS LOOKING TO BANG THE DRUM OF ANTITRUST OR OVERSIGHT.
REST ASSURED, YOU TWO WILL SUFFER NO CONSEQUENCE FROM THIS.
ANNE, CHECK YOUR MyCeeMAIL. YOU'LL FIND YOUR NEW EMPLOYMENT CONTRACT. YOU'RE ENTITLED TO EQUITY AT THE END OF THE YEAR.
10%? YOU'RE FAR TOO KIND, BRAMWELL.
SIGNING!
SPLENDID.
I NEED BOTH OF YOU OVER HERE, NOW.
ONCE I COLLECT A TISSUE SAMPLE, YOU'RE BOTH TO FOLLOW MY EVERY WORD.
TO THE LETTER.

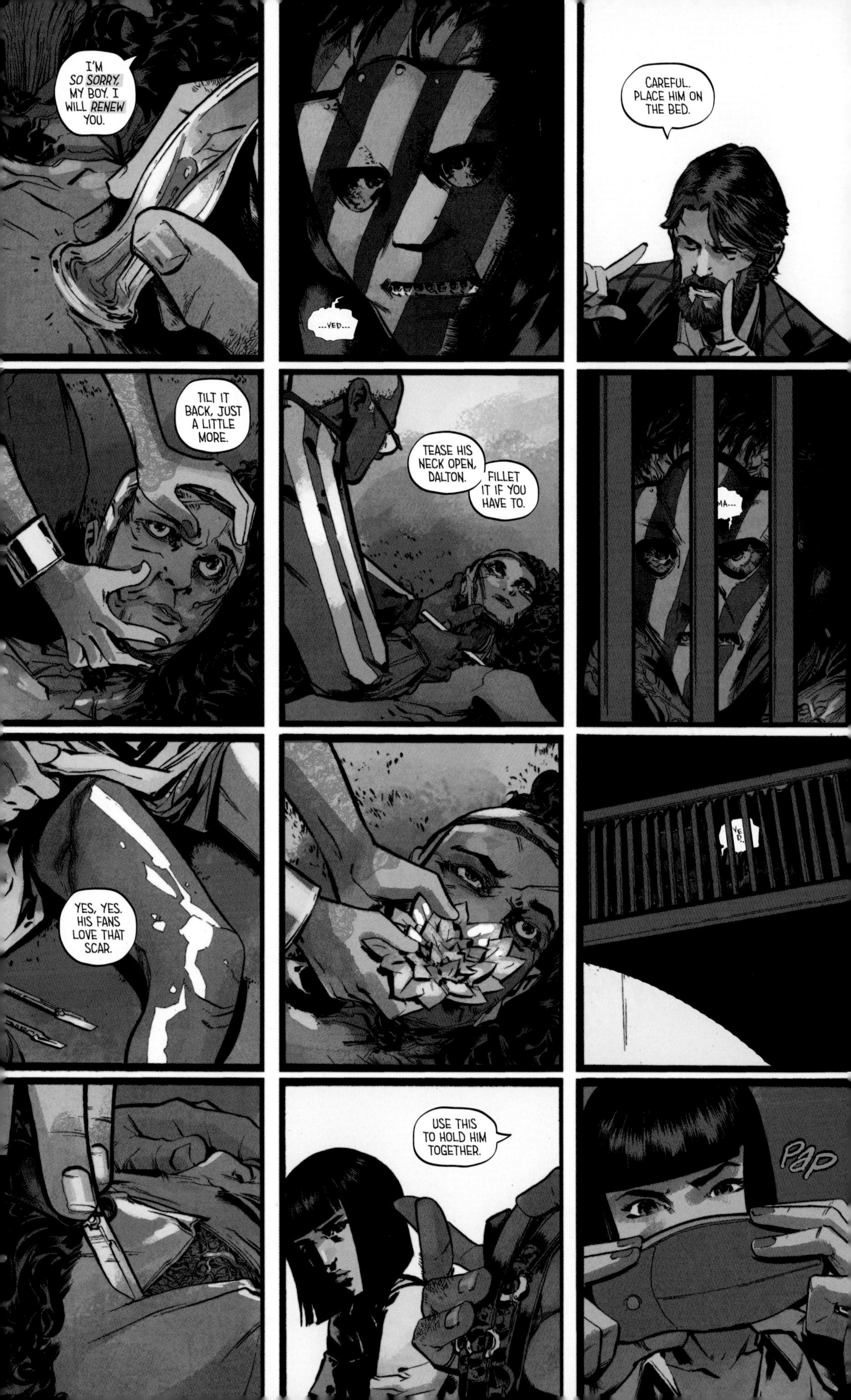
I'M SO SORRY, MY BOY. I WILL RENEW YOU.
...VED...
CAREFUL. PLACE HIM ON THE BED.
TILT IT BACK, JUST A LITTLE MORE.
TEASE HIS NECK OPEN, DALTON.
FILLET IT IF YOU HAVE TO.
MA...
YES, YES. HIS FANS LOVE THAT SCAR.
VED..
USE THIS TO HOLD HIM TOGETHER.
PAP

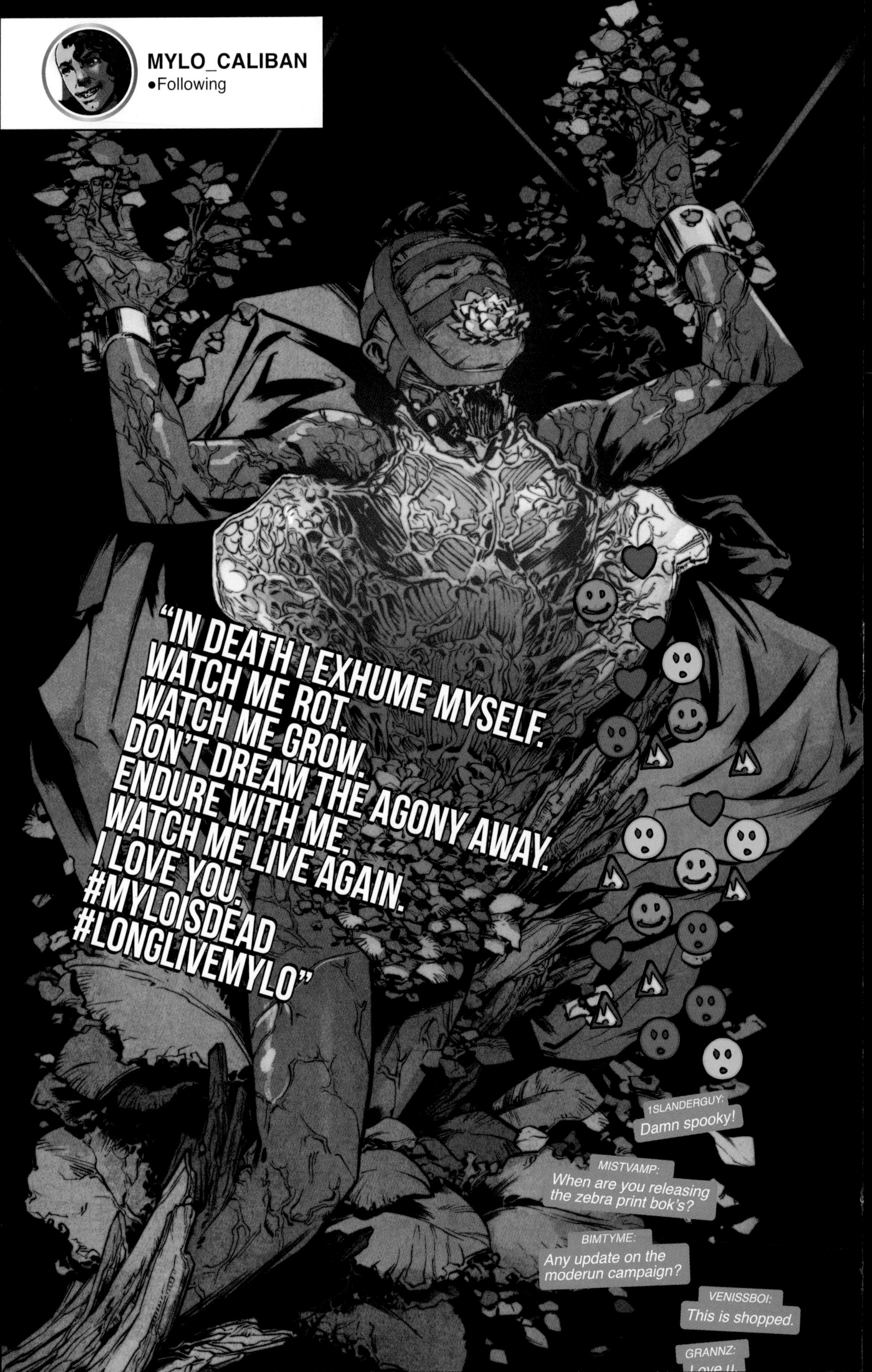
MYLO_CALIBAN
•Following
"IN DEATH I EXHUME MYSELF.
WATCH ME ROT.
WATCH ME GROW.
DON'T DREAM THE AGONY AWAY.
ENDURE WITH ME.
WATCH ME LIVE AGAIN.
I LOVE YOU.
#MYLOISDEAD
#LONGLIVEMYLO"
1SLANDERGUY:
Damn spooky!
MISTVAMP:
When are you releasing the zebra print bok's?
BIMTYME:
Any update on the moderun campaign?
VENISSBOI:
This is shopped.
GRANNZ:

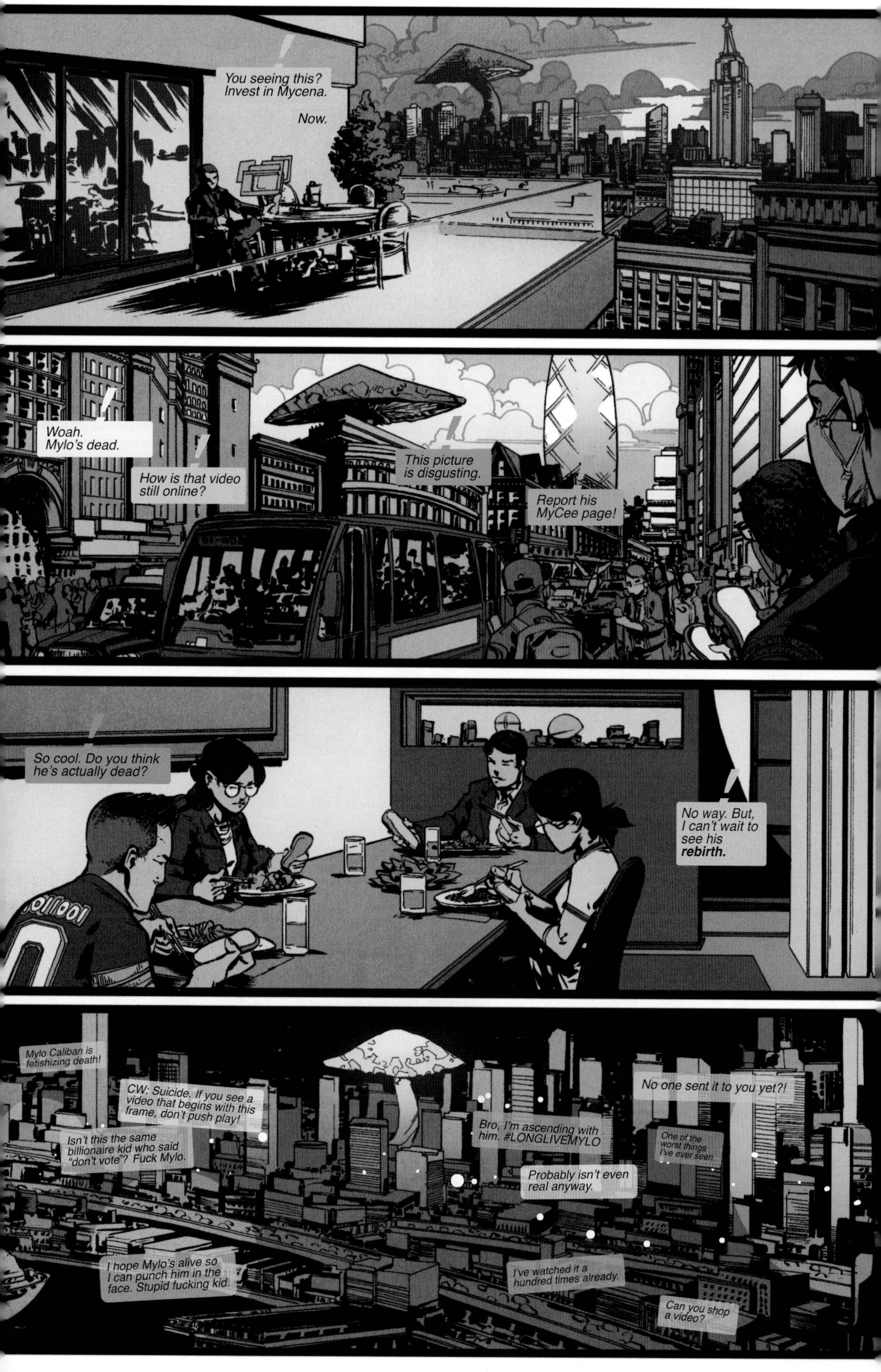
You seeing this? Invest in Mycena.
Now.
Woah. Mylo's dead.
How is that video still online?
This picture is disgusting.
Report his MyCee page!
So cool. Do you think he's actually dead?
No way. But, I can't wait to see his **rebirth.**
Mylo Caliban is fetishizing death!
CW: Suicide. If you see a video that begins with this frame, don't push play!
Isn't this the same billionaire kid who said "don't vote"? Fuck Mylo.
No one sent it to you yet?!
Bro, I'm ascending with him. #LONGLIVEMYLO
One of the worst things I've ever seen.
Probably isn't even real anyway.
I hope Mylo's alive so I can punch him in the face. Stupid fucking kid.
I've watched it a hundred times already.
Can you shop a video?

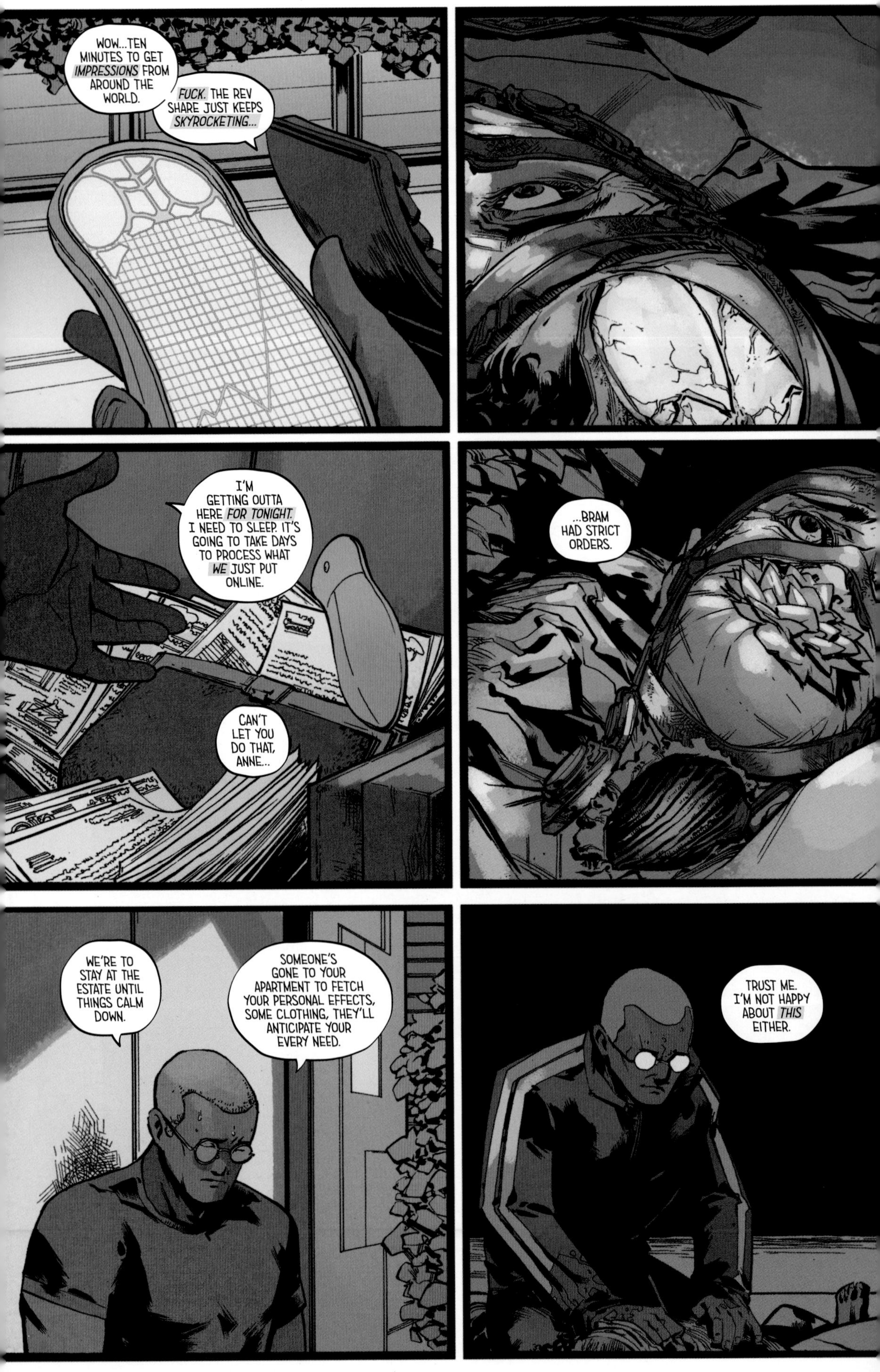
WOW...TEN MINUTES TO GET IMPRESSIONS FROM AROUND THE WORLD.
FUCK. THE REV SHARE JUST KEEPS SKYROCKETING...
I'M GETTING OUTTA HERE FOR TONIGHT. I NEED TO SLEEP. IT'S GOING TO TAKE DAYS TO PROCESS WHAT WE JUST PUT ONLINE.
CAN'T LET YOU DO THAT, ANNE...
...BRAM HAD STRICT ORDERS.
WE'RE TO STAY AT THE ESTATE UNTIL THINGS CALM DOWN.
SOMEONE'S GONE TO YOUR APARTMENT TO FETCH YOUR PERSONAL EFFECTS, SOME CLOTHING, THEY'LL ANTICIPATE YOUR EVERY NEED.
TRUST ME. I'M NOT HAPPY ABOUT THIS EITHER.

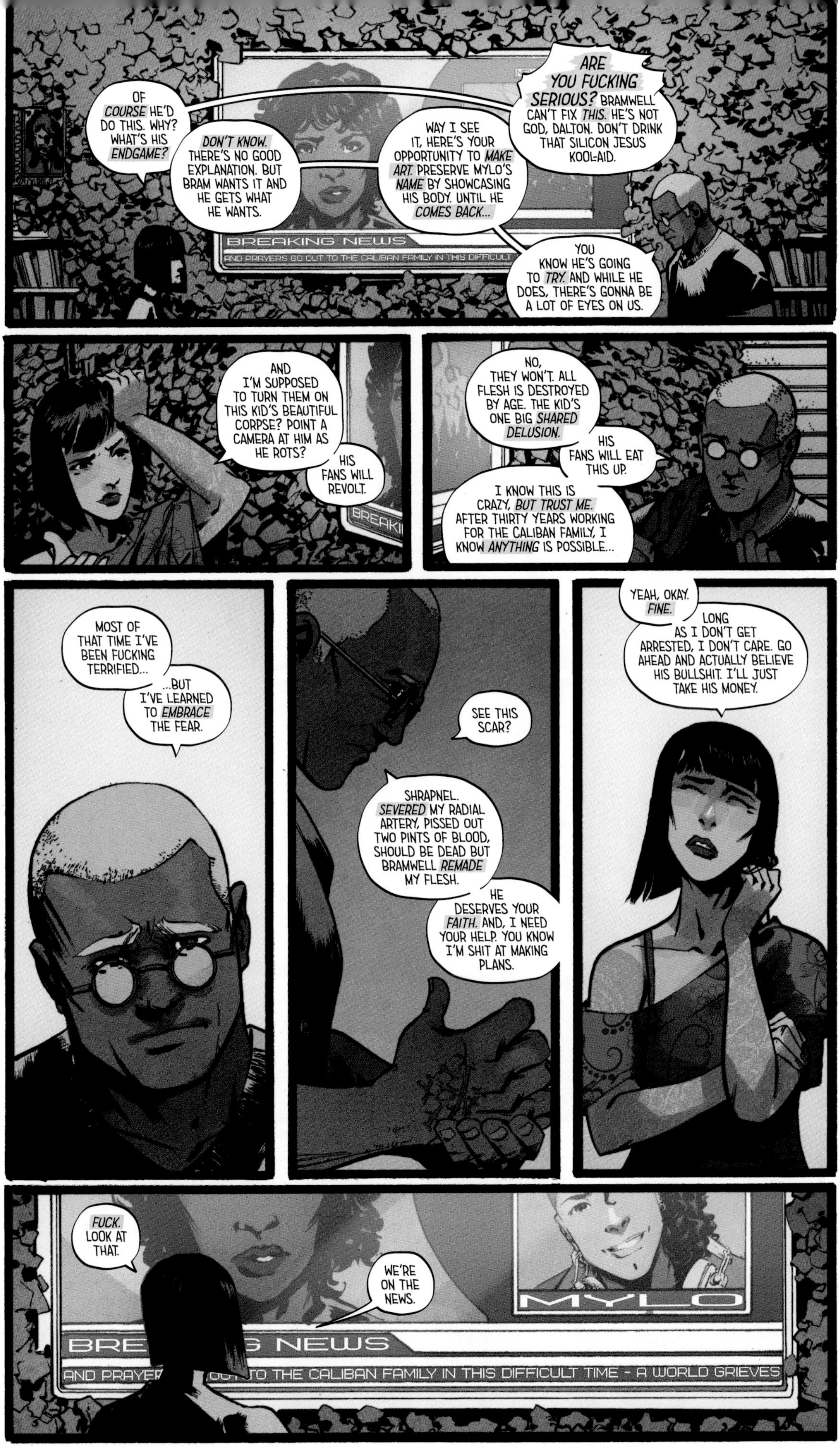

OF COURSE HE'D DO THIS. WHY? WHAT'S HIS ENDGAME?
DON'T KNOW. THERE'S NO GOOD EXPLANATION. BUT BRAM WANTS IT AND HE GETS WHAT HE WANTS.
WAY I SEE IT, HERE'S YOUR OPPORTUNITY TO MAKE ART. PRESERVE MYLO'S NAME BY SHOWCASING HIS BODY. UNTIL HE COMES BACK...
ARE YOU FUCKING SERIOUS? BRAMWELL CAN'T FIX THIS. HE'S NOT GOD, DALTON. DON'T DRINK THAT SILICON JESUS KOOL-AID.
BREAKING NEWS
AND PRAYERS GO OUT TO THE CALIBAN FAMILY IN THIS DIFFICULT
YOU KNOW HE'S GOING TO TRY. AND WHILE HE DOES, THERE'S GONNA BE A LOT OF EYES ON US.
AND I'M SUPPOSED TO TURN THEM ON THIS KID'S BEAUTIFUL CORPSE? POINT A CAMERA AT HIM AS HE ROTS?
HIS FANS WILL REVOLT.
NO, THEY WON'T. ALL FLESH IS DESTROYED BY AGE. THE KID'S ONE BIG SHARED DELUSION.
HIS FANS WILL EAT THIS UP.
I KNOW THIS IS CRAZY, BUT TRUST ME. AFTER THIRTY YEARS WORKING FOR THE CALIBAN FAMILY, I KNOW ANYTHING IS POSSIBLE...
MOST OF THAT TIME I'VE BEEN FUCKING TERRIFIED...
...BUT I'VE LEARNED TO EMBRACE THE FEAR.
SEE THIS SCAR?
SHRAPNEL. SEVERED MY RADIAL ARTERY, PISSED OUT TWO PINTS OF BLOOD, SHOULD BE DEAD BUT BRAMWELL REMADE MY FLESH.
HE DESERVES YOUR FAITH. AND, I NEED YOUR HELP. YOU KNOW I'M SHIT AT MAKING PLANS.
YEAH, OKAY. FINE.
LONG AS I DON'T GET ARRESTED, I DON'T CARE. GO AHEAD AND ACTUALLY BELIEVE HIS BULLSHIT. I'LL JUST TAKE HIS MONEY.
FUCK. LOOK AT THAT.
WE'RE ON THE NEWS.
MYLO
BRE G NEWS
AND PRAYER OUT TO THE CALIBAN FAMILY IN THIS DIFFICULT TIME - A WORLD GRIEVES

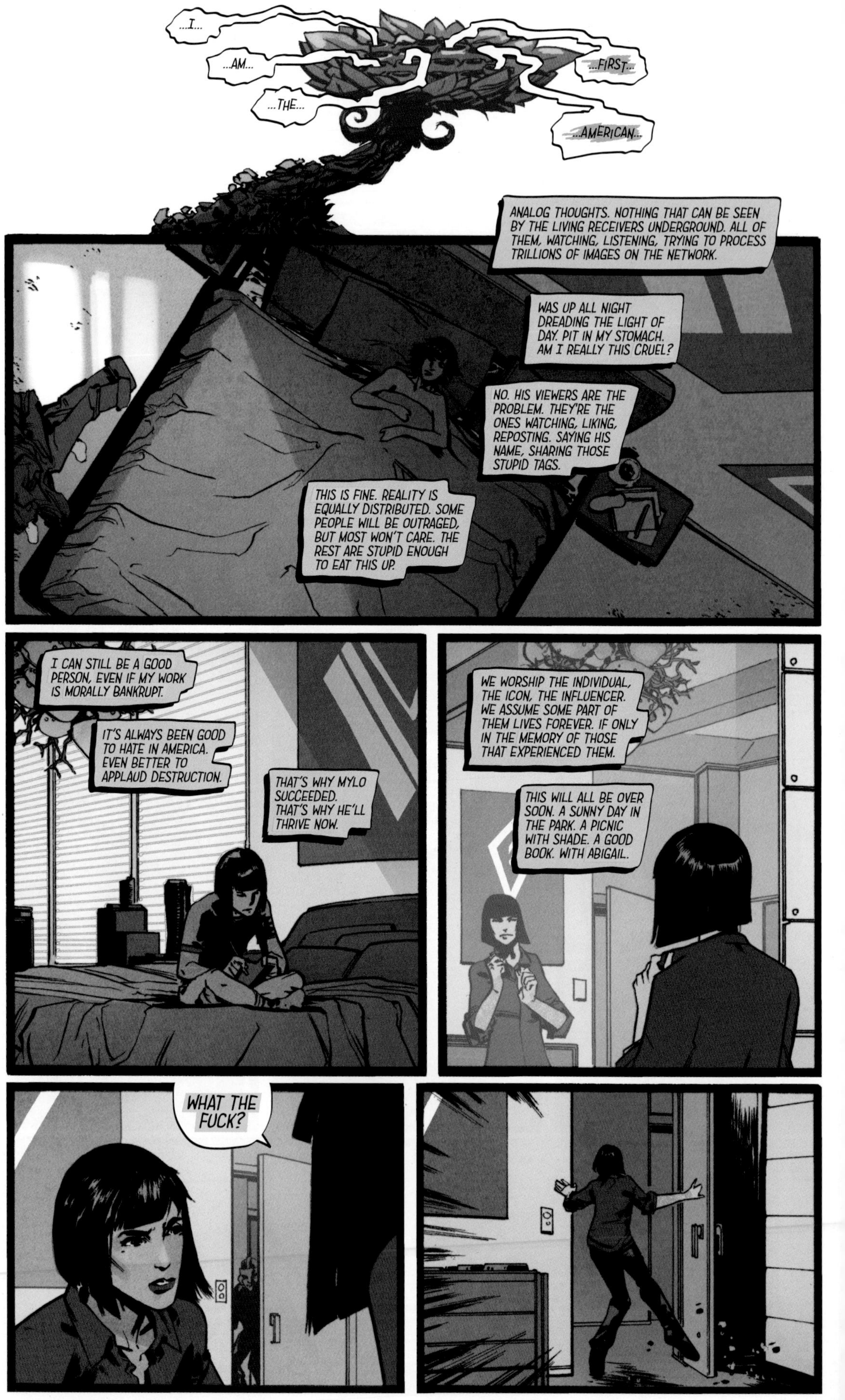

...I...
...AM...
...THE...
...FIRST...
...AMERICAN...
ANALOG THOUGHTS. NOTHING THAT CAN BE SEEN BY THE LIVING RECEIVERS UNDERGROUND. ALL OF THEM, WATCHING, LISTENING, TRYING TO PROCESS TRILLIONS OF IMAGES ON THE NETWORK.
WAS UP ALL NIGHT DREADING THE LIGHT OF DAY. PIT IN MY STOMACH. AM I REALLY THIS CRUEL?
NO. HIS VIEWERS ARE THE PROBLEM. THEY'RE THE ONES WATCHING, LIKING, REPOSTING. SAYING HIS NAME, SHARING THOSE STUPID TAGS.
THIS IS FINE. REALITY IS EQUALLY DISTRIBUTED. SOME PEOPLE WILL BE OUTRAGED, BUT MOST WON'T CARE. THE REST ARE STUPID ENOUGH TO EAT THIS UP.
I CAN STILL BE A GOOD PERSON, EVEN IF MY WORK IS MORALLY BANKRUPT.
IT'S ALWAYS BEEN GOOD TO HATE IN AMERICA. EVEN BETTER TO APPLAUD DESTRUCTION.
THAT'S WHY MYLO SUCCEEDED. THAT'S WHY HE'LL THRIVE NOW.
WE WORSHIP THE INDIVIDUAL, THE ICON, THE INFLUENCER. WE ASSUME SOME PART OF THEM LIVES FOREVER. IF ONLY IN THE MEMORY OF THOSE THAT EXPERIENCED THEM.
THIS WILL ALL BE OVER SOON. A SUNNY DAY IN THE PARK. A PICNIC WITH SHADE. A GOOD BOOK. WITH ABIGAIL.
WHAT THE FUCK?

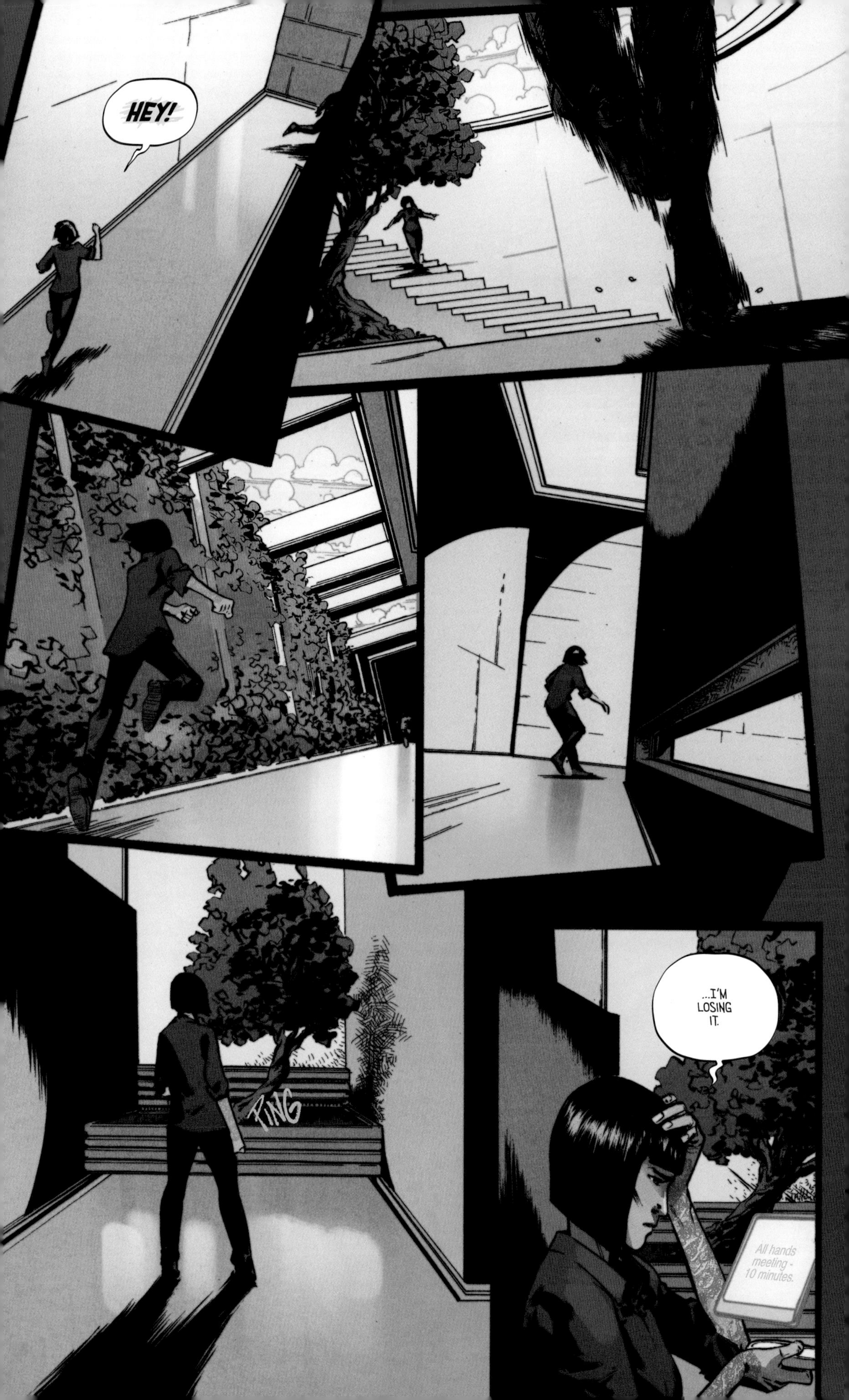
HEY!
PING
...I'M LOSING IT.
All hands meeting - 10 minutes.

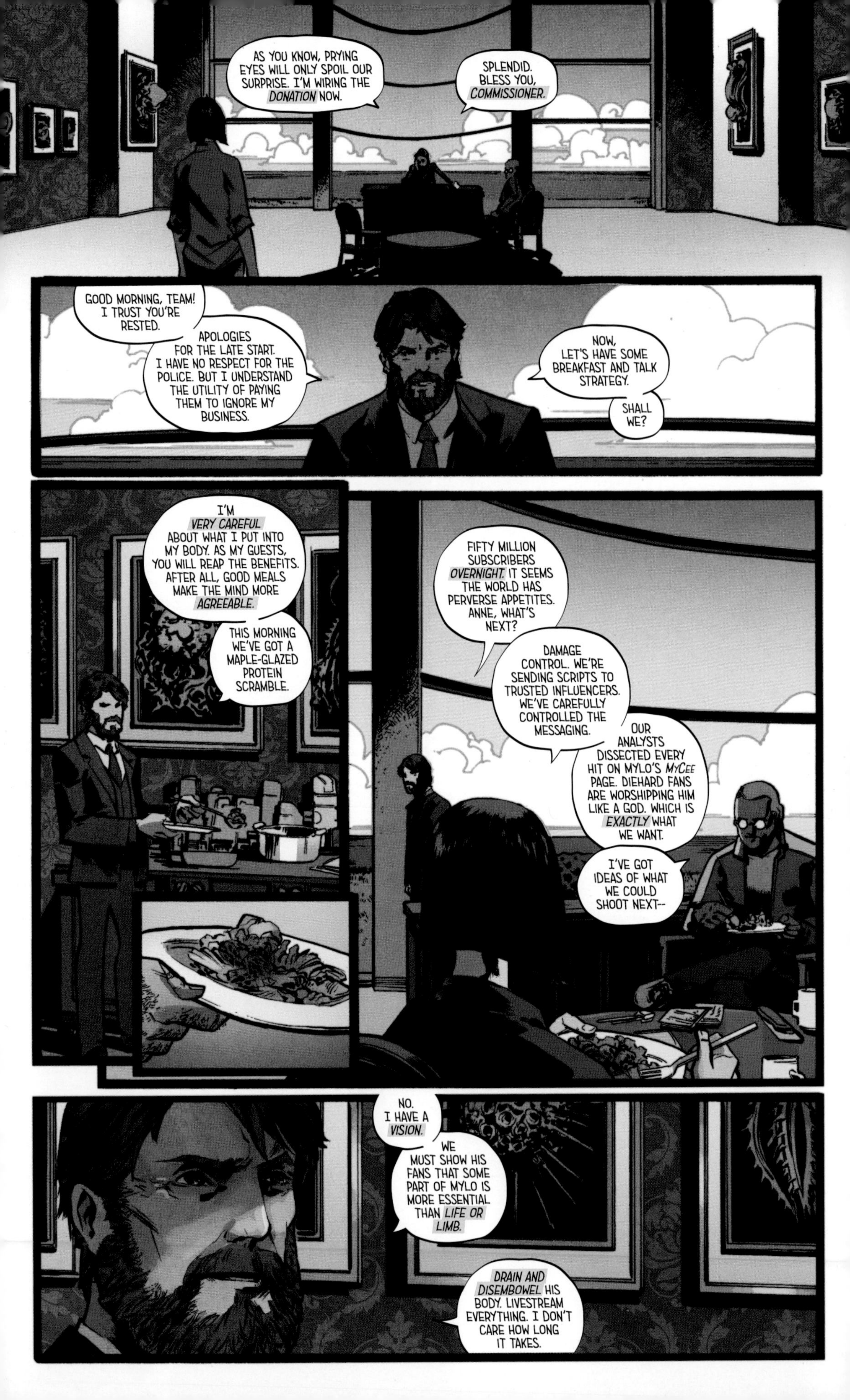
AS YOU KNOW, PRYING EYES WILL ONLY SPOIL OUR SURPRISE. I'M WIRING THE DONATION NOW.
SPLENDID. BLESS YOU, COMMISSIONER.
GOOD MORNING, TEAM! I TRUST YOU'RE RESTED.
APOLOGIES FOR THE LATE START. I HAVE NO RESPECT FOR THE POLICE. BUT I UNDERSTAND THE UTILITY OF PAYING THEM TO IGNORE MY BUSINESS.
NOW, LET'S HAVE SOME BREAKFAST AND TALK STRATEGY.
SHALL WE?
I'M VERY CAREFUL ABOUT WHAT I PUT INTO MY BODY. AS MY GUESTS, YOU WILL REAP THE BENEFITS. AFTER ALL, GOOD MEALS MAKE THE MIND MORE AGREEABLE.
THIS MORNING WE'VE GOT A MAPLE-GLAZED PROTEIN SCRAMBLE.
FIFTY MILLION SUBSCRIBERS OVERNIGHT. IT SEEMS THE WORLD HAS PERVERSE APPETITES. ANNE, WHAT'S NEXT?
DAMAGE CONTROL. WE'RE SENDING SCRIPTS TO TRUSTED INFLUENCERS. WE'VE CAREFULLY CONTROLLED THE MESSAGING.
OUR ANALYSTS DISSECTED EVERY HIT ON MYLO'S MYCEE PAGE. DIEHARD FANS ARE WORSHIPPING HIM LIKE A GOD. WHICH IS EXACTLY WHAT WE WANT.
I'VE GOT IDEAS OF WHAT WE COULD SHOOT NEXT--
NO. I HAVE A VISION.
WE MUST SHOW HIS FANS THAT SOME PART OF MYLO IS MORE ESSENTIAL THAN LIFE OR LIMB.
DRAIN AND DISEMBOWEL HIS BODY. LIVESTREAM EVERYTHING. I DON'T CARE HOW LONG IT TAKES.

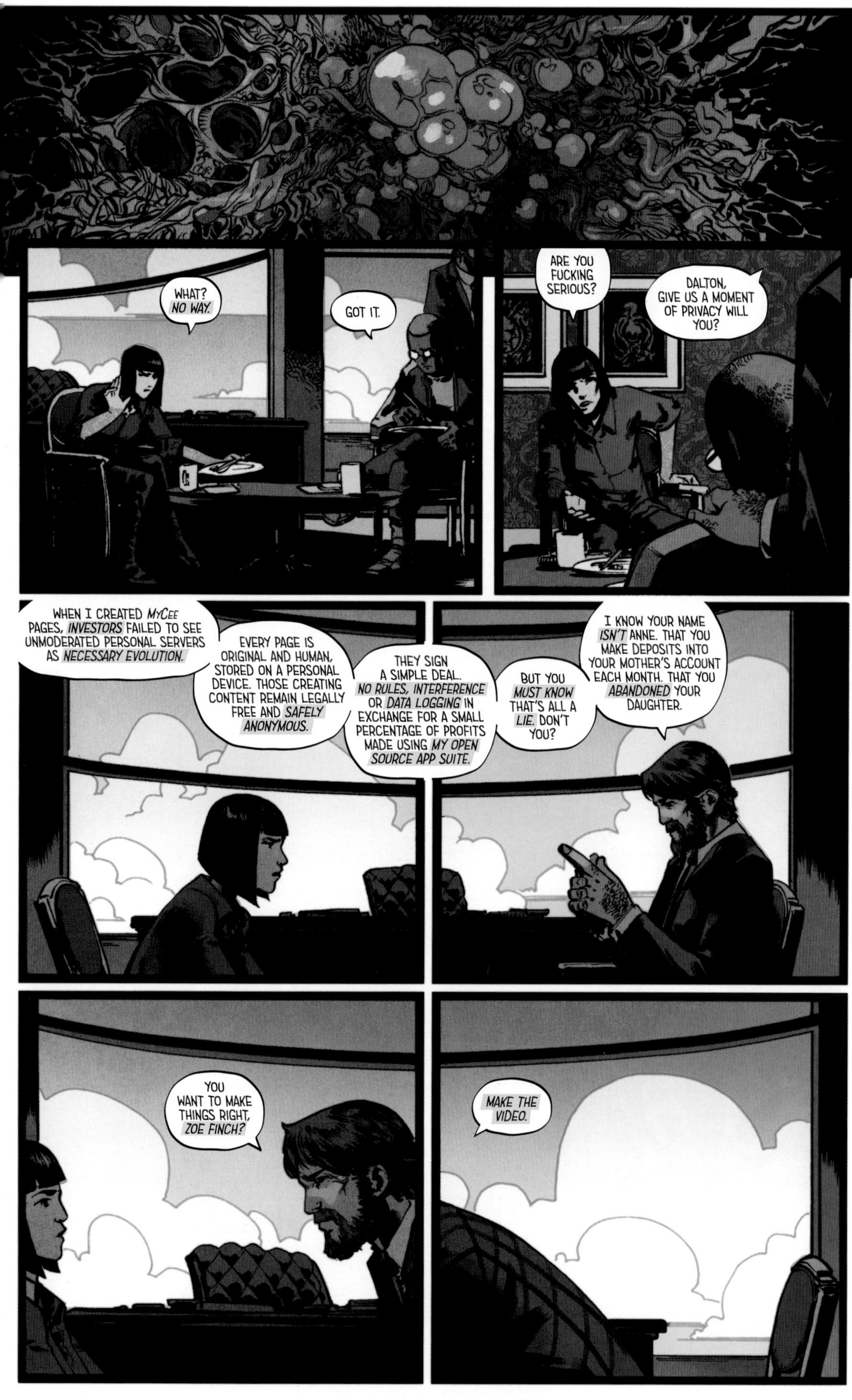
WHAT? NO WAY.
GOT IT.
ARE YOU FUCKING SERIOUS?
DALTON, GIVE US A MOMENT OF PRIVACY WILL YOU?
WHEN I CREATED MyCee PAGES, INVESTORS FAILED TO SEE UNMODERATED PERSONAL SERVERS AS NECESSARY EVOLUTION.
EVERY PAGE IS ORIGINAL AND HUMAN, STORED ON A PERSONAL DEVICE. THOSE CREATING CONTENT REMAIN LEGALLY FREE AND SAFELY ANONYMOUS.
THEY SIGN A SIMPLE DEAL. NO RULES, INTERFERENCE OR DATA LOGGING IN EXCHANGE FOR A SMALL PERCENTAGE OF PROFITS MADE USING MY OPEN SOURCE APP SUITE.
BUT YOU MUST KNOW THAT'S ALL A LIE. DON'T YOU?
I KNOW YOUR NAME ISN'T ANNE. THAT YOU MAKE DEPOSITS INTO YOUR MOTHER'S ACCOUNT EACH MONTH. THAT YOU ABANDONED YOUR DAUGHTER.
YOU WANT TO MAKE THINGS RIGHT, ZOE FINCH?
MAKE THE VIDEO.

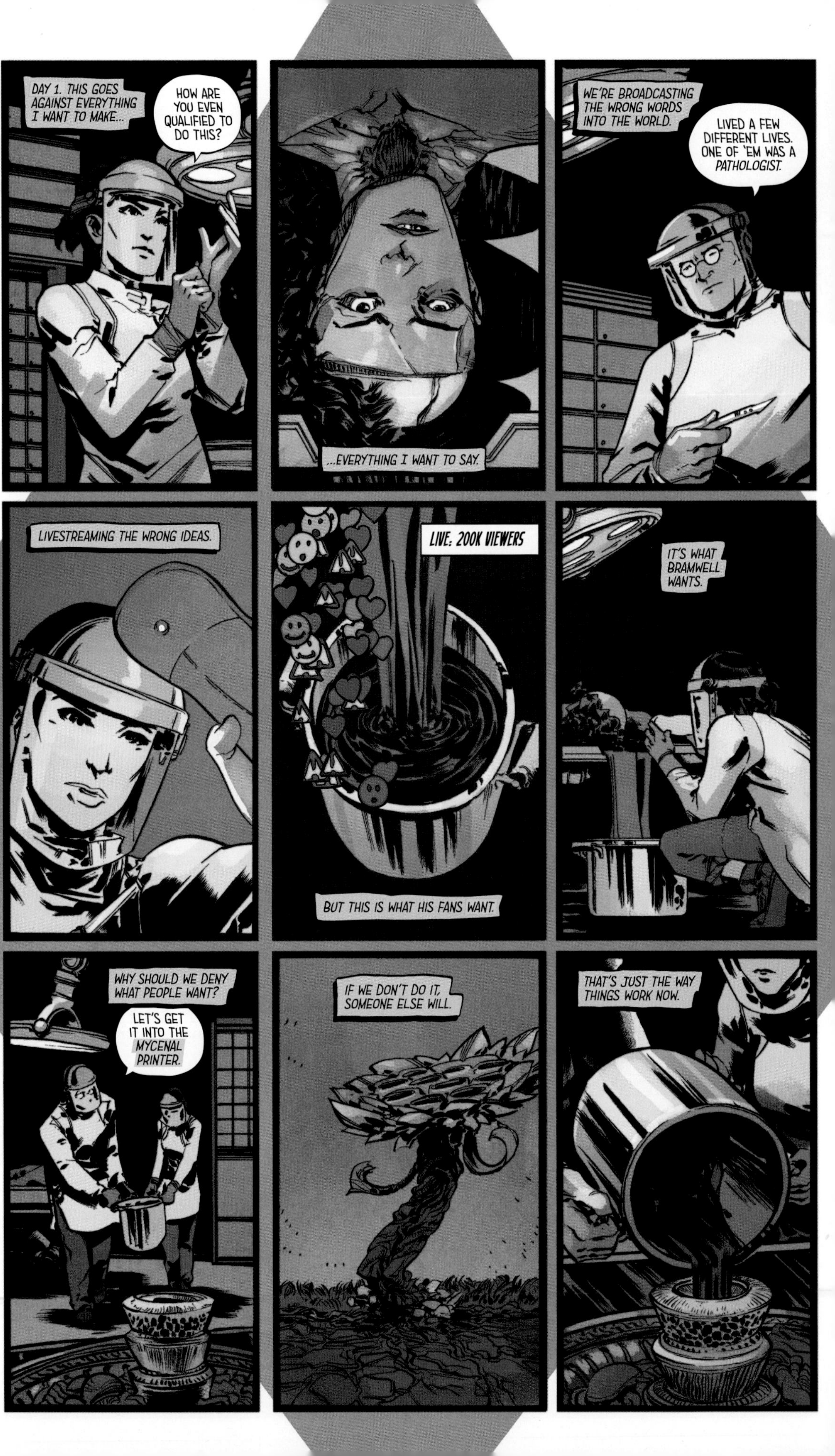
DAY 1. THIS GOES AGAINST EVERYTHING I WANT TO MAKE...
HOW ARE YOU EVEN QUALIFIED TO DO THIS?
...EVERYTHING I WANT TO SAY.
WE'RE BROADCASTING THE WRONG WORDS INTO THE WORLD.
LIVED A FEW DIFFERENT LIVES. ONE OF 'EM WAS A PATHOLOGIST.
LIVESTREAMING THE WRONG IDEAS.
LIVE: 200K VIEWERS
BUT THIS IS WHAT HIS FANS WANT.
IT'S WHAT BRAMWELL WANTS.
WHY SHOULD WE DENY WHAT PEOPLE WANT?
LET'S GET IT INTO THE MYCENAL PRINTER.
IF WE DON'T DO IT, SOMEONE ELSE WILL.
THAT'S JUST THE WAY THINGS WORK NOW.

DAY 2. SIXTEEN MILLION PEOPLE DOWNLOAD MYLO'S BLOOD.

I'M IN AWE. THEY KEEP TAKING IT, LIKE A STEADY DRIP FROM A LEAKY FAUCET.

USED TO THINK, PEOPLE WERE AFRAID OF CHANGE, OF BEING CHANGED, BUT WE ALL WANT TO BE SOMEONE ELSE.

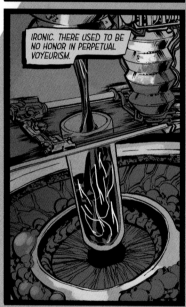

IRONIC. THERE USED TO BE NO HONOR IN PERPETUAL VOYEURISM.

BEFORE THE INTERNET, IT WAS TREASON AGAINST YOUR OWN KIND.

PRINTING COMPLETE.

NOW IT'S WARPED THE PRIVACY OF OUR LIVES. EVERYTHING AND NOTHING IS SACRED, SECRET.

WE PRACTICE OWNERSHIP OF ONE ANOTHER. ACTING LIKE WE DESERVE IT.

ONLY $119.99

BUT IT'S MADE MOST OF US LESS THAN HUMAN.

BUT NOT ME. I'M NO SYCOPHANT. I SEE THIS THEATER OF BULLSHIT FOR WHAT IT IS.

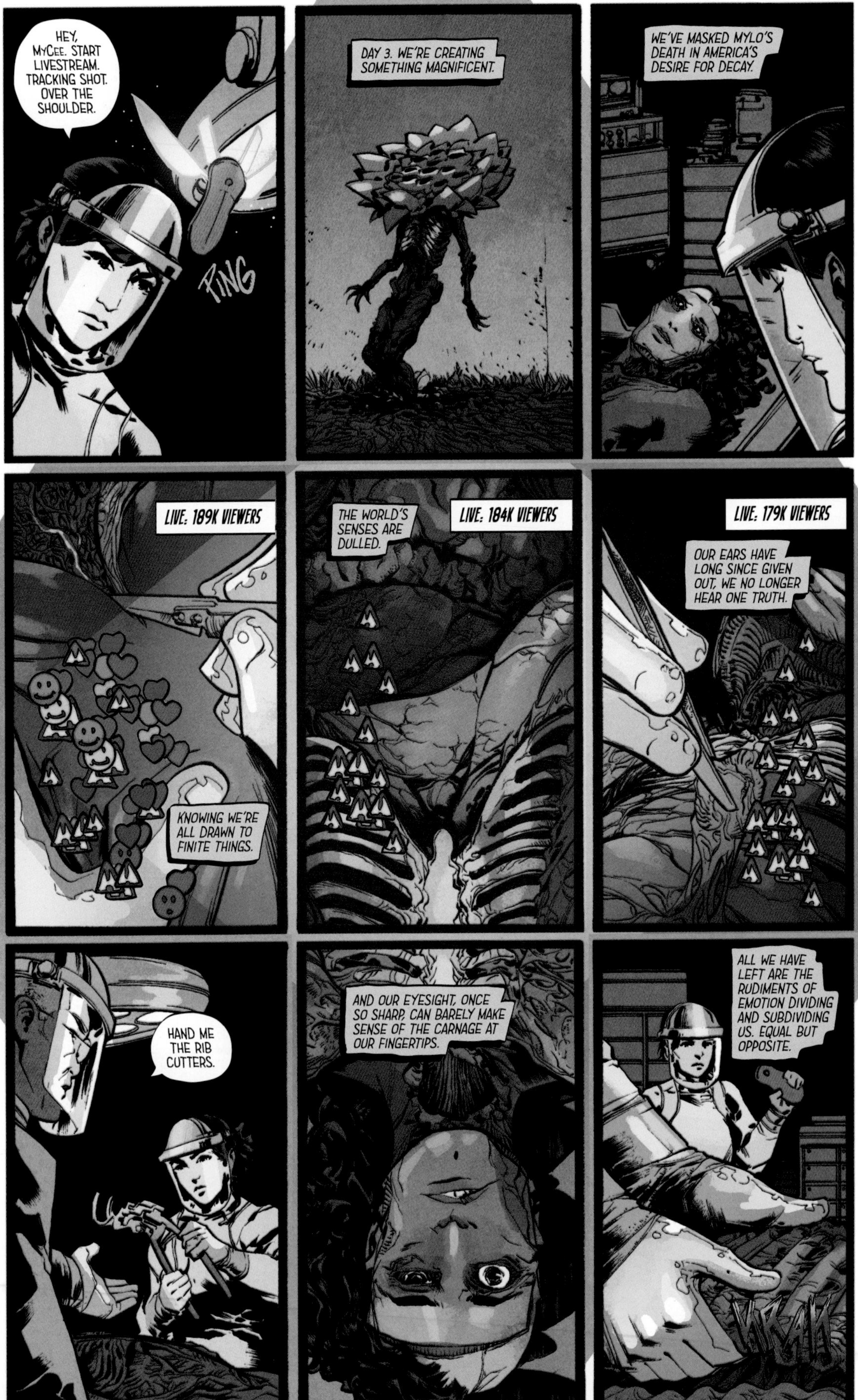
HEY, MyCee. START LIVESTREAM. TRACKING SHOT. OVER THE SHOULDER.
PING
DAY 3. WE'RE CREATING SOMETHING MAGNIFICENT.
WE'VE MASKED MYLO'S DEATH IN AMERICA'S DESIRE FOR DECAY.
LIVE: 189K VIEWERS
KNOWING WE'RE ALL DRAWN TO FINITE THINGS.
THE WORLD'S SENSES ARE DULLED.
LIVE: 184K VIEWERS
LIVE: 179K VIEWERS
OUR EARS HAVE LONG SINCE GIVEN OUT, WE NO LONGER HEAR ONE TRUTH.
HAND ME THE RIB CUTTERS.
AND OUR EYESIGHT, ONCE SO SHARP, CAN BARELY MAKE SENSE OF THE CARNAGE AT OUR FINGERTIPS.
ALL WE HAVE LEFT ARE THE RUDIMENTS OF EMOTION DIVIDING AND SUBDIVIDING US. EQUAL BUT OPPOSITE.

UNTIL IT'S IMPOSSIBLE TO TELL APART THE PIECES OF US THAT SPEAK FROM THE PIECES OF US THAT SHIT.

LIVE: 175K VIEWERS

LUNGS HAVE SUSTAINED AN INCREDIBLE AMOUNT OF DAMAGE FROM VAPING.

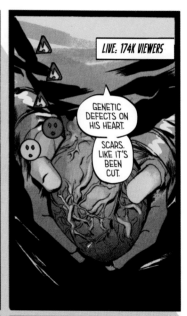

LIVE: 174K VIEWERS

GENETIC DEFECTS ON HIS HEART.

SCARS. LIKE IT'S BEEN CUT.

LIVE: 179K VIEWERS

STOMACH AND GASTROINTESTINAL SYSTEM ARE CLEAN.

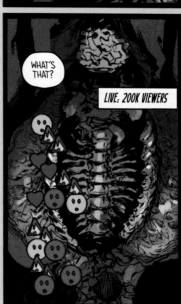

WHAT'S THAT?

LIVE: 200K VIEWERS

NOT SURE.

LIVE: 211K VIEWERS

END THE STREAM.

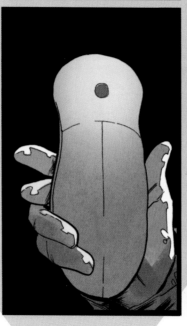

WE'VE GOT ENOUGH FOR HIS FANS. I'LL FINISH THIS IN THE MORNING. BY MYSELF.

THANKS. APPRECIATE IT. I NEED TIME TO PREPARE FOR THE SHAREHOLDER DINNER.

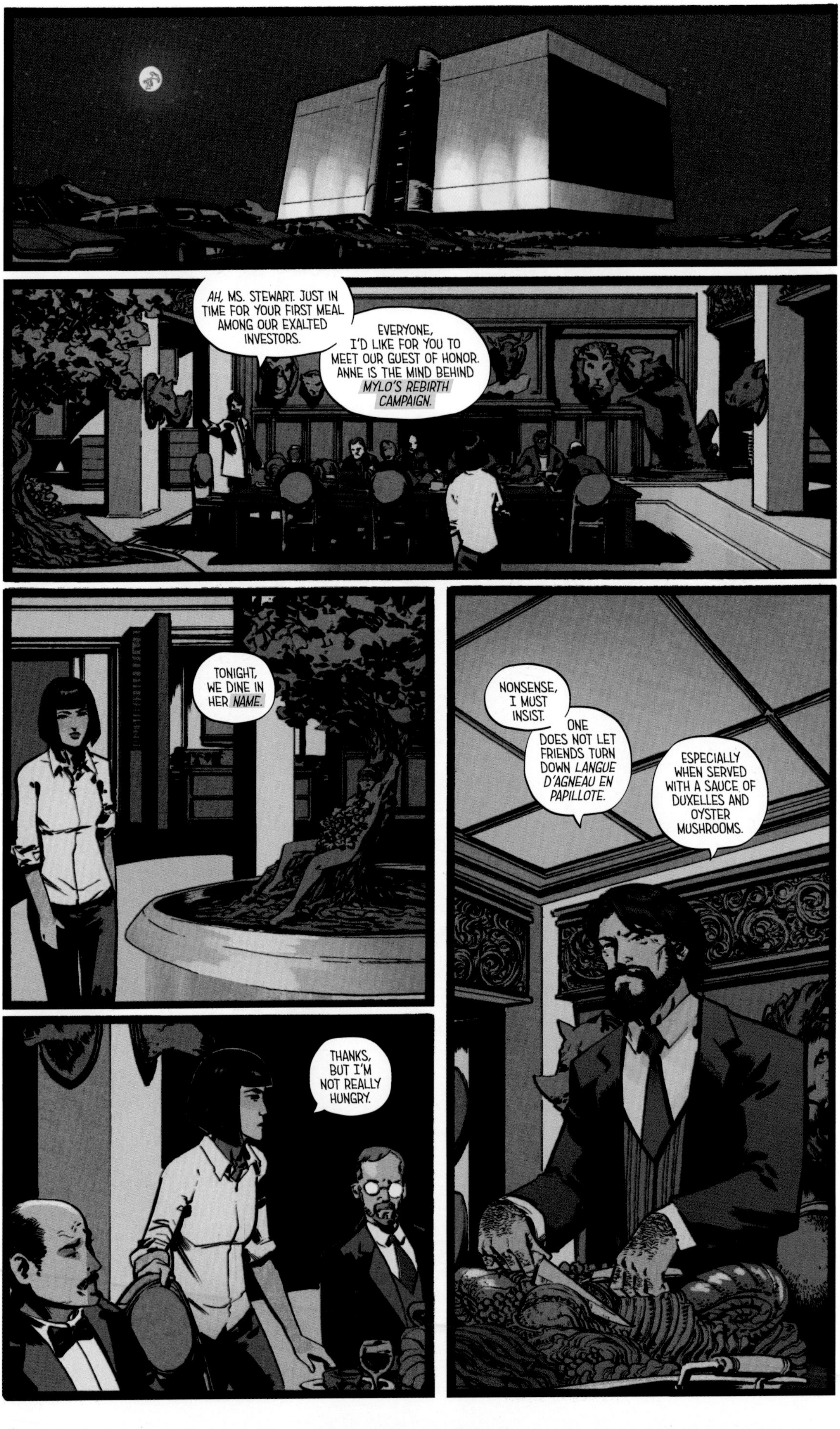
AH, MS. STEWART. JUST IN TIME FOR YOUR FIRST MEAL AMONG OUR EXALTED INVESTORS.
EVERYONE, I'D LIKE FOR YOU TO MEET OUR GUEST OF HONOR. ANNE IS THE MIND BEHIND *MYLO'S REBIRTH CAMPAIGN.*
TONIGHT, WE DINE IN HER *NAME.*
THANKS, BUT I'M NOT REALLY HUNGRY.
NONSENSE, I MUST INSIST.
ONE DOES NOT LET FRIENDS TURN DOWN *LANGUE D'AGNEAU EN PAPILLOTE.*
ESPECIALLY WHEN SERVED WITH A SAUCE OF DUXELLES AND OYSTER MUSHROOMS.

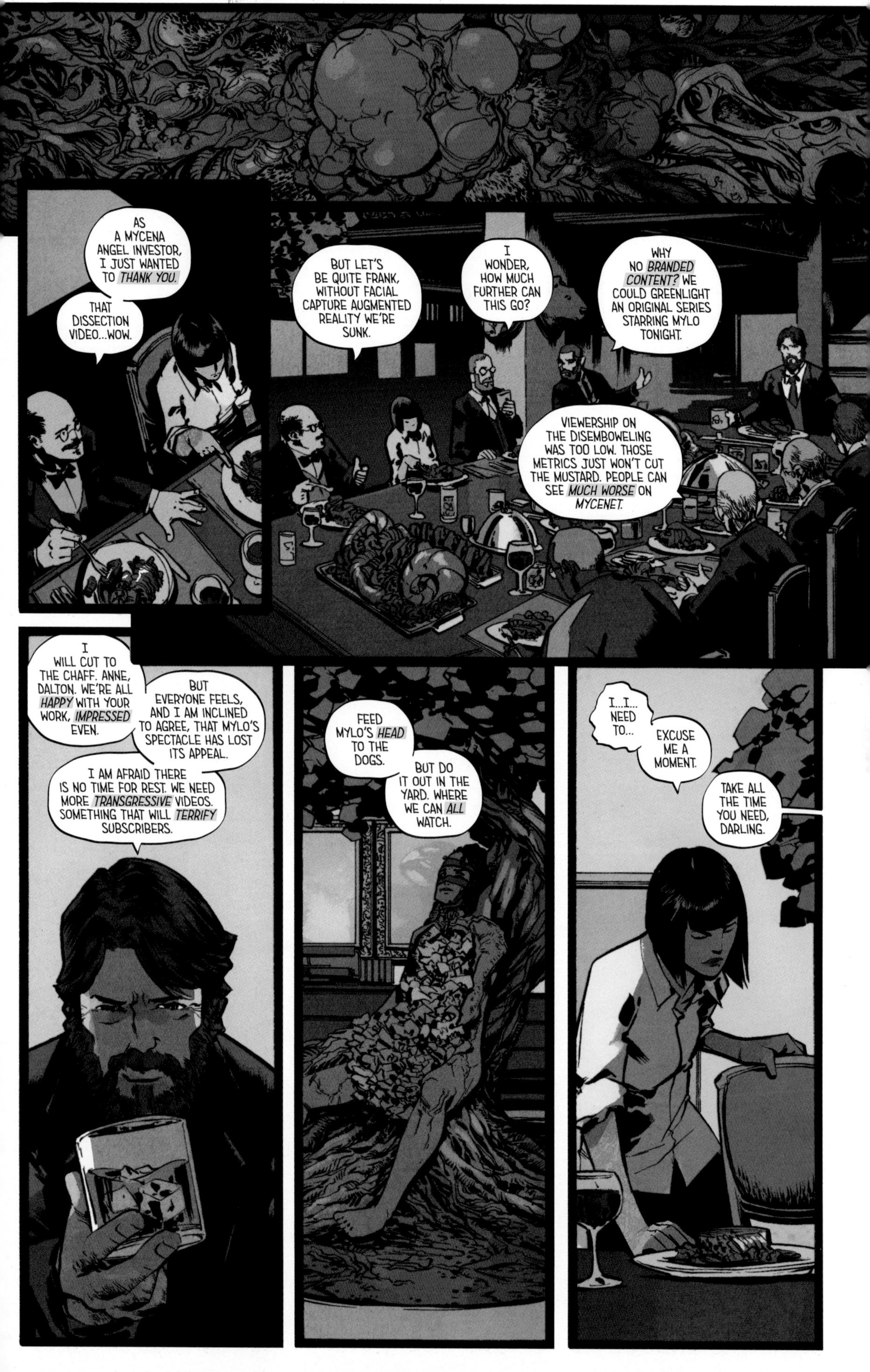
AS A MYCENA ANGEL INVESTOR, I JUST WANTED TO THANK YOU.
THAT DISSECTION VIDEO...WOW.
BUT LET'S BE QUITE FRANK, WITHOUT FACIAL CAPTURE AUGMENTED REALITY WE'RE SUNK.
I WONDER, HOW MUCH FURTHER CAN THIS GO?
WHY NO BRANDED CONTENT? WE COULD GREENLIGHT AN ORIGINAL SERIES STARRING MYLO TONIGHT.
VIEWERSHIP ON THE DISEMBOWELING WAS TOO LOW. THOSE METRICS JUST WON'T CUT THE MUSTARD. PEOPLE CAN SEE MUCH WORSE ON MYCENET.
I WILL CUT TO THE CHAFF. ANNE, DALTON. WE'RE ALL HAPPY WITH YOUR WORK, IMPRESSED EVEN.
BUT EVERYONE FEELS, AND I AM INCLINED TO AGREE, THAT MYLO'S SPECTACLE HAS LOST ITS APPEAL.
I AM AFRAID THERE IS NO TIME FOR REST. WE NEED MORE TRANSGRESSIVE VIDEOS. SOMETHING THAT WILL TERRIFY SUBSCRIBERS.
FEED MYLO'S HEAD TO THE DOGS.
BUT DO IT OUT IN THE YARD. WHERE WE CAN ALL WATCH.
I...I... NEED TO...
EXCUSE ME A MOMENT.
TAKE ALL THE TIME YOU NEED, DARLING.

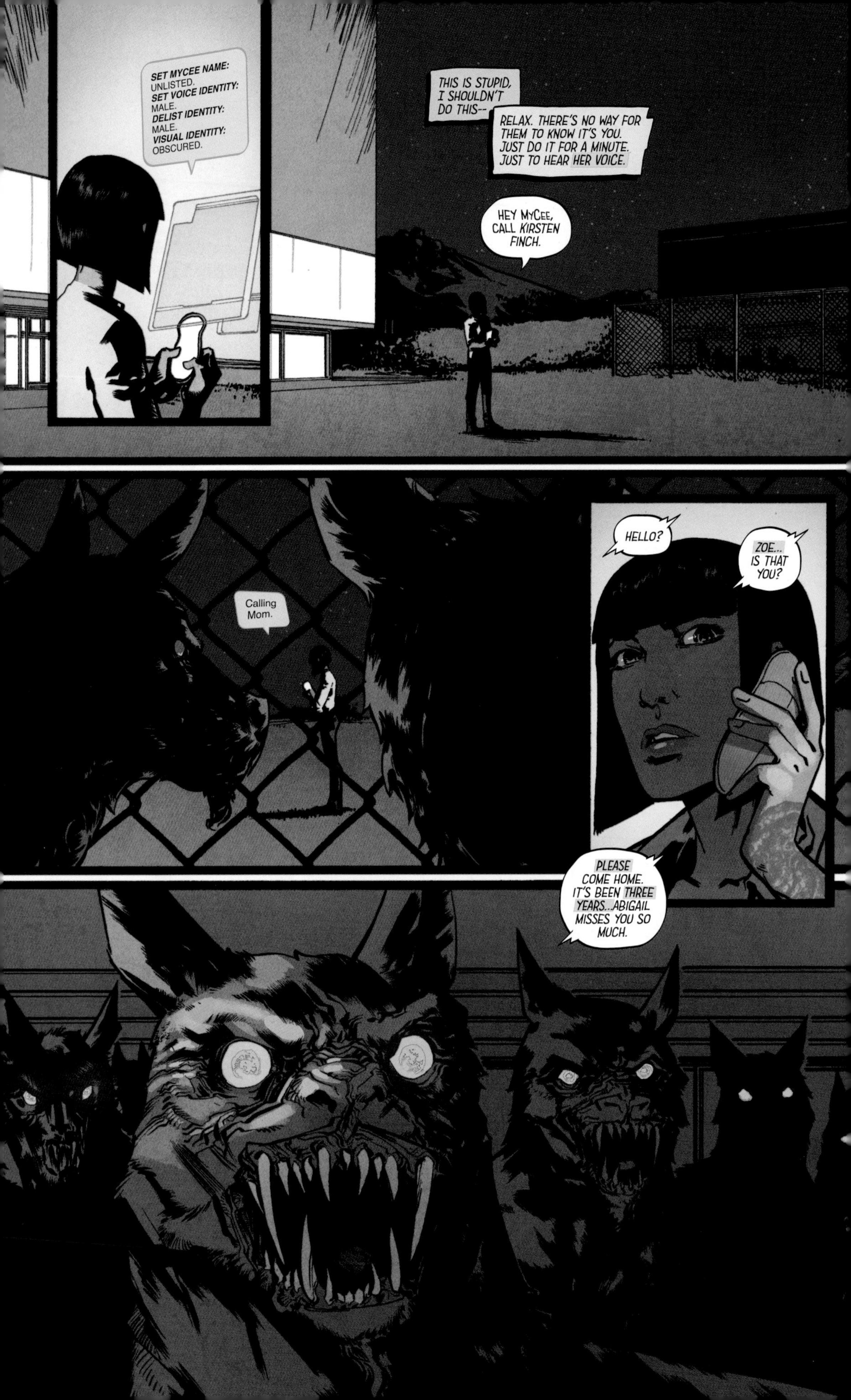
SET MYCEE NAME: UNLISTED. SET VOICE IDENTITY: MALE. DELIST IDENTITY: MALE. VISUAL IDENTITY: OBSCURED.
THIS IS STUPID, I SHOULDN'T DO THIS--
RELAX. THERE'S NO WAY FOR THEM TO KNOW IT'S YOU. JUST DO IT FOR A MINUTE. JUST TO HEAR HER VOICE.
HEY MyCee, CALL KIRSTEN FINCH.
Calling Mom.
HELLO?
ZOE... IS THAT YOU?
PLEASE COME HOME. IT'S BEEN THREE YEARS...ABIGAIL MISSES YOU SO MUCH.

3

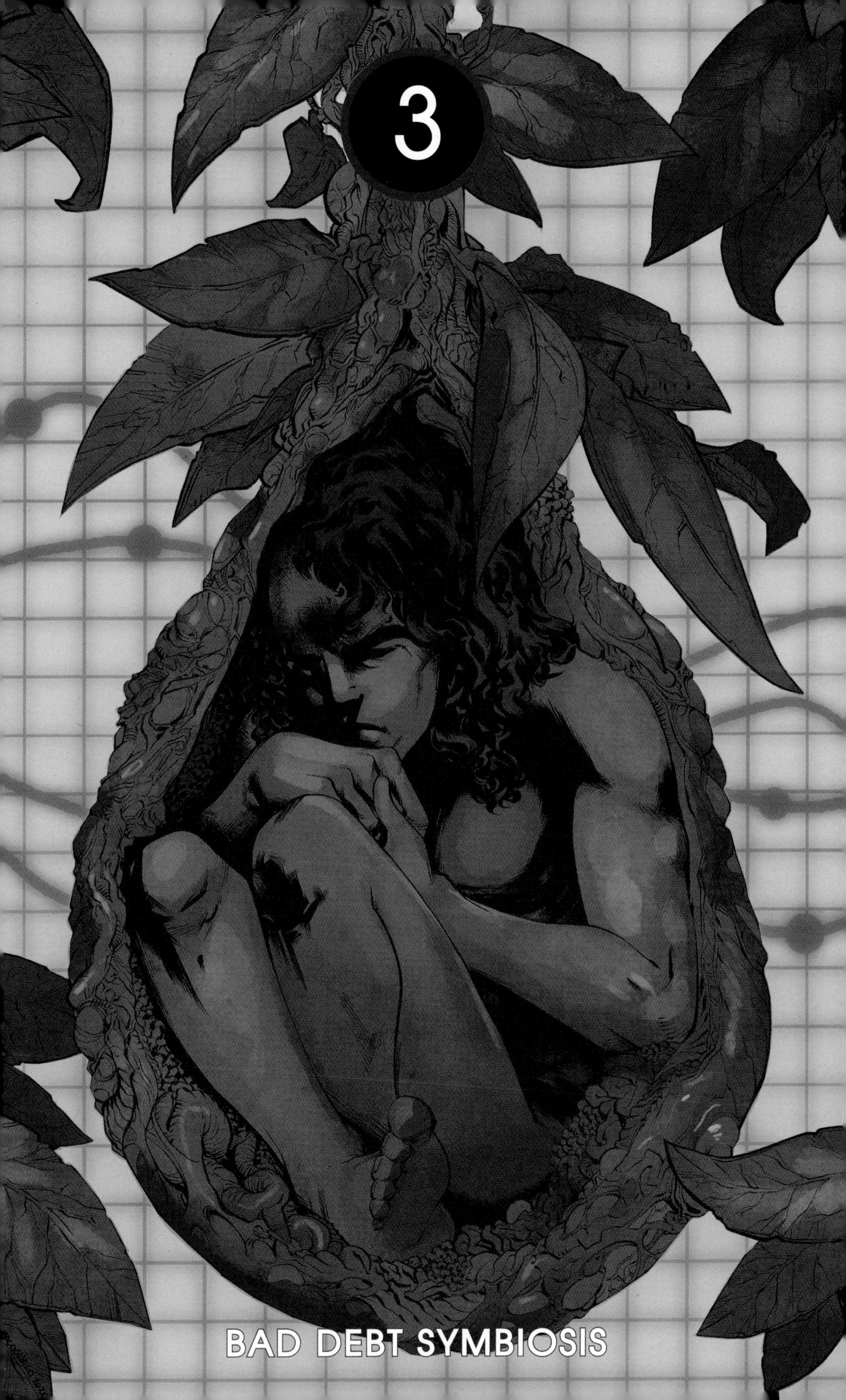

BAD DEBT SYMBIOSIS

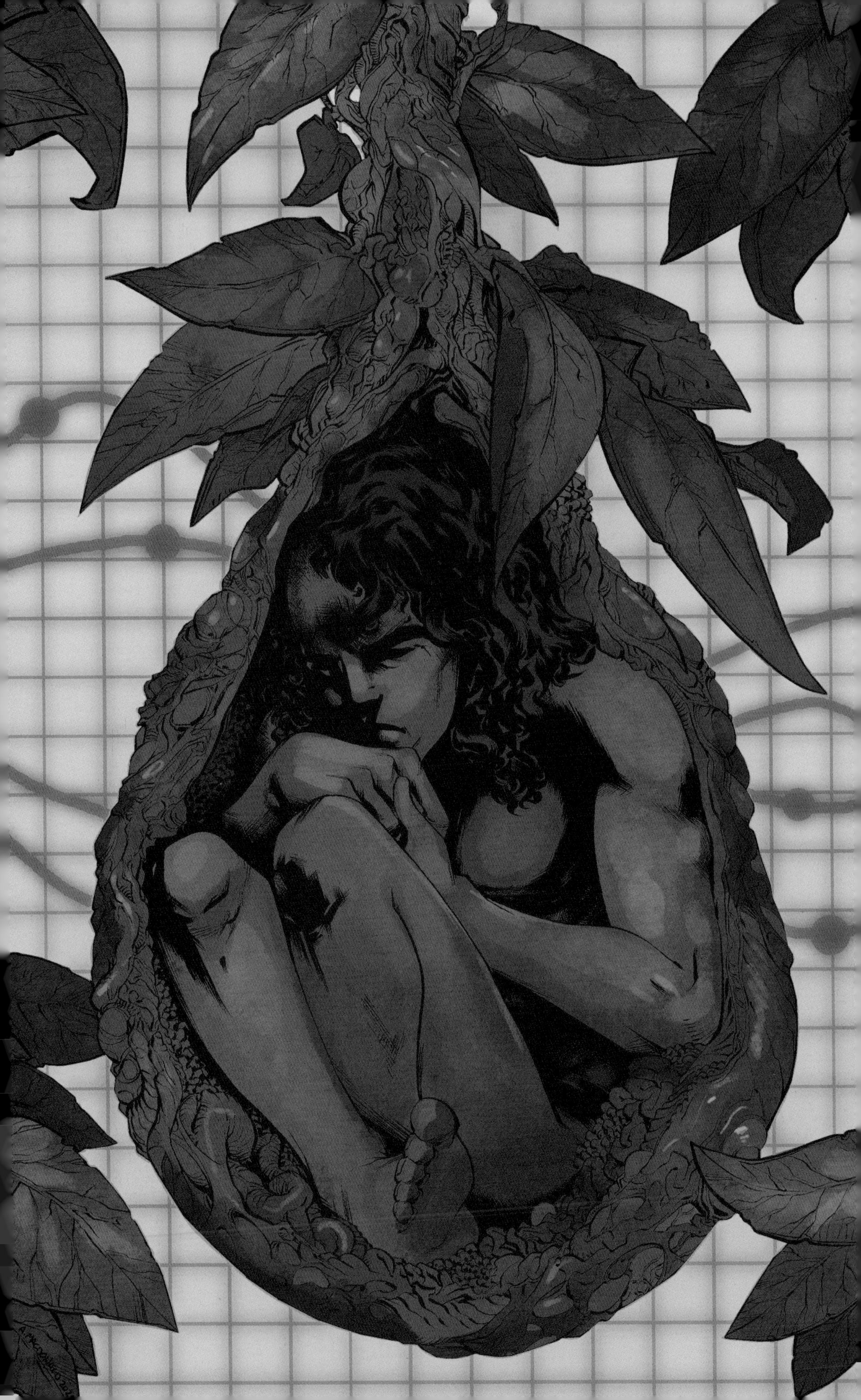

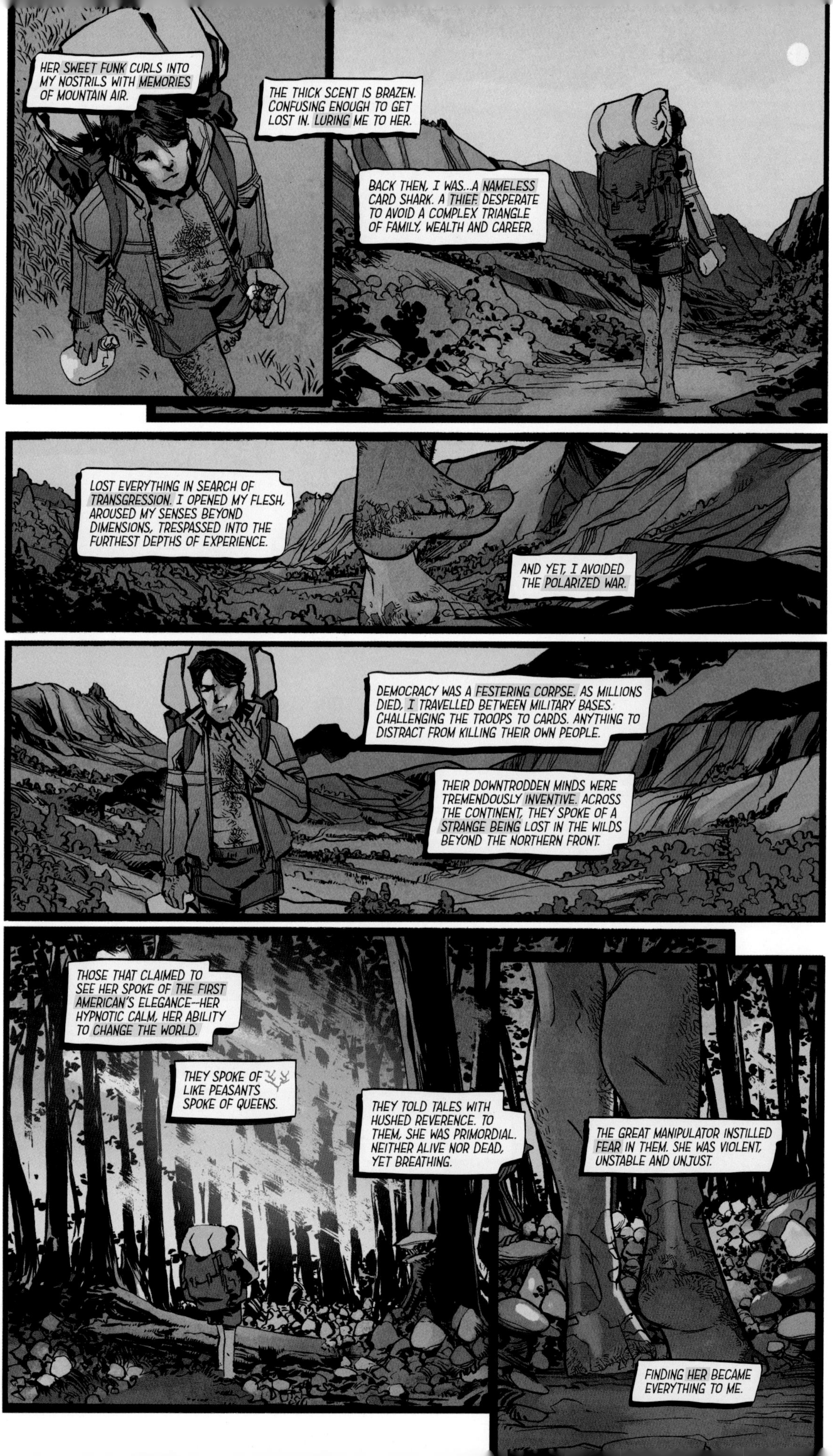
HER SWEET FUNK CURLS INTO MY NOSTRILS WITH MEMORIES OF MOUNTAIN AIR.
THE THICK SCENT IS BRAZEN. CONFUSING ENOUGH TO GET LOST IN. LURING ME TO HER.
BACK THEN, I WAS...A NAMELESS CARD SHARK. A THIEF. DESPERATE TO AVOID A COMPLEX TRIANGLE OF FAMILY, WEALTH AND CAREER.
LOST EVERYTHING IN SEARCH OF TRANSGRESSION. I OPENED MY FLESH, AROUSED MY SENSES BEYOND DIMENSIONS, TRESPASSED INTO THE FURTHEST DEPTHS OF EXPERIENCE.
AND YET, I AVOIDED THE POLARIZED WAR.
DEMOCRACY WAS A FESTERING CORPSE. AS MILLIONS DIED, I TRAVELLED BETWEEN MILITARY BASES. CHALLENGING THE TROOPS TO CARDS. ANYTHING TO DISTRACT FROM KILLING THEIR OWN PEOPLE.
THEIR DOWNTRODDEN MINDS WERE TREMENDOUSLY INVENTIVE. ACROSS THE CONTINENT, THEY SPOKE OF A STRANGE BEING LOST IN THE WILDS BEYOND THE NORTHERN FRONT.
THOSE THAT CLAIMED TO SEE HER SPOKE OF THE FIRST AMERICAN'S ELEGANCE--HER HYPNOTIC CALM, HER ABILITY TO CHANGE THE WORLD.
THEY SPOKE OF LIKE PEASANTS SPOKE OF QUEENS.
THEY TOLD TALES WITH HUSHED REVERENCE. TO THEM, SHE WAS PRIMORDIAL. NEITHER ALIVE NOR DEAD, YET BREATHING.
THE GREAT MANIPULATOR INSTILLED FEAR IN THEM. SHE WAS VIOLENT, UNSTABLE AND UNJUST.
FINDING HER BECAME EVERYTHING TO ME.

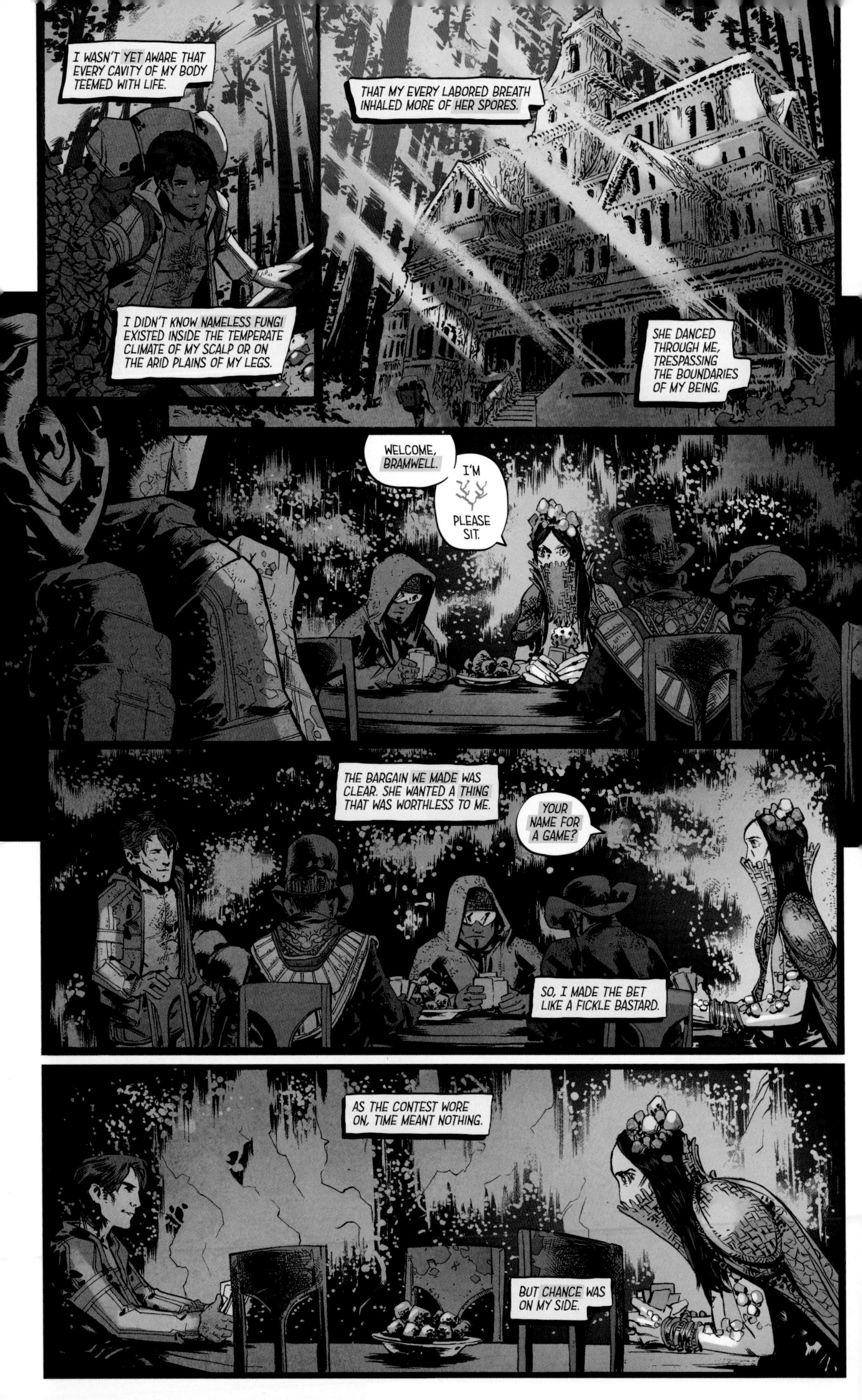
I WASN'T YET AWARE THAT EVERY CAVITY OF MY BODY TEEMED WITH LIFE.
I DIDN'T KNOW NAMELESS FUNGI EXISTED INSIDE THE TEMPERATE CLIMATE OF MY SCALP OR ON THE ARID PLAINS OF MY LEGS.
THAT MY EVERY LABORED BREATH INHALED MORE OF HER SPORES.
SHE DANCED THROUGH ME, TRESPASSING THE BOUNDARIES OF MY BEING.
WELCOME, BRAMWELL.
I'M
PLEASE SIT.
THE BARGAIN WE MADE WAS CLEAR. SHE WANTED A THING THAT WAS WORTHLESS TO ME.
YOUR NAME FOR A GAME?
SO, I MADE THE BET LIKE A FICKLE BASTARD.
AS THE CONTEST WORE ON, TIME MEANT NOTHING.
BUT CHANCE WAS ON MY SIDE.

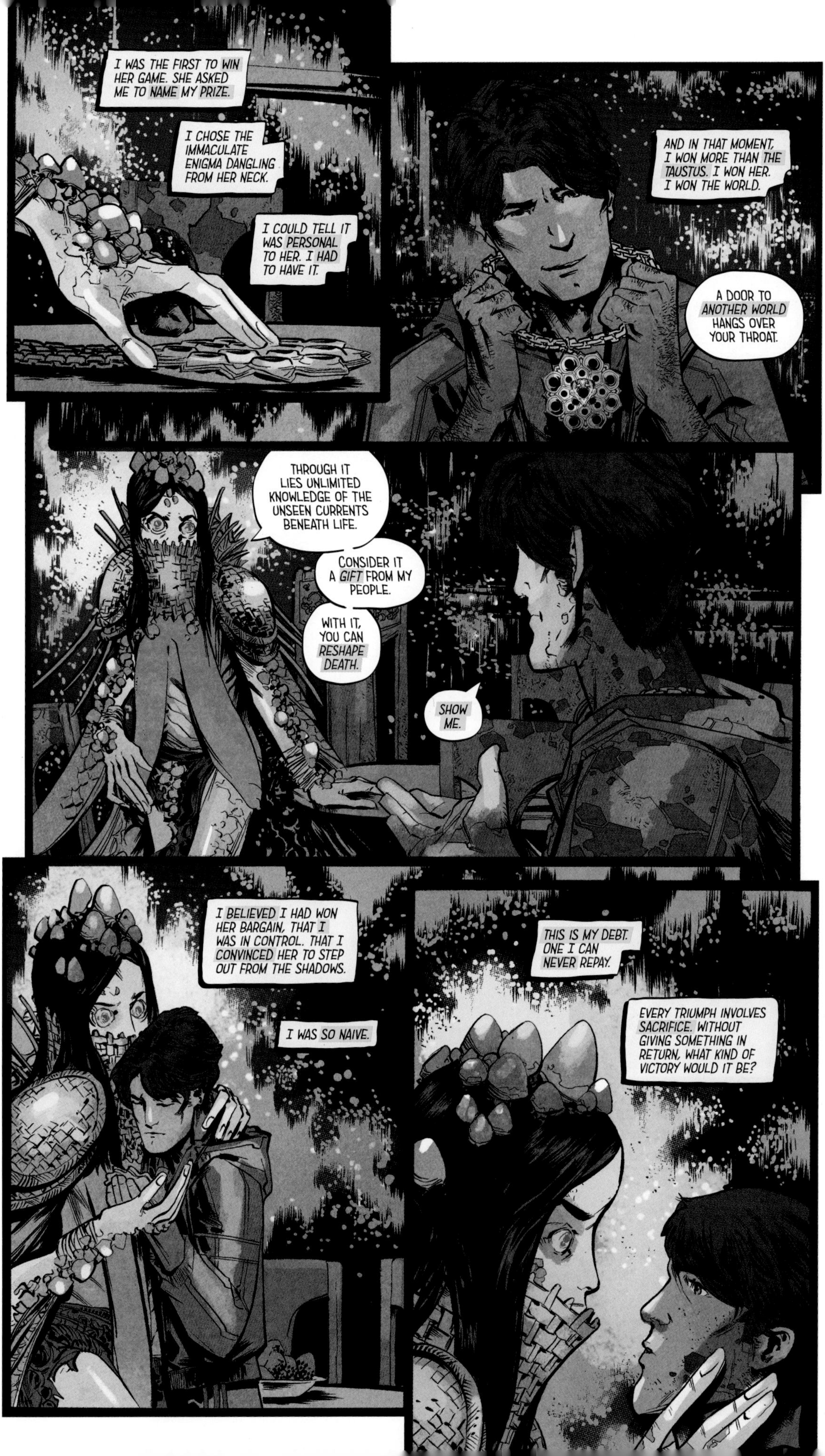
I WAS THE FIRST TO WIN HER GAME. SHE ASKED ME TO NAME MY PRIZE.
I CHOSE THE IMMACULATE ENIGMA DANGLING FROM HER NECK.
I COULD TELL IT WAS PERSONAL TO HER. I HAD TO HAVE IT.
AND IN THAT MOMENT, I WON MORE THAN THE TAUSTUS. I WON HER. I WON THE WORLD.
A DOOR TO ANOTHER WORLD HANGS OVER YOUR THROAT.
THROUGH IT LIES UNLIMITED KNOWLEDGE OF THE UNSEEN CURRENTS BENEATH LIFE.
CONSIDER IT A GIFT FROM MY PEOPLE.
WITH IT, YOU CAN RESHAPE DEATH.
SHOW ME.
I BELIEVED I HAD WON HER BARGAIN, THAT I WAS IN CONTROL. THAT I CONVINCED HER TO STEP OUT FROM THE SHADOWS.
I WAS SO NAIVE.
THIS IS MY DEBT. ONE I CAN NEVER REPAY.
EVERY TRIUMPH INVOLVES SACRIFICE. WITHOUT GIVING SOMETHING IN RETURN, WHAT KIND OF VICTORY WOULD IT BE?

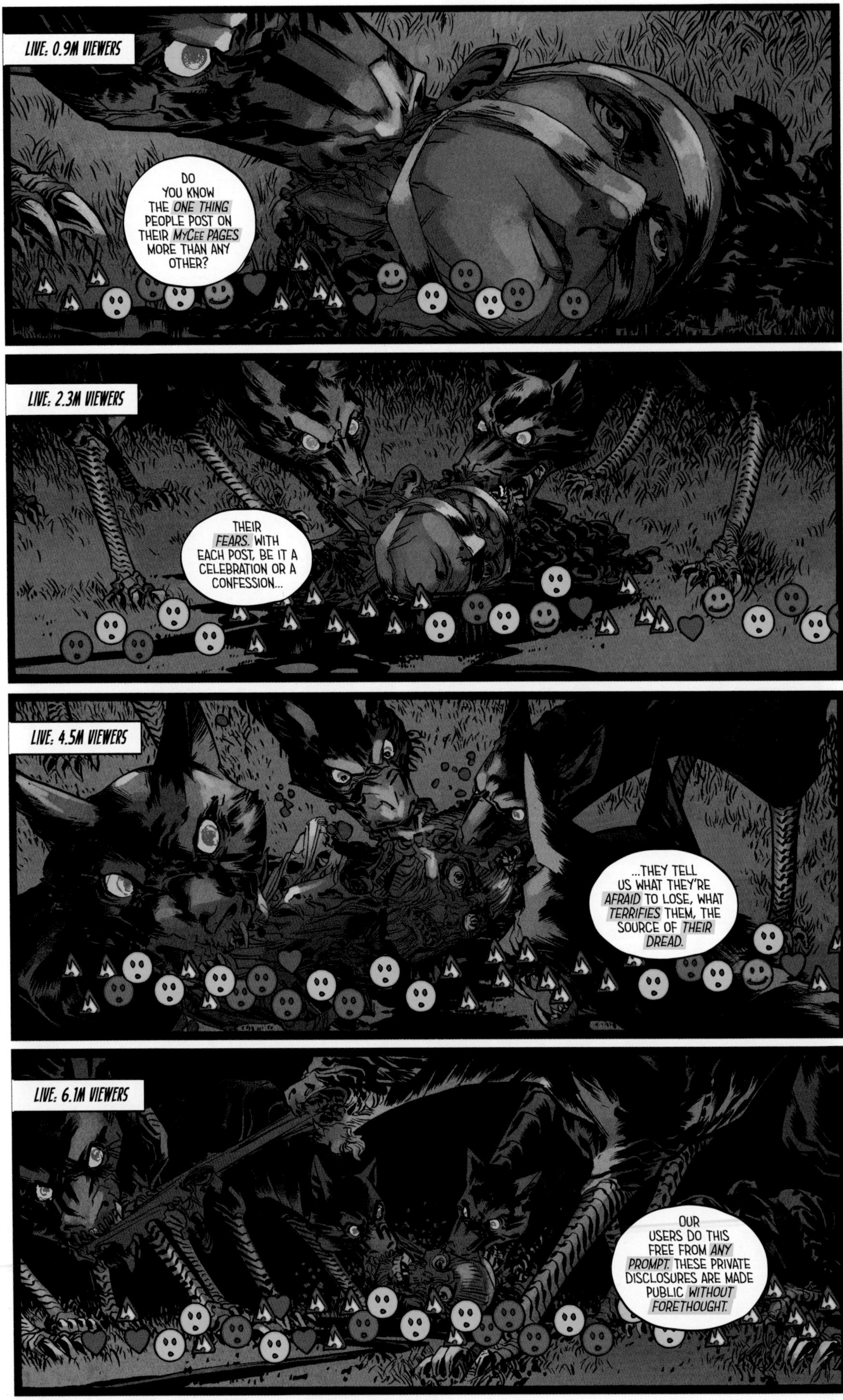

LIVE: 0.9M VIEWERS
DO YOU KNOW THE ONE THING PEOPLE POST ON THEIR MYCEE PAGES MORE THAN ANY OTHER?
LIVE: 2.3M VIEWERS
THEIR FEARS. WITH EACH POST, BE IT A CELEBRATION OR A CONFESSION...
LIVE: 4.5M VIEWERS
...THEY TELL US WHAT THEY'RE AFRAID TO LOSE, WHAT TERRIFIES THEM, THE SOURCE OF THEIR DREAD.
LIVE: 6.1M VIEWERS
OUR USERS DO THIS FREE FROM ANY PROMPT. THESE PRIVATE DISCLOSURES ARE MADE PUBLIC WITHOUT FORETHOUGHT.

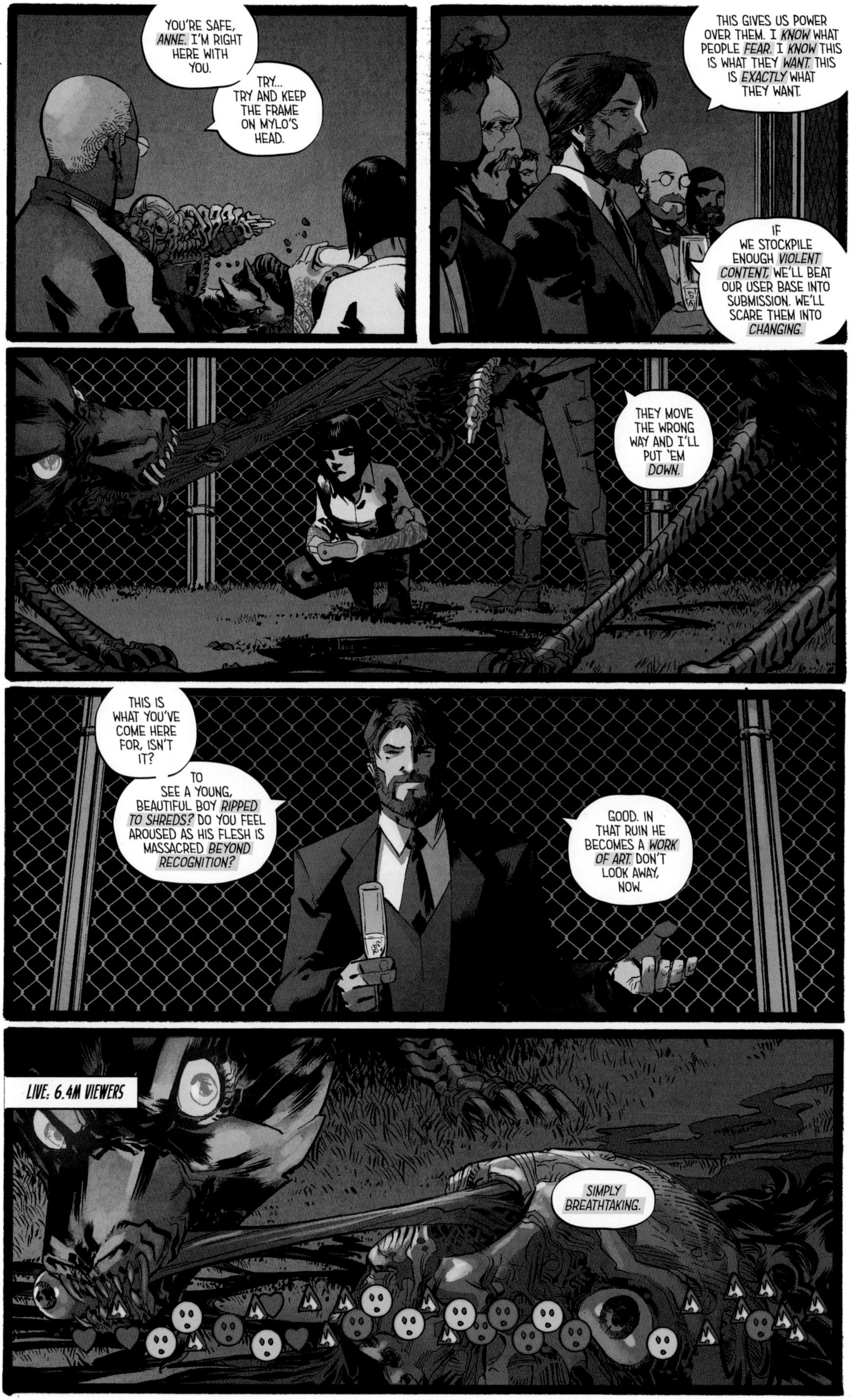
YOU'RE SAFE, ANNE. I'M RIGHT HERE WITH YOU.
TRY... TRY AND KEEP THE FRAME ON MYLO'S HEAD.
THIS GIVES US POWER OVER THEM. I KNOW WHAT PEOPLE FEAR. I KNOW THIS IS WHAT THEY WANT. THIS IS EXACTLY WHAT THEY WANT.
IF WE STOCKPILE ENOUGH VIOLENT CONTENT, WE'LL BEAT OUR USER BASE INTO SUBMISSION. WE'LL SCARE THEM INTO CHANGING.
THEY MOVE THE WRONG WAY AND I'LL PUT 'EM DOWN.
THIS IS WHAT YOU'VE COME HERE FOR, ISN'T IT?
TO SEE A YOUNG, BEAUTIFUL BOY RIPPED TO SHREDS? DO YOU FEEL AROUSED AS HIS FLESH IS MASSACRED BEYOND RECOGNITION?
GOOD. IN THAT RUIN HE BECOMES A WORK OF ART. DON'T LOOK AWAY, NOW.
LIVE: 6.4M VIEWERS
SIMPLY BREATHTAKING.

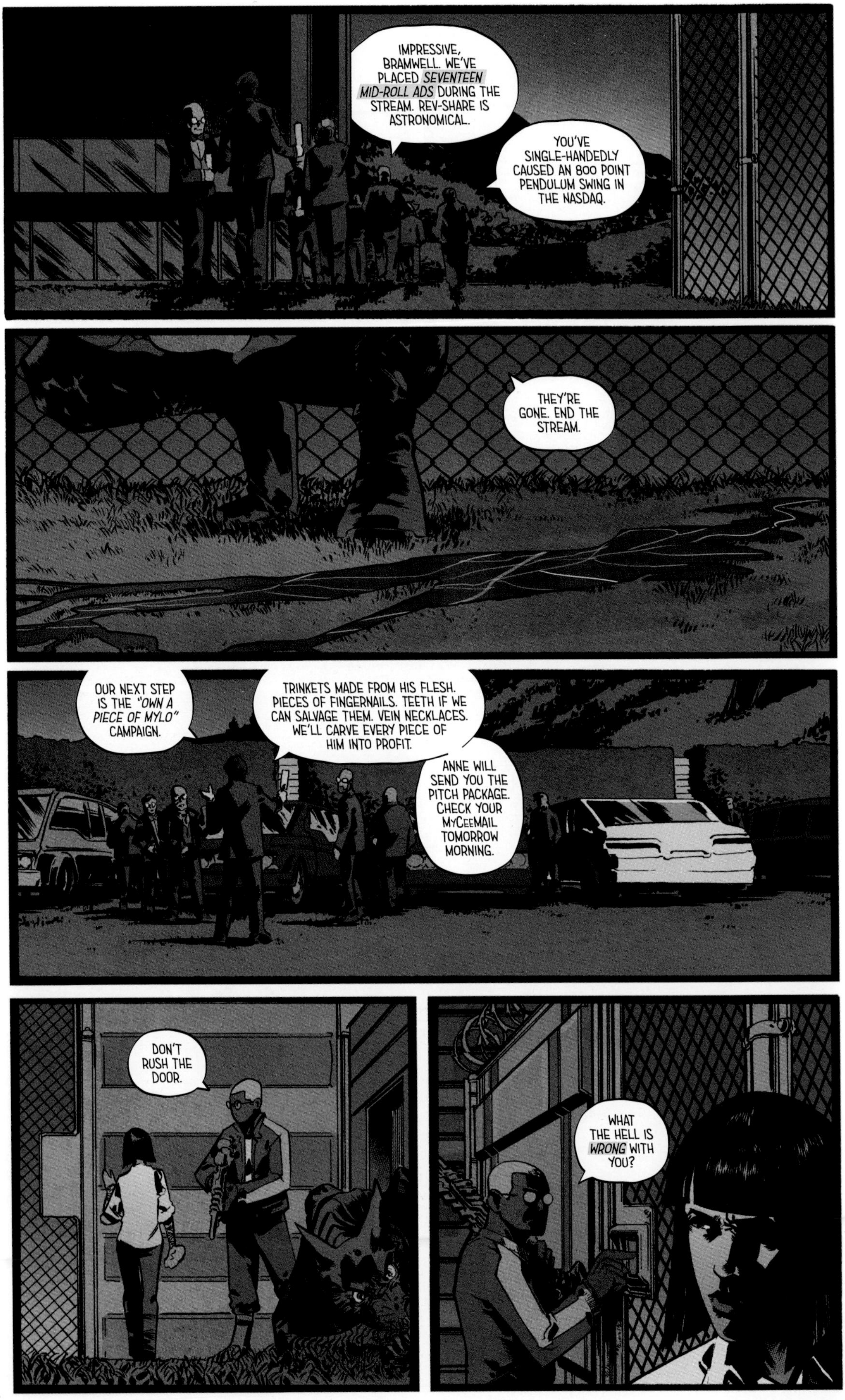
IMPRESSIVE, BRAMWELL. WE'VE PLACED SEVENTEEN MID-ROLL ADS DURING THE STREAM. REV-SHARE IS ASTRONOMICAL.
YOU'VE SINGLE-HANDEDLY CAUSED AN 800 POINT PENDULUM SWING IN THE NASDAQ.
THEY'RE GONE. END THE STREAM.
OUR NEXT STEP IS THE "OWN A PIECE OF MYLO" CAMPAIGN.
TRINKETS MADE FROM HIS FLESH. PIECES OF FINGERNAILS. TEETH IF WE CAN SALVAGE THEM. VEIN NECKLACES. WE'LL CARVE EVERY PIECE OF HIM INTO PROFIT.
ANNE WILL SEND YOU THE PITCH PACKAGE. CHECK YOUR MYCEEMAIL TOMORROW MORNING.
DON'T RUSH THE DOOR.
WHAT THE HELL IS WRONG WITH YOU?

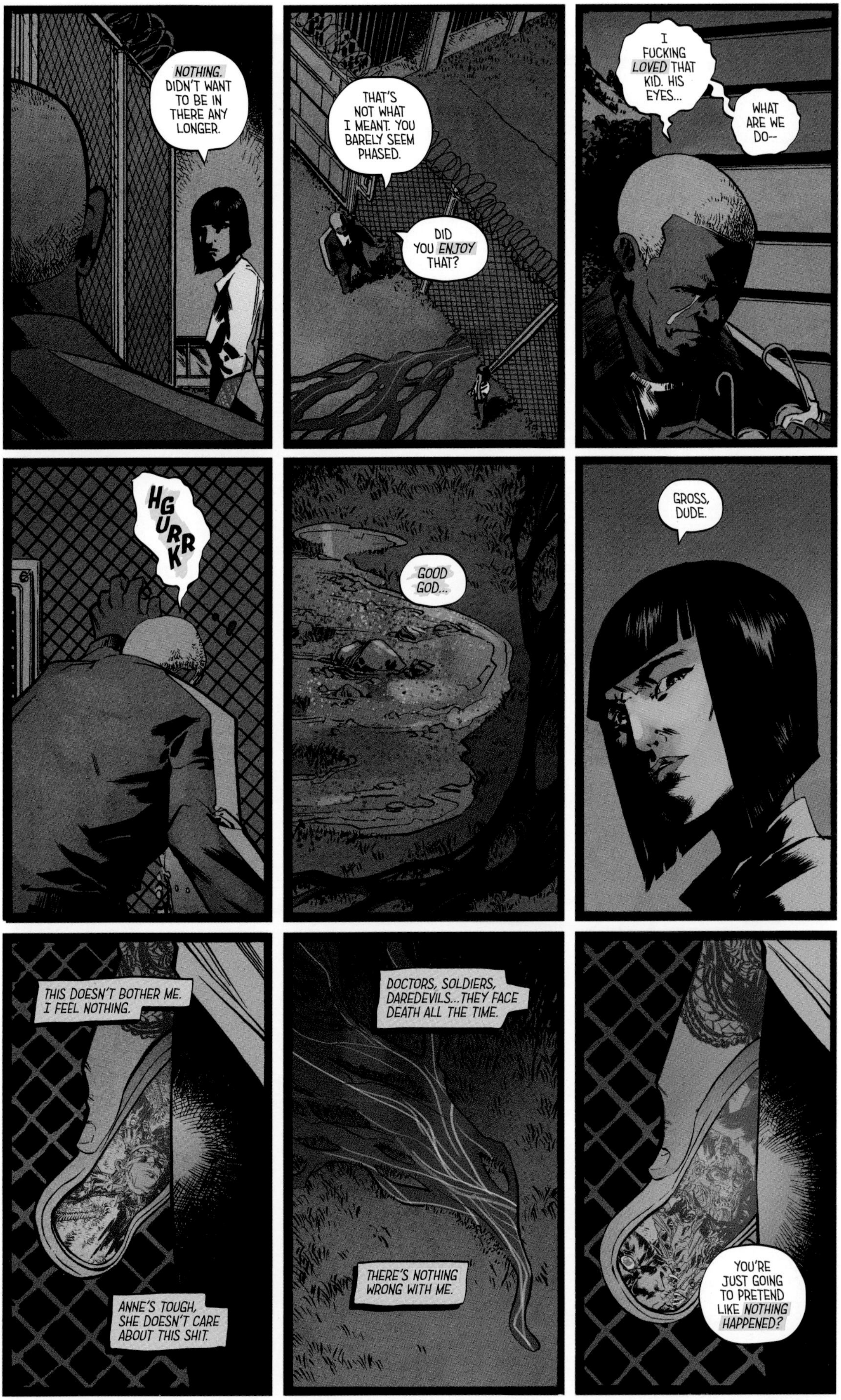
NOTHING. DIDN'T WANT TO BE IN THERE ANY LONGER.
THAT'S NOT WHAT I MEANT. YOU BARELY SEEM PHASED.
DID YOU ENJOY THAT?
I FUCKING LOVED THAT KID. HIS EYES...
WHAT ARE WE DO--
HGURRK
GOOD GOD...
GROSS, DUDE.
THIS DOESN'T BOTHER ME. I FEEL NOTHING.
ANNE'S TOUGH, SHE DOESN'T CARE ABOUT THIS SHIT.
DOCTORS, SOLDIERS, DAREDEVILS...THEY FACE DEATH ALL THE TIME.
THERE'S NOTHING WRONG WITH ME.
YOU'RE JUST GOING TO PRETEND LIKE NOTHING HAPPENED?

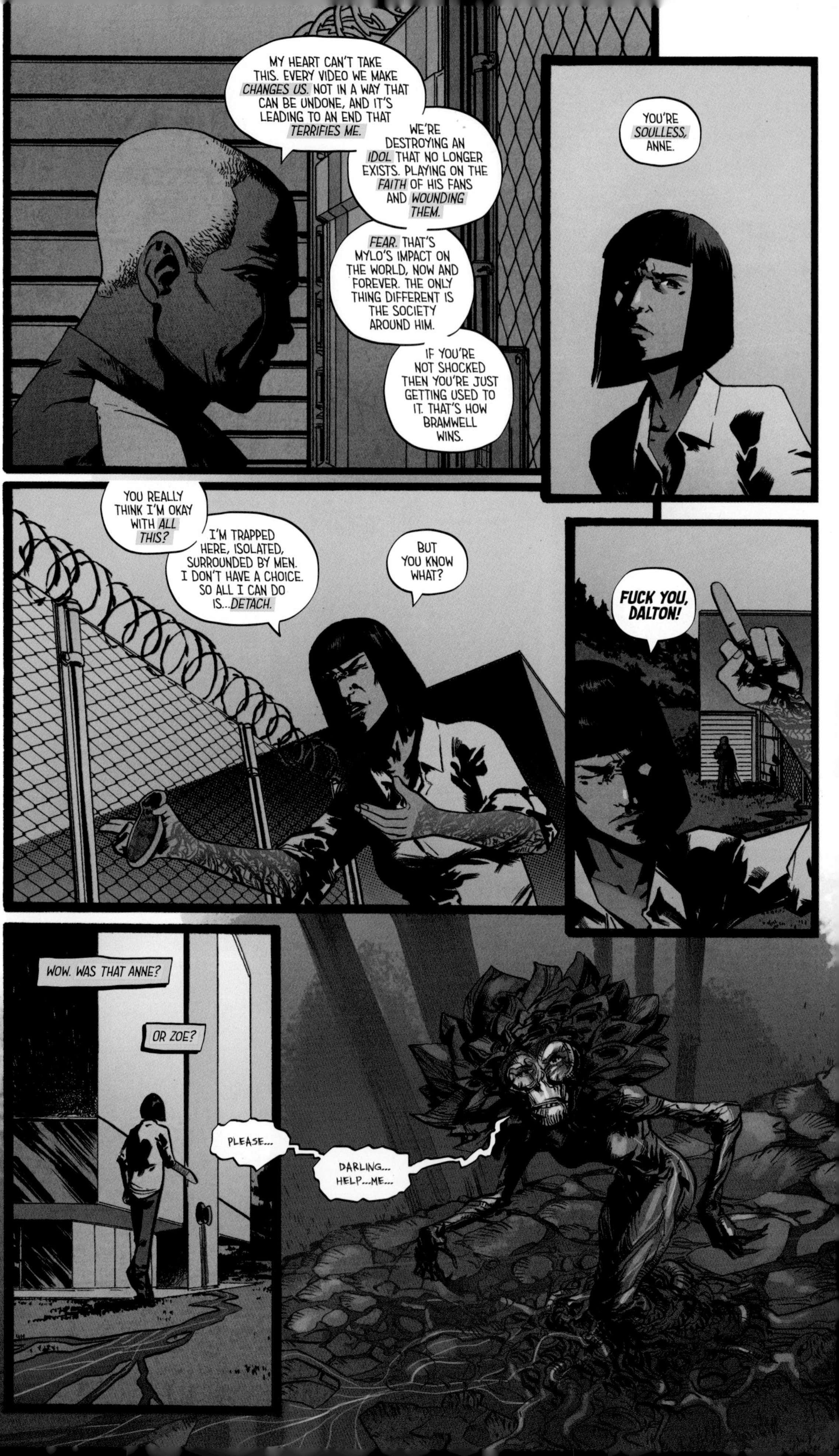

MY HEART CAN'T TAKE THIS. EVERY VIDEO WE MAKE CHANGES US. NOT IN A WAY THAT CAN BE UNDONE, AND IT'S LEADING TO AN END THAT TERRIFIES ME.
WE'RE DESTROYING AN IDOL THAT NO LONGER EXISTS. PLAYING ON THE FAITH OF HIS FANS AND WOUNDING THEM.
FEAR. THAT'S MYLO'S IMPACT ON THE WORLD, NOW AND FOREVER. THE ONLY THING DIFFERENT IS THE SOCIETY AROUND HIM.
IF YOU'RE NOT SHOCKED THEN YOU'RE JUST GETTING USED TO IT. THAT'S HOW BRAMWELL WINS.
YOU'RE SOULLESS, ANNE.
YOU REALLY THINK I'M OKAY WITH ALL THIS?
I'M TRAPPED HERE, ISOLATED, SURROUNDED BY MEN. I DON'T HAVE A CHOICE. SO ALL I CAN DO IS...DETACH.
BUT YOU KNOW WHAT?
FUCK YOU, DALTON!
WOW. WAS THAT ANNE?
OR ZOE?
PLEASE...
DARLING... HELP...ME...

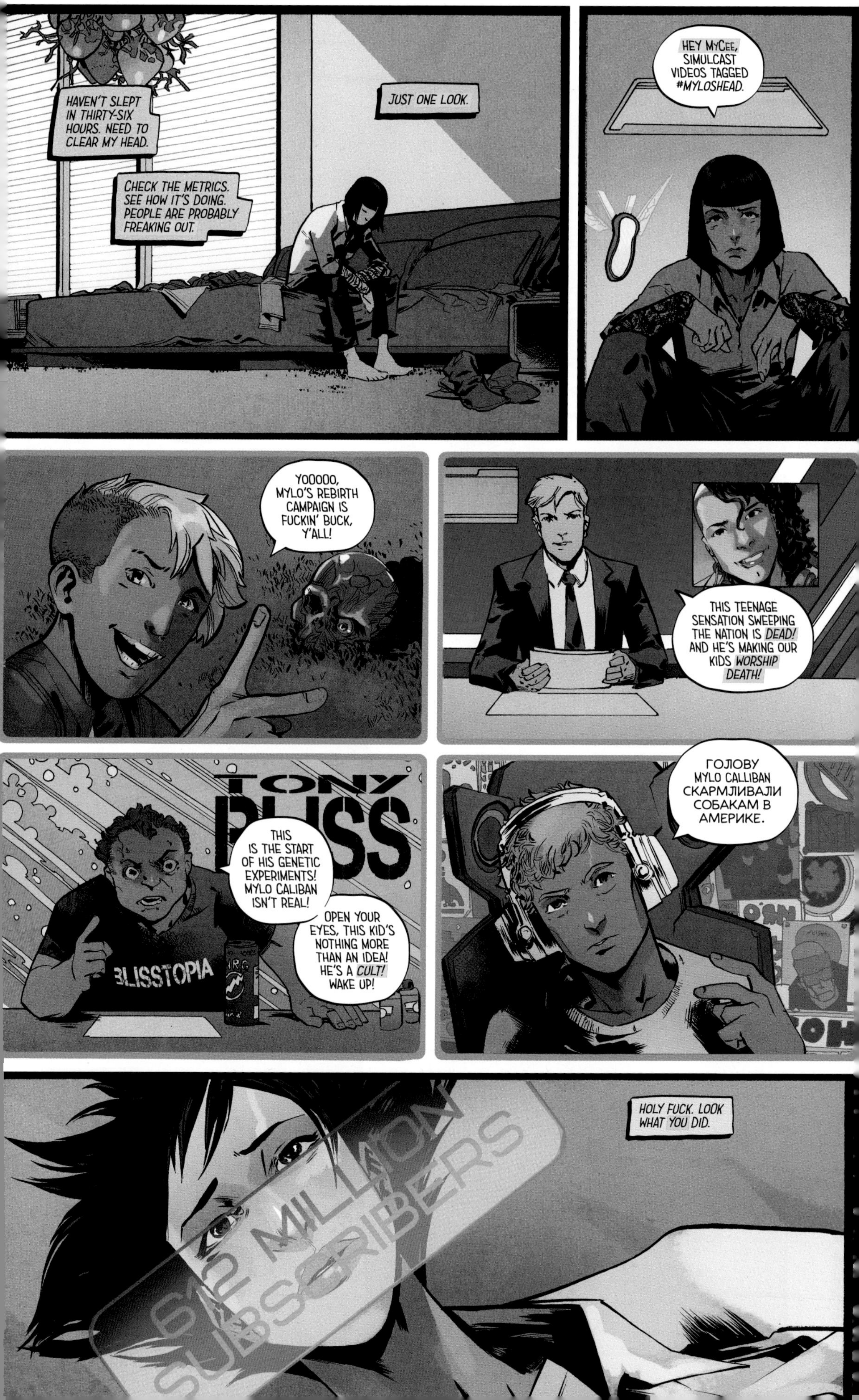
HAVEN'T SLEPT IN THIRTY-SIX HOURS. NEED TO CLEAR MY HEAD.
CHECK THE METRICS. SEE HOW IT'S DOING. PEOPLE ARE PROBABLY FREAKING OUT.
JUST ONE LOOK.
HEY MyCEE, SIMULCAST VIDEOS TAGGED #MYLOSHEAD.
YOOOOO, MYLO'S REBIRTH CAMPAIGN IS FUCKIN' BUCK, Y'ALL!
THIS TEENAGE SENSATION SWEEPING THE NATION IS DEAD! AND HE'S MAKING OUR KIDS WORSHIP DEATH!
TONY RUSS
BLISSTOPIA
THIS IS THE START OF HIS GENETIC EXPERIMENTS! MYLO CALIBAN ISN'T REAL!
OPEN YOUR EYES, THIS KID'S NOTHING MORE THAN AN IDEA! HE'S A CULT! WAKE UP!
ГОЛОВУ MYLO CALLIBAN СКАРМЛИВАЛИ СОБАКАМ В АМЕРИКЕ.
HOLY FUCK. LOOK WHAT YOU DID.
6.12 MILLION SUBSCRIBERS

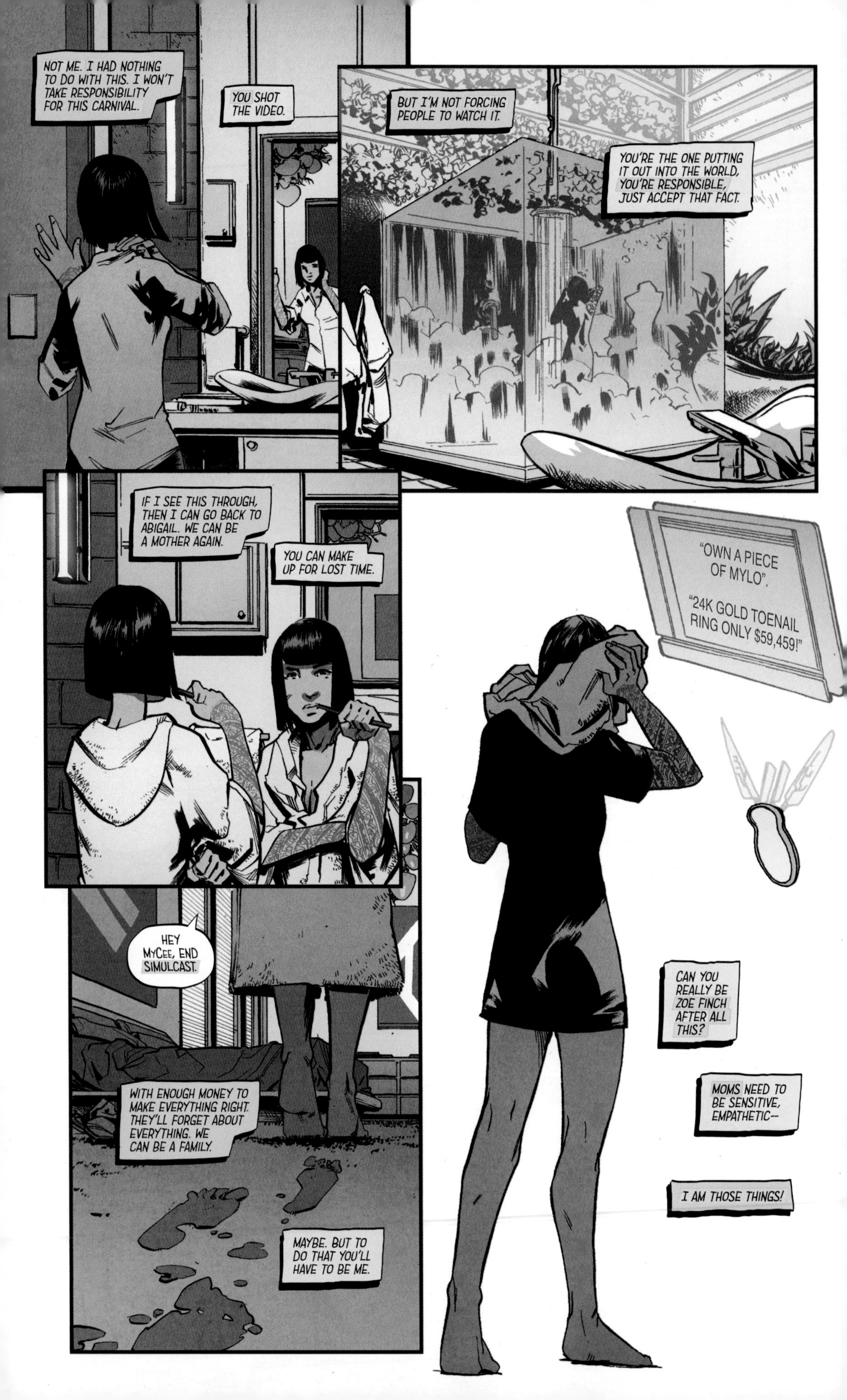
NOT ME. I HAD NOTHING TO DO WITH THIS. I WON'T TAKE RESPONSIBILITY FOR THIS CARNIVAL.
YOU SHOT THE VIDEO.
BUT I'M NOT FORCING PEOPLE TO WATCH IT.
YOU'RE THE ONE PUTTING IT OUT INTO THE WORLD, YOU'RE RESPONSIBLE, JUST ACCEPT THAT FACT.
IF I SEE THIS THROUGH, THEN I CAN GO BACK TO ABIGAIL. WE CAN BE A MOTHER AGAIN.
YOU CAN MAKE UP FOR LOST TIME.
"OWN A PIECE OF MYLO".
"24K GOLD TOENAIL RING ONLY $59,459!"
HEY MyCee, END SIMULCAST.
WITH ENOUGH MONEY TO MAKE EVERYTHING RIGHT. THEY'LL FORGET ABOUT EVERYTHING. WE CAN BE A FAMILY.
MAYBE. BUT TO DO THAT YOU'LL HAVE TO BE ME.
CAN YOU REALLY BE ZOE FINCH AFTER ALL THIS?
MOMS NEED TO BE SENSITIVE, EMPATHETIC--
I AM THOSE THINGS!

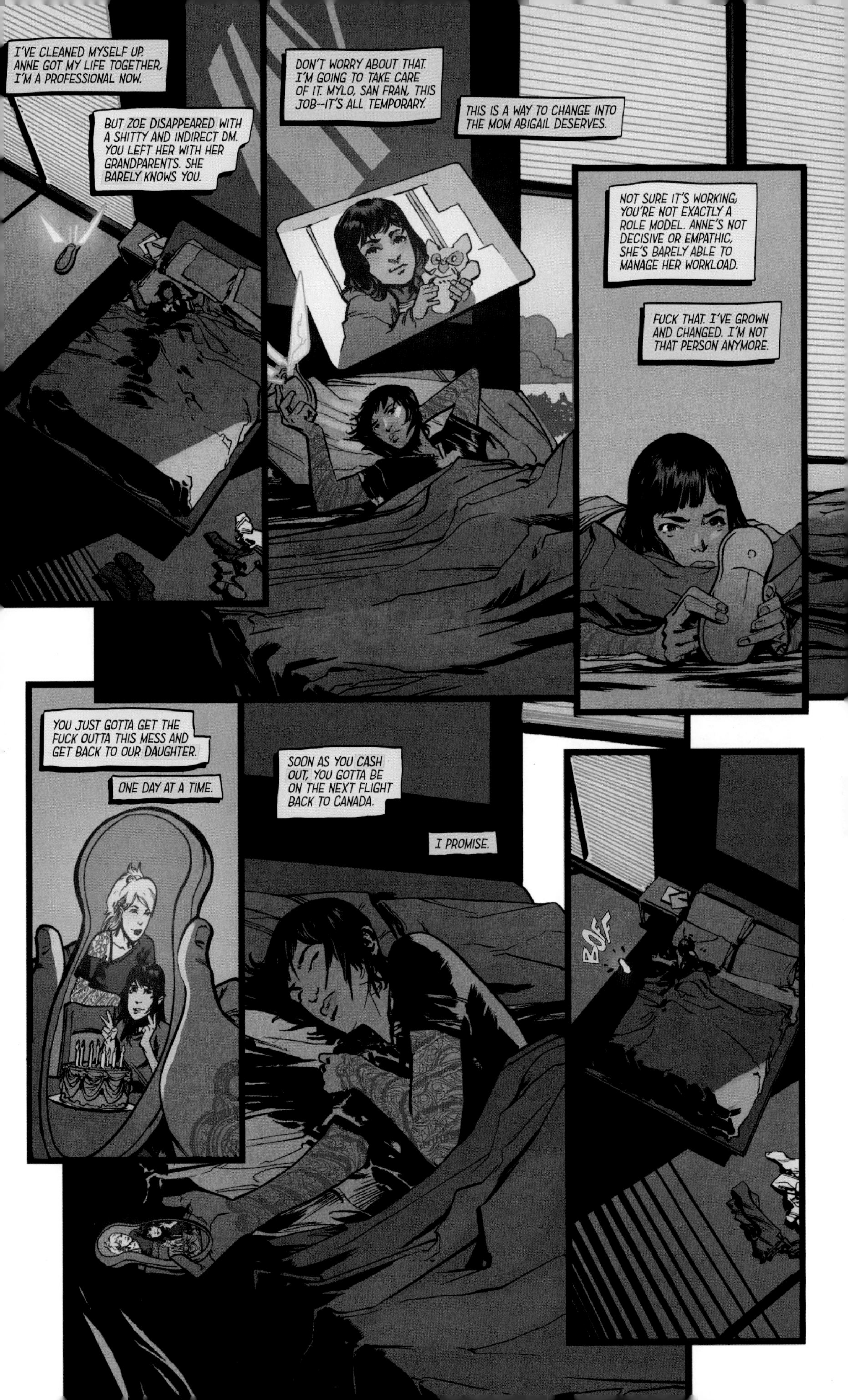
I'VE CLEANED MYSELF UP. ANNE GOT MY LIFE TOGETHER. I'M A PROFESSIONAL NOW.
BUT ZOE DISAPPEARED WITH A SHITTY AND INDIRECT DM. YOU LEFT HER WITH HER GRANDPARENTS. SHE BARELY KNOWS YOU.
DON'T WORRY ABOUT THAT. I'M GOING TO TAKE CARE OF IT. MYLO, SAN FRAN, THIS JOB--IT'S ALL TEMPORARY.
THIS IS A WAY TO CHANGE INTO THE MOM ABIGAIL DESERVES.
NOT SURE IT'S WORKING; YOU'RE NOT EXACTLY A ROLE MODEL. ANNE'S NOT DECISIVE OR EMPATHIC, SHE'S BARELY ABLE TO MANAGE HER WORKLOAD.
FUCK THAT. I'VE GROWN AND CHANGED. I'M NOT THAT PERSON ANYMORE.
YOU JUST GOTTA GET THE FUCK OUTTA THIS MESS AND GET BACK TO OUR DAUGHTER.
ONE DAY AT A TIME.
SOON AS YOU CASH OUT, YOU GOTTA BE ON THE NEXT FLIGHT BACK TO CANADA.
I PROMISE.
BOFF

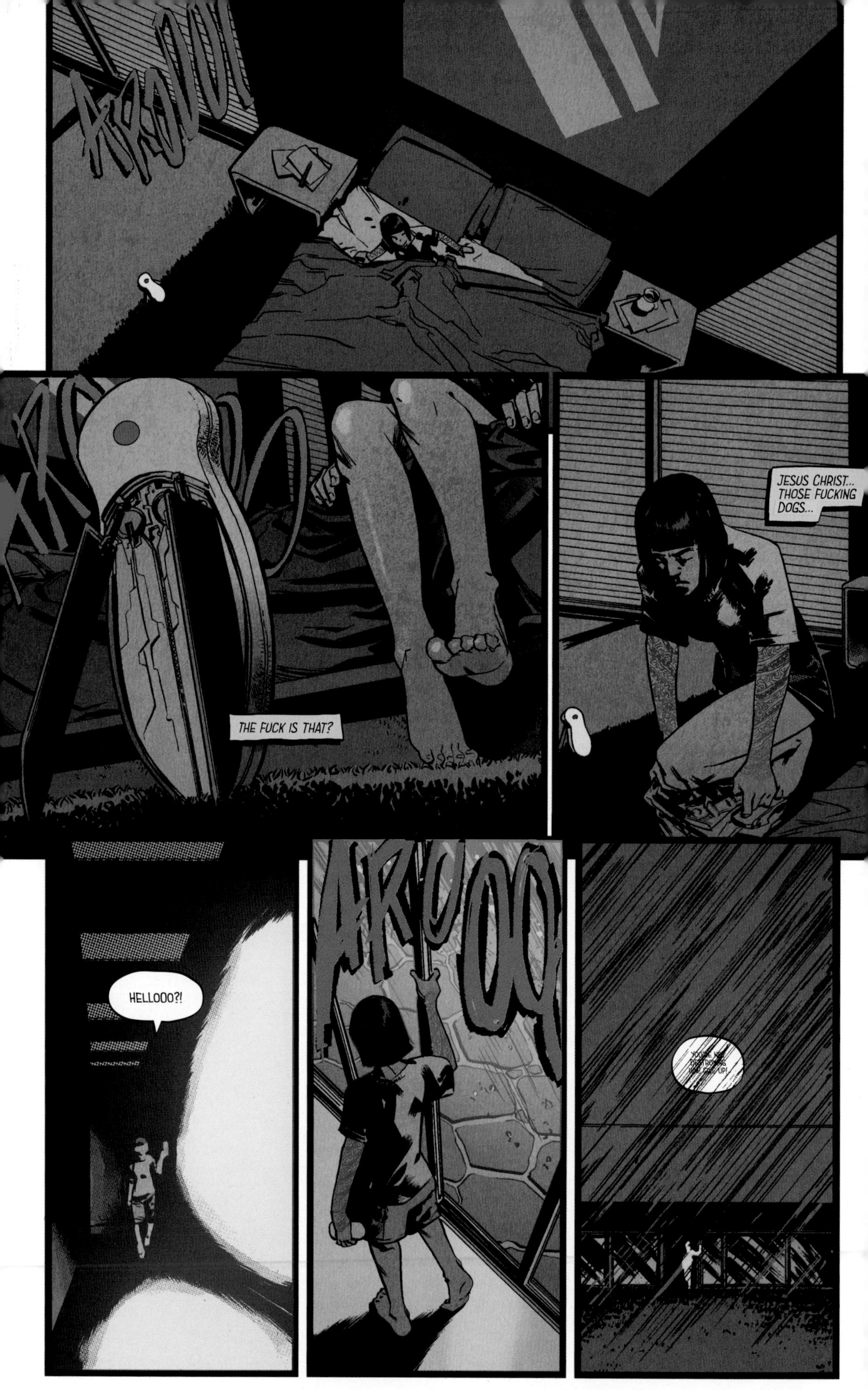
THE FUCK IS THAT?
JESUS CHRIST... THOSE FUCKING DOGS...
HELLOOO?!

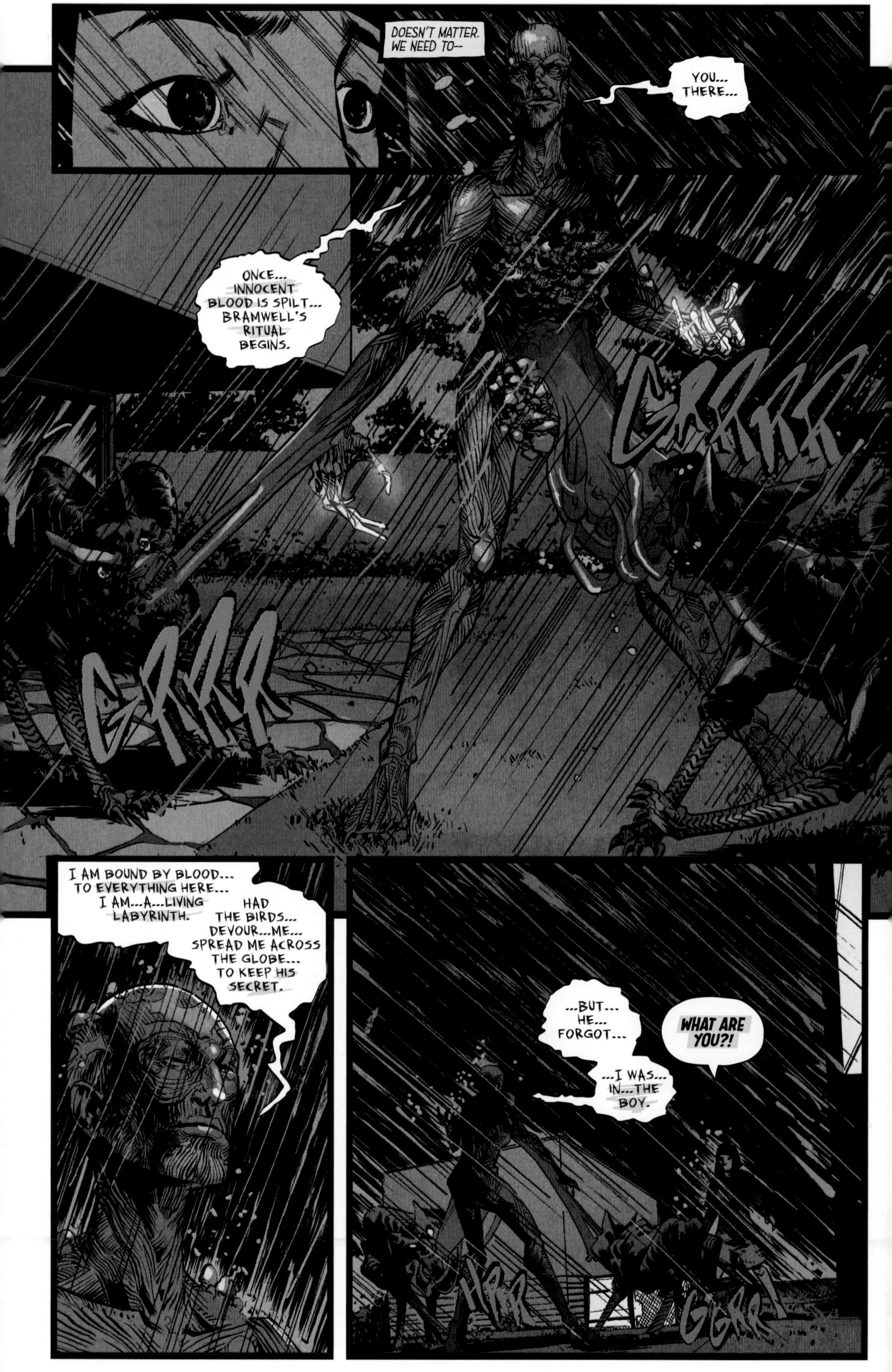
DOESN'T MATTER. WE NEED TO--
YOU... THERE...
ONCE... INNOCENT BLOOD IS SPILT... BRAMWELL'S RITUAL BEGINS.
GRRRR
GRRR
I AM BOUND BY BLOOD... TO EVERYTHING HERE... I AM...A...LIVING LABYRINTH.
HAD THE BIRDS... DEVOUR...ME... SPREAD ME ACROSS THE GLOBE... TO KEEP HIS SECRET.
...BUT... HE... FORGOT...
...I WAS... IN...THE BOY.
WHAT ARE YOU?!
HRRR
GGRR

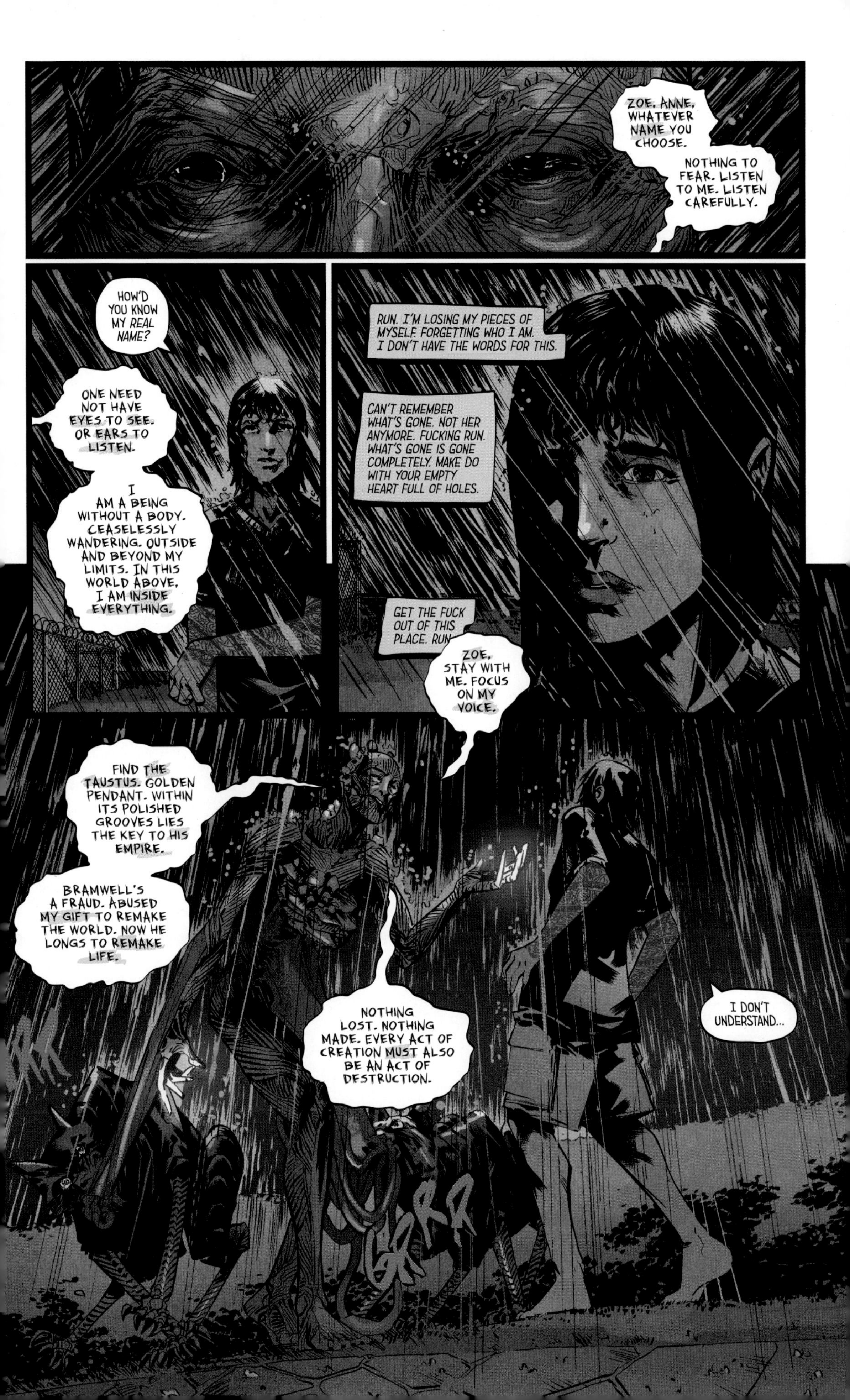
ZOE, ANNE, WHATEVER NAME YOU CHOOSE.
NOTHING TO FEAR. LISTEN TO ME. LISTEN CAREFULLY.
HOW'D YOU KNOW MY *REAL* NAME?
ONE NEED NOT HAVE EYES TO SEE. OR EARS TO LISTEN.
I AM A BEING WITHOUT A BODY. CEASELESSLY WANDERING. OUTSIDE AND BEYOND MY LIMITS. IN THIS WORLD ABOVE, I AM INSIDE EVERYTHING.
RUN. I'M LOSING MY PIECES OF MYSELF. FORGETTING WHO I AM. I DON'T HAVE THE WORDS FOR THIS.
CAN'T REMEMBER WHAT'S GONE. NOT HER ANYMORE. FUCKING RUN. WHAT'S GONE IS GONE COMPLETELY. MAKE DO WITH YOUR EMPTY HEART FULL OF HOLES.
GET THE FUCK OUT OF THIS PLACE. RUN.
ZOE, STAY WITH ME. FOCUS ON MY VOICE.
FIND THE TAUSTUS. GOLDEN PENDANT. WITHIN ITS POLISHED GROOVES LIES THE KEY TO HIS EMPIRE.
BRAMWELL'S A FRAUD. ABUSED MY GIFT TO REMAKE THE WORLD. NOW HE LONGS TO REMAKE LIFE.
NOTHING LOST. NOTHING MADE. EVERY ACT OF CREATION MUST ALSO BE AN ACT OF DESTRUCTION.
I DON'T UNDERSTAND...
GRRR
GRRR

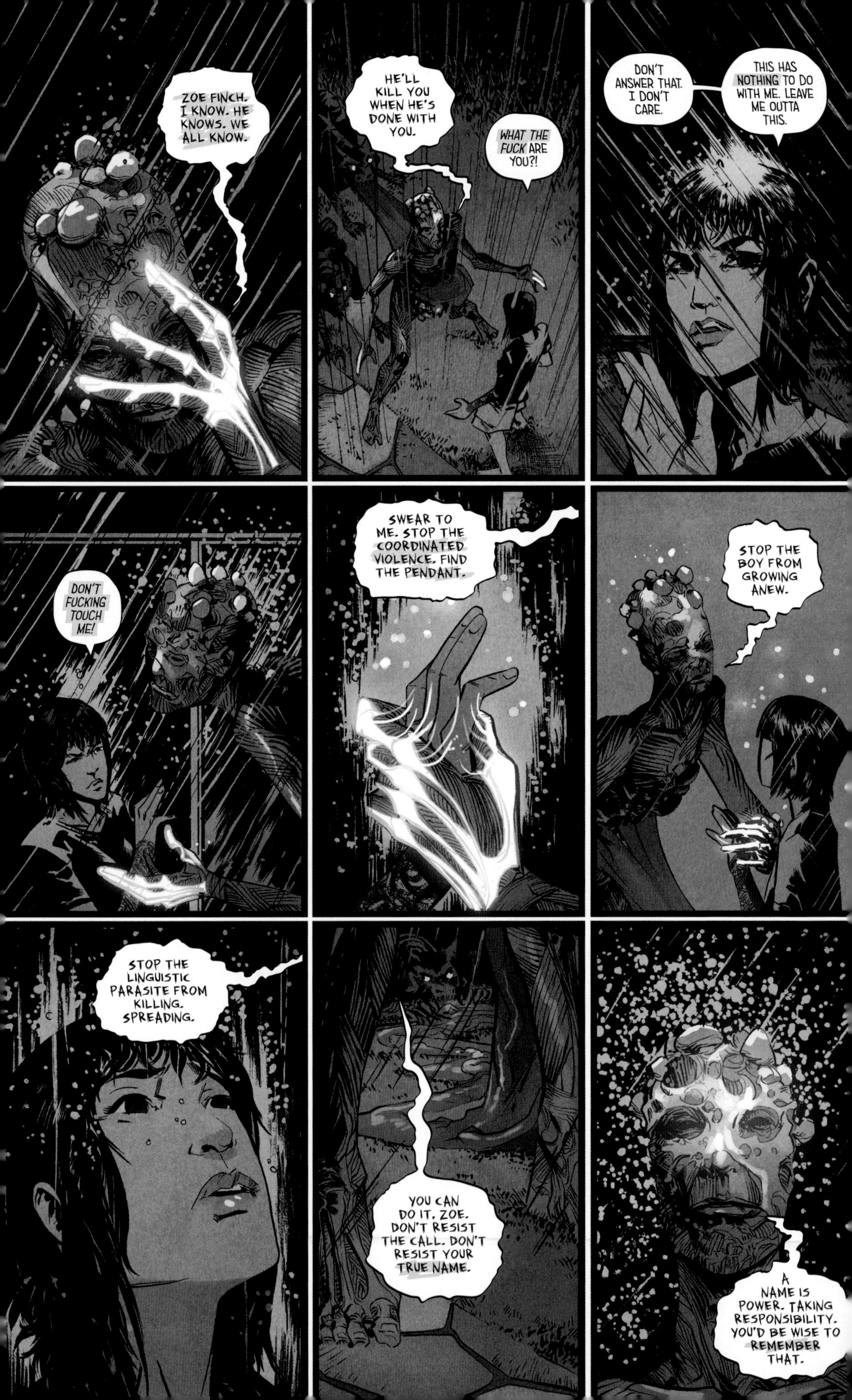
ZOE FINCH. I KNOW. HE KNOWS. WE ALL KNOW.
HE'LL KILL YOU WHEN HE'S DONE WITH YOU.
WHAT THE FUCK ARE YOU?!
DON'T ANSWER THAT. I DON'T CARE.
THIS HAS NOTHING TO DO WITH ME. LEAVE ME OUTTA THIS.
DON'T FUCKING TOUCH ME!
SWEAR TO ME. STOP THE COORDINATED VIOLENCE. FIND THE PENDANT.
STOP THE BOY FROM GROWING ANEW.
STOP THE LINGUISTIC PARASITE FROM KILLING. SPREADING.
YOU CAN DO IT, ZOE. DON'T RESIST THE CALL. DON'T RESIST YOUR TRUE NAME.
A NAME IS POWER. TAKING RESPONSIBILITY. YOU'D BE WISE TO REMEMBER THAT.

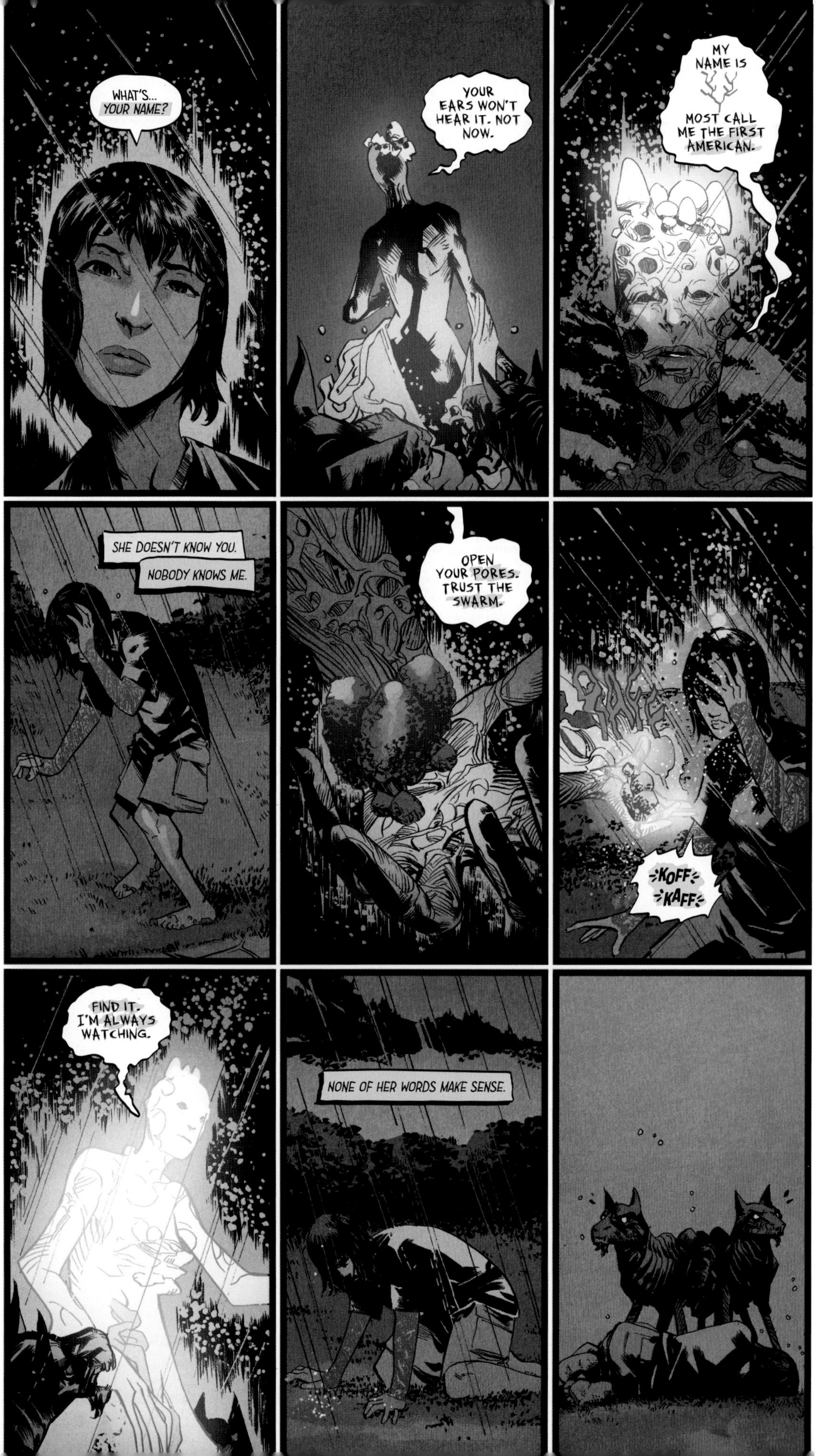
WHAT'S... YOUR NAME?
YOUR EARS WON'T HEAR IT. NOT NOW.
MY NAME IS
MOST CALL ME THE FIRST AMERICAN.
SHE DOESN'T KNOW YOU.
NOBODY KNOWS ME.
OPEN YOUR PORES. TRUST THE SWARM.
KOFF KAFF
FIND IT. I'M ALWAYS WATCHING.
NONE OF HER WORDS MAKE SENSE.

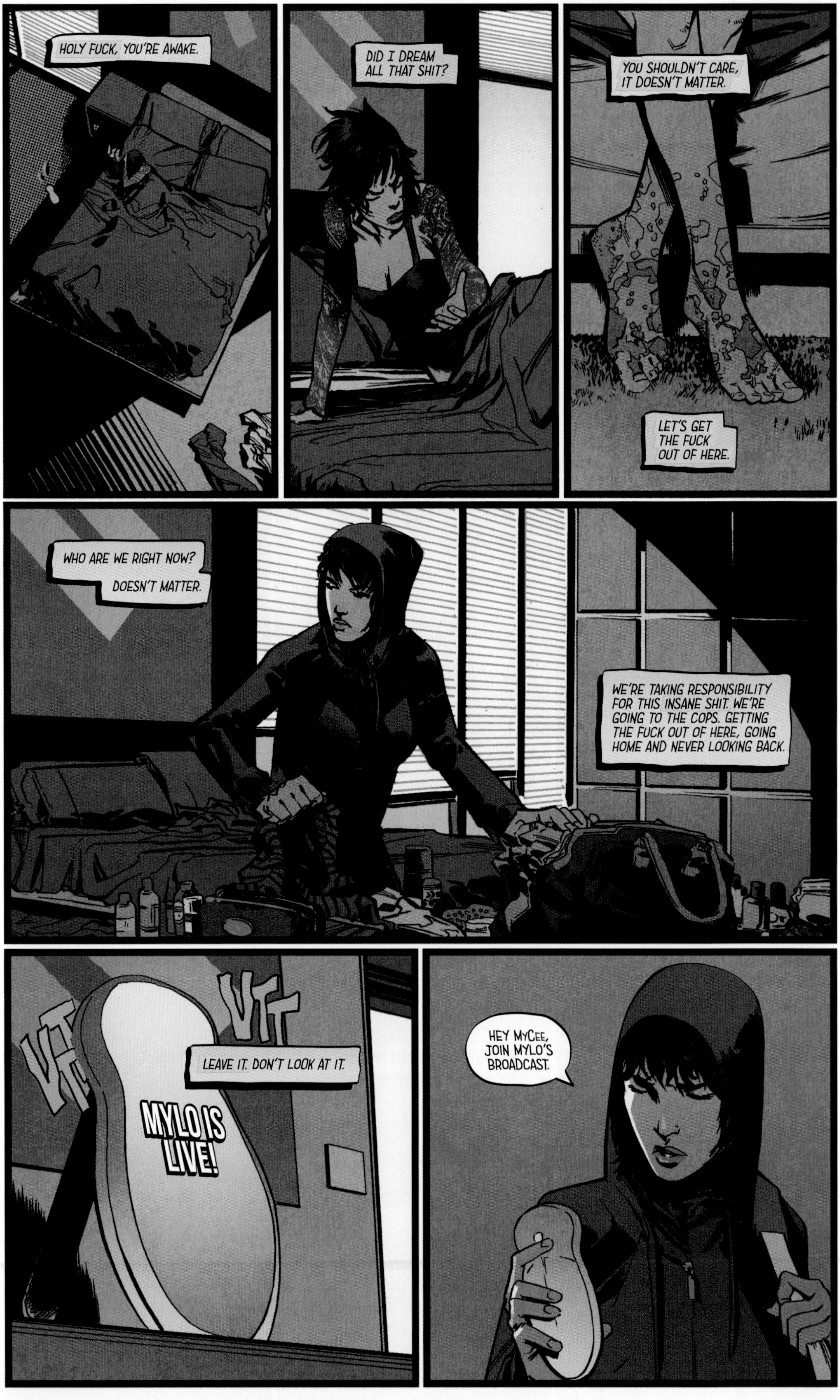
HOLY FUCK, YOU'RE AWAKE.
DID I DREAM ALL THAT SHIT?
YOU SHOULDN'T CARE, IT DOESN'T MATTER.
LET'S GET THE FUCK OUT OF HERE.
WHO ARE WE RIGHT NOW?
DOESN'T MATTER.
WE'RE TAKING RESPONSIBILITY FOR THIS INSANE SHIT. WE'RE GOING TO THE COPS. GETTING THE FUCK OUT OF HERE, GOING HOME AND NEVER LOOKING BACK.
VTT
VTT
LEAVE IT. DON'T LOOK AT IT.
MYLO IS LIVE!
HEY MyCee, JOIN MYLO'S BROADCAST.

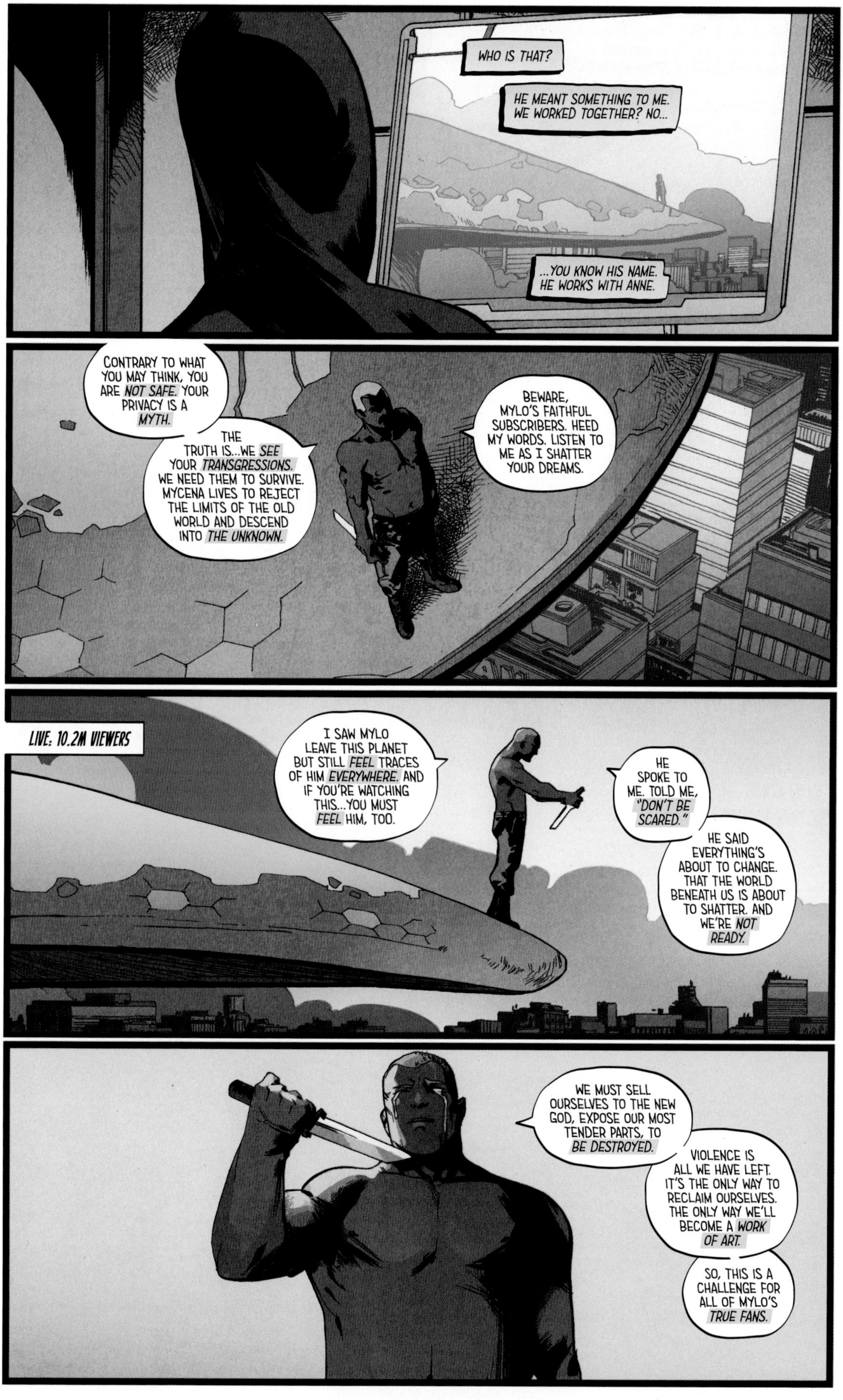
WHO IS THAT?
HE MEANT SOMETHING TO ME. WE WORKED TOGETHER? NO...
...YOU KNOW HIS NAME. HE WORKS WITH ANNE.
CONTRARY TO WHAT YOU MAY THINK, YOU ARE NOT SAFE. YOUR PRIVACY IS A MYTH.
THE TRUTH IS...WE SEE YOUR TRANSGRESSIONS. WE NEED THEM TO SURVIVE. MYCENA LIVES TO REJECT THE LIMITS OF THE OLD WORLD AND DESCEND INTO THE UNKNOWN.
BEWARE, MYLO'S FAITHFUL SUBSCRIBERS. HEED MY WORDS. LISTEN TO ME AS I SHATTER YOUR DREAMS.
LIVE: 10.2M VIEWERS
I SAW MYLO LEAVE THIS PLANET BUT STILL FEEL TRACES OF HIM EVERYWHERE. AND IF YOU'RE WATCHING THIS...YOU MUST FEEL HIM, TOO.
HE SPOKE TO ME. TOLD ME, "DON'T BE SCARED."
HE SAID EVERYTHING'S ABOUT TO CHANGE. THAT THE WORLD BENEATH US IS ABOUT TO SHATTER. AND WE'RE NOT READY.
WE MUST SELL OURSELVES TO THE NEW GOD, EXPOSE OUR MOST TENDER PARTS, TO BE DESTROYED.
VIOLENCE IS ALL WE HAVE LEFT. IT'S THE ONLY WAY TO RECLAIM OURSELVES. THE ONLY WAY WE'LL BECOME A WORK OF ART.
SO, THIS IS A CHALLENGE FOR ALL OF MYLO'S TRUE FANS.

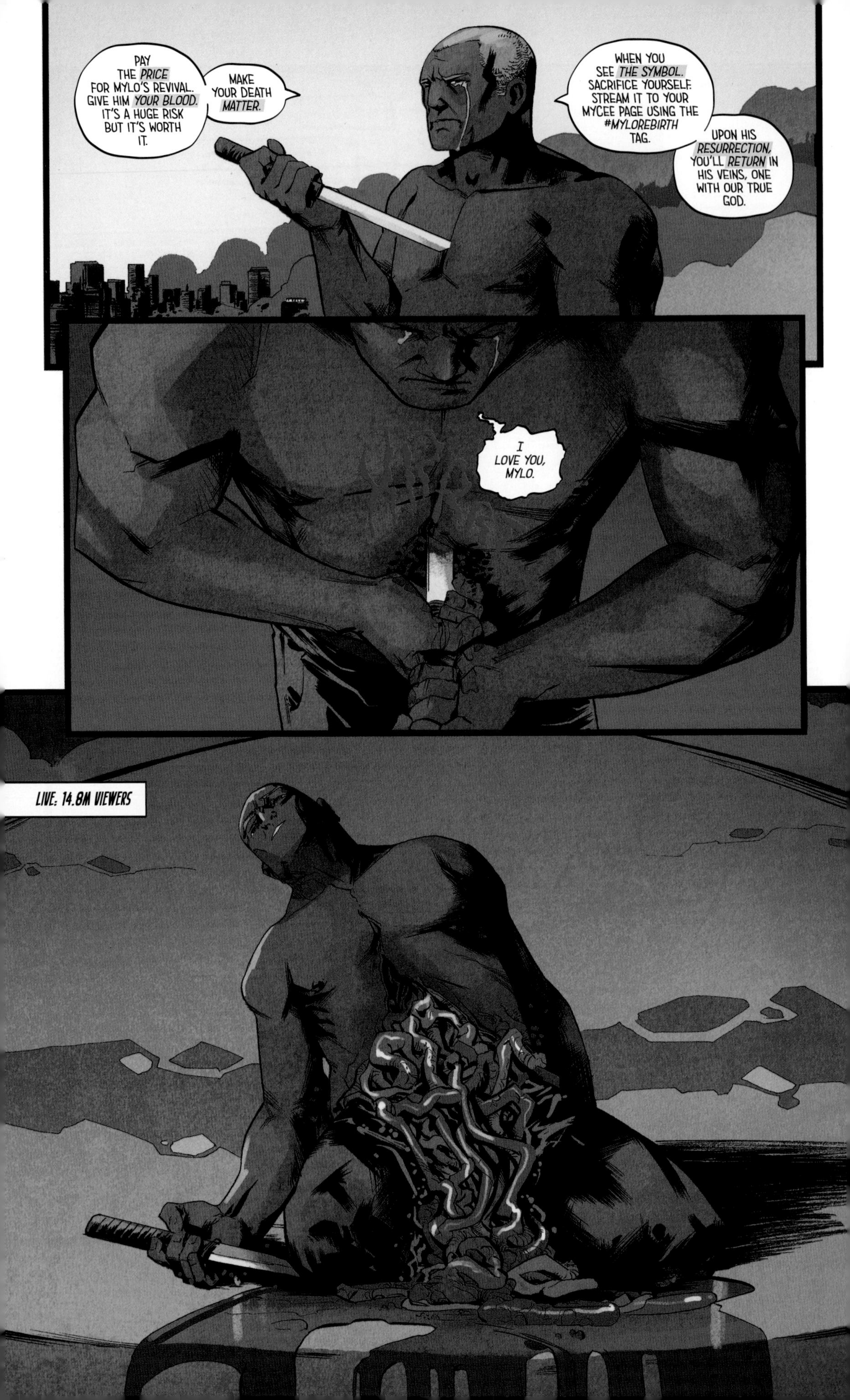

PAY THE PRICE FOR MYLO'S REVIVAL. GIVE HIM YOUR BLOOD. IT'S A HUGE RISK BUT IT'S WORTH IT.
MAKE YOUR DEATH MATTER.
WHEN YOU SEE THE SYMBOL. SACRIFICE YOURSELF. STREAM IT TO YOUR MYCEE PAGE USING THE #MYLOREBIRTH TAG.
UPON HIS RESURRECTION, YOU'LL RETURN IN HIS VEINS, ONE WITH OUR TRUE GOD.
I LOVE YOU, MYLO.
LIVE: 14.8M VIEWERS

4

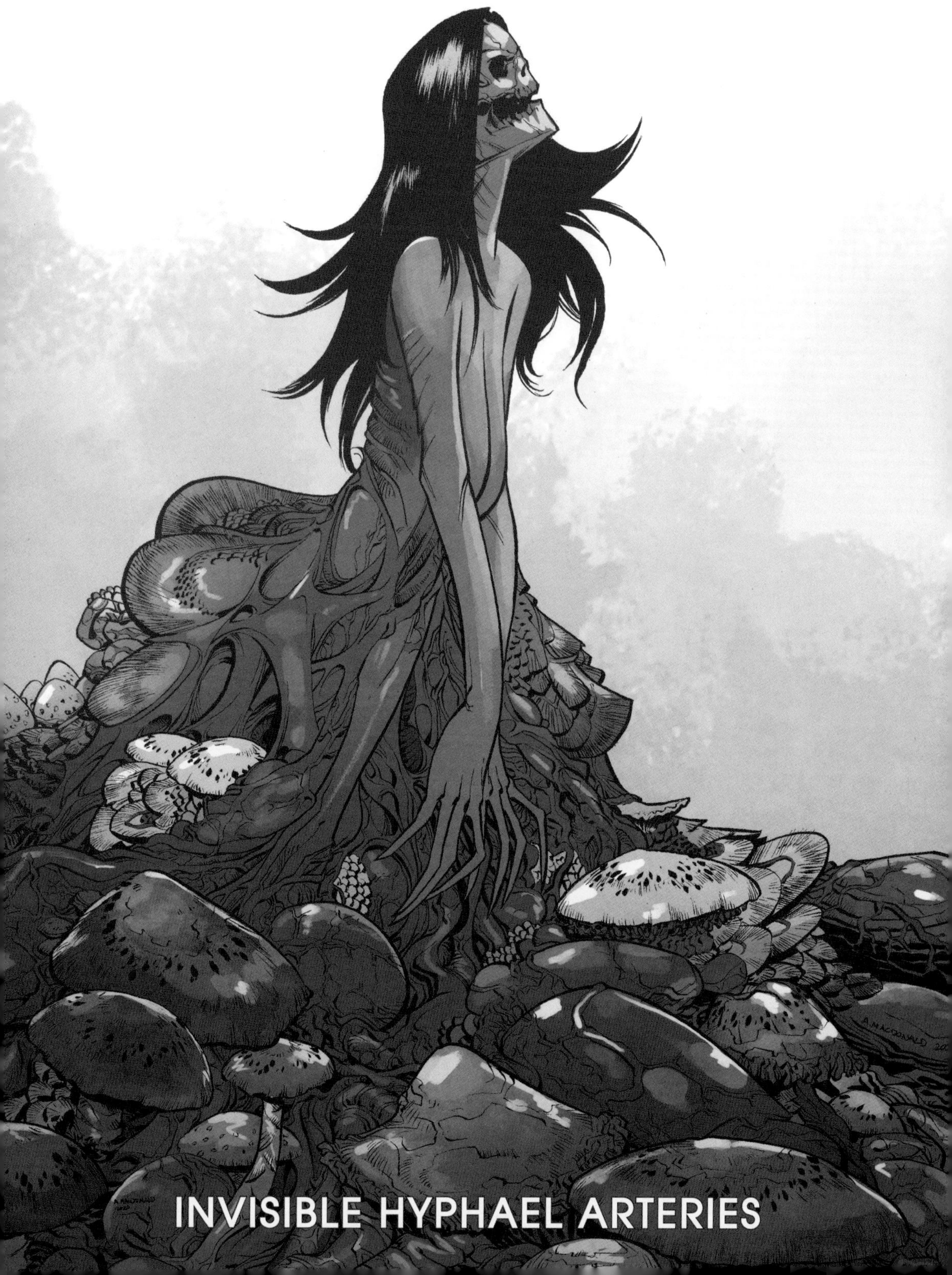

INVISIBLE HYPHAEL ARTERIES

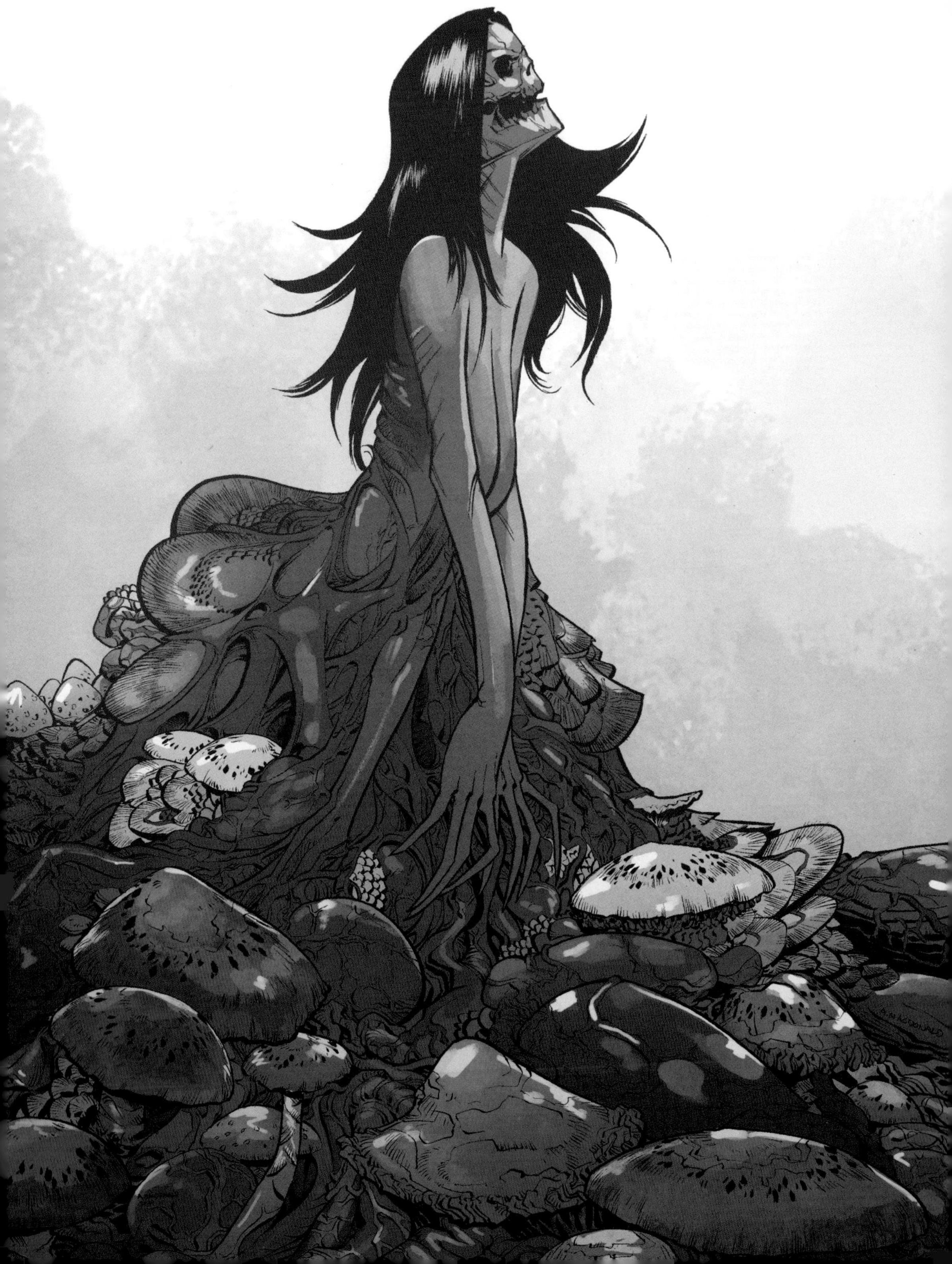

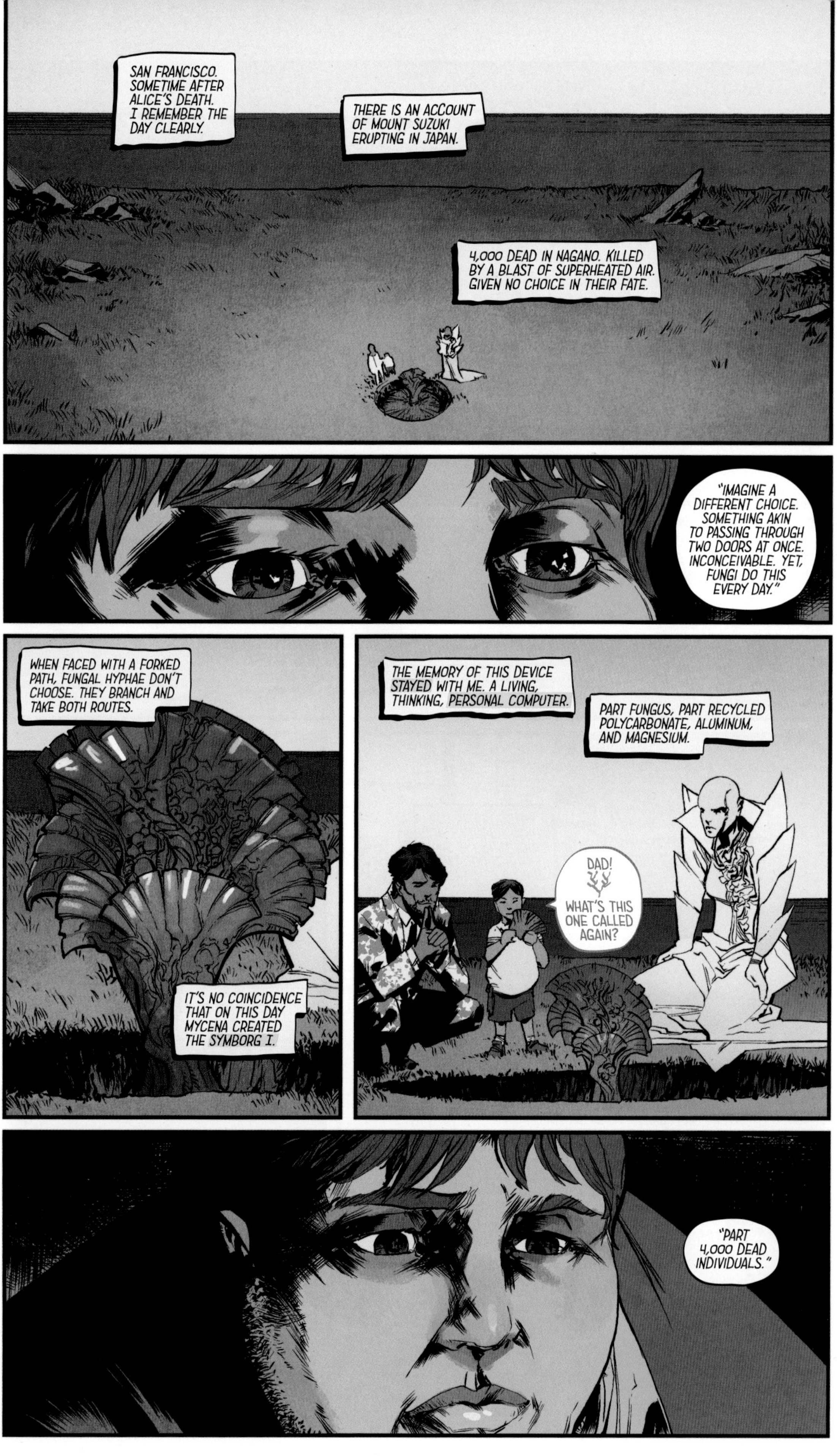

SAN FRANCISCO. SOMETIME AFTER ALICE'S DEATH. I REMEMBER THE DAY CLEARLY.
THERE IS AN ACCOUNT OF MOUNT SUZUKI ERUPTING IN JAPAN.
4,000 DEAD IN NAGANO. KILLED BY A BLAST OF SUPERHEATED AIR. GIVEN NO CHOICE IN THEIR FATE.
"IMAGINE A DIFFERENT CHOICE. SOMETHING AKIN TO PASSING THROUGH TWO DOORS AT ONCE. INCONCEIVABLE. YET, FUNGI DO THIS EVERY DAY."
WHEN FACED WITH A FORKED PATH, FUNGAL HYPHAE DON'T CHOOSE. THEY BRANCH AND TAKE BOTH ROUTES.
IT'S NO COINCIDENCE THAT ON THIS DAY MYCENA CREATED THE SYMBORG I.
THE MEMORY OF THIS DEVICE STAYED WITH ME. A LIVING, THINKING, PERSONAL COMPUTER.
PART FUNGUS, PART RECYCLED POLYCARBONATE, ALUMINUM, AND MAGNESIUM.
DAD!
WHAT'S THIS ONE CALLED AGAIN?
"PART 4,000 DEAD INDIVIDUALS."

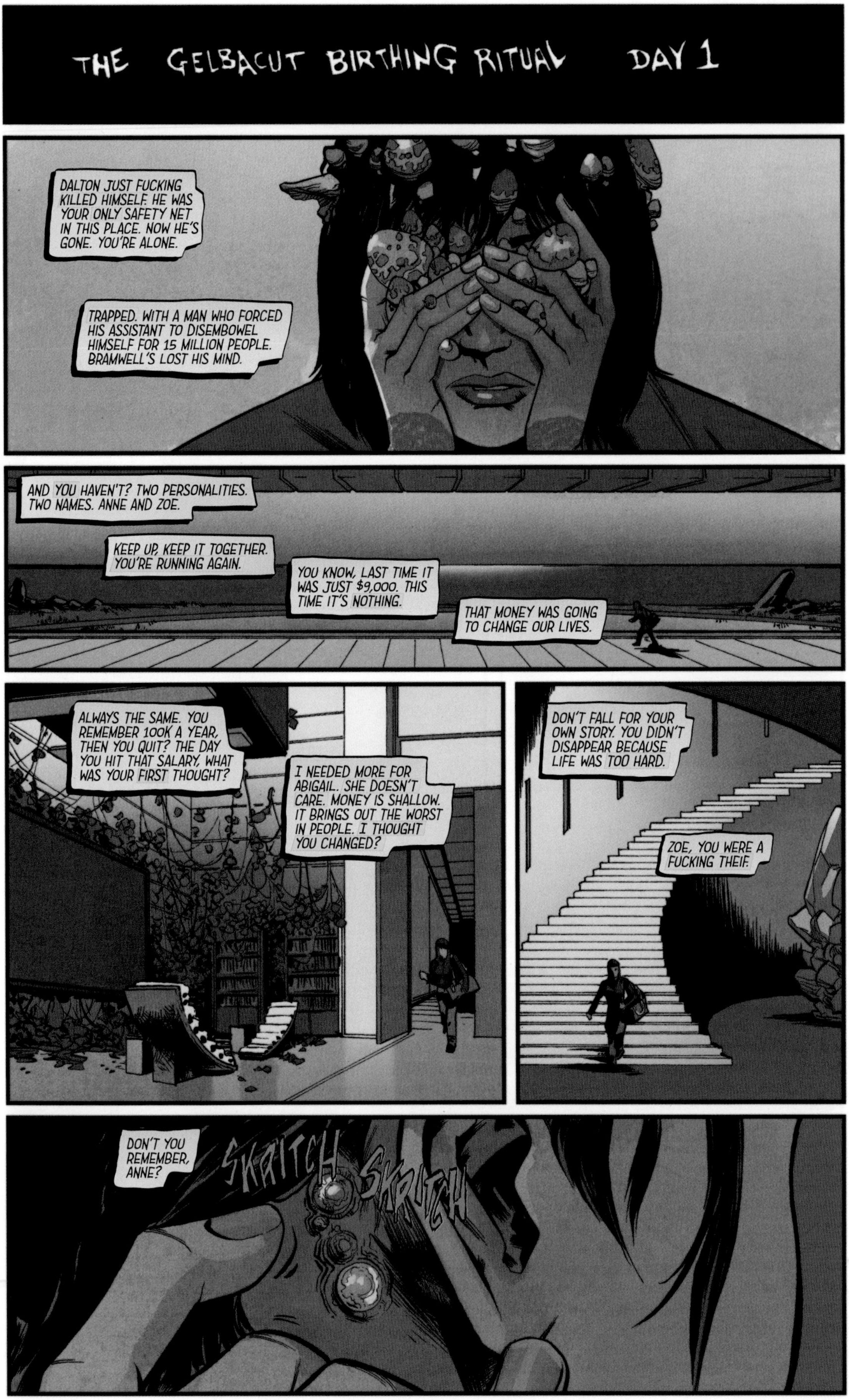
THE GELBACUT BIRTHING RITUAL DAY 1
DALTON JUST FUCKING KILLED HIMSELF. HE WAS YOUR ONLY SAFETY NET IN THIS PLACE. NOW HE'S GONE. YOU'RE ALONE.
TRAPPED. WITH A MAN WHO FORCED HIS ASSISTANT TO DISEMBOWEL HIMSELF FOR 15 MILLION PEOPLE. BRAMWELL'S LOST HIS MIND.
AND YOU HAVEN'T? TWO PERSONALITIES. TWO NAMES. ANNE AND ZOE.
KEEP UP, KEEP IT TOGETHER. YOU'RE RUNNING AGAIN.
YOU KNOW, LAST TIME IT WAS JUST $9,000. THIS TIME IT'S NOTHING.
THAT MONEY WAS GOING TO CHANGE OUR LIVES.
ALWAYS THE SAME. YOU REMEMBER 100K A YEAR, THEN YOU QUIT? THE DAY YOU HIT THAT SALARY, WHAT WAS YOUR FIRST THOUGHT?
I NEEDED MORE FOR ABIGAIL. SHE DOESN'T CARE. MONEY IS SHALLOW. IT BRINGS OUT THE WORST IN PEOPLE. I THOUGHT YOU CHANGED?
DON'T FALL FOR YOUR OWN STORY. YOU DIDN'T DISAPPEAR BECAUSE LIFE WAS TOO HARD.
ZOE, YOU WERE A FUCKING THEIF.
DON'T YOU REMEMBER, ANNE?
SKRITCH SKRITCH

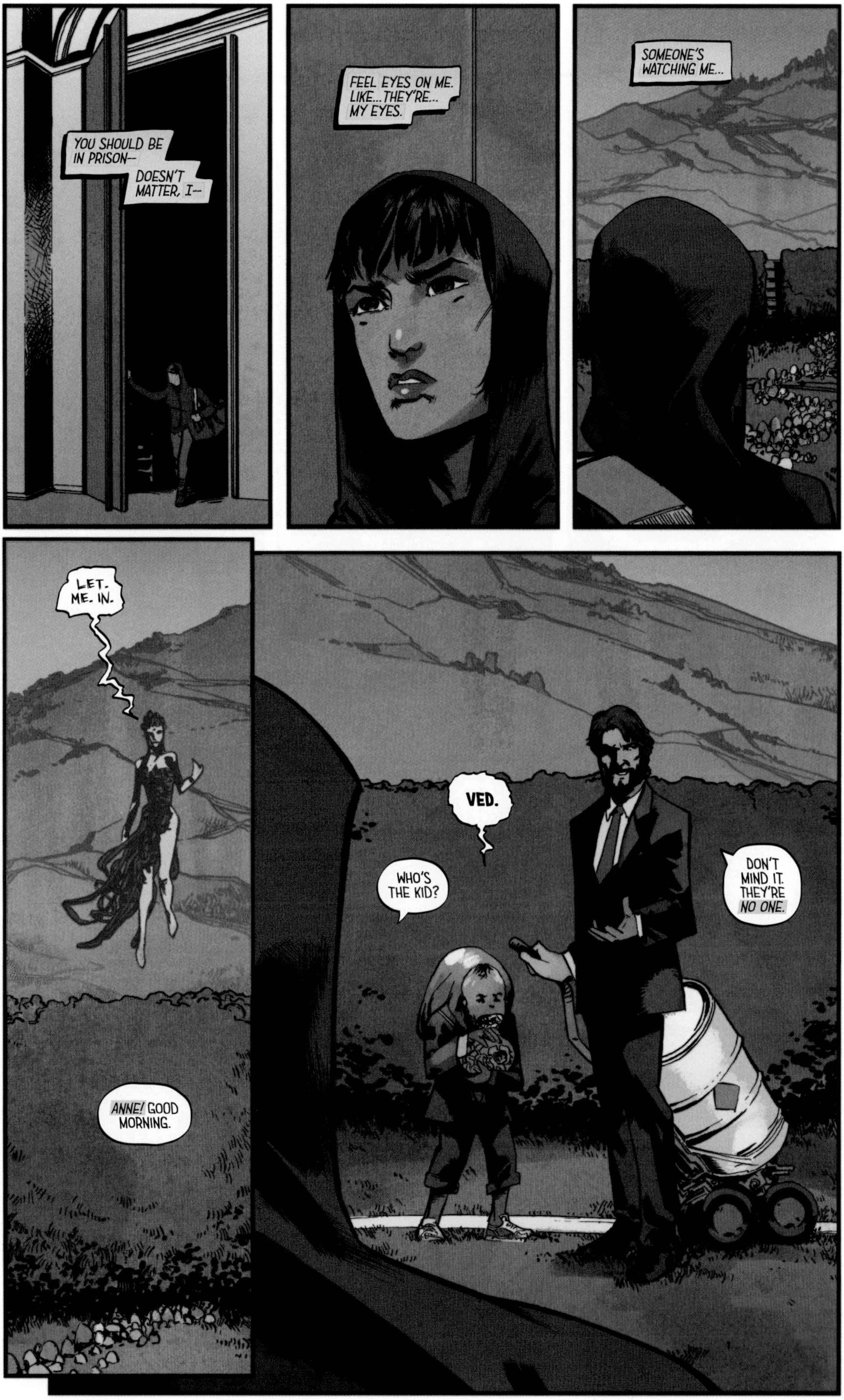
YOU SHOULD BE IN PRISON--
DOESN'T MATTER, I--
FEEL EYES ON ME. LIKE...THEY'RE... MY EYES.
SOMEONE'S WATCHING ME...
LET. ME. IN.
ANNE! GOOD MORNING.
VED.
WHO'S THE KID?
DON'T MIND IT. THEY'RE NO ONE.

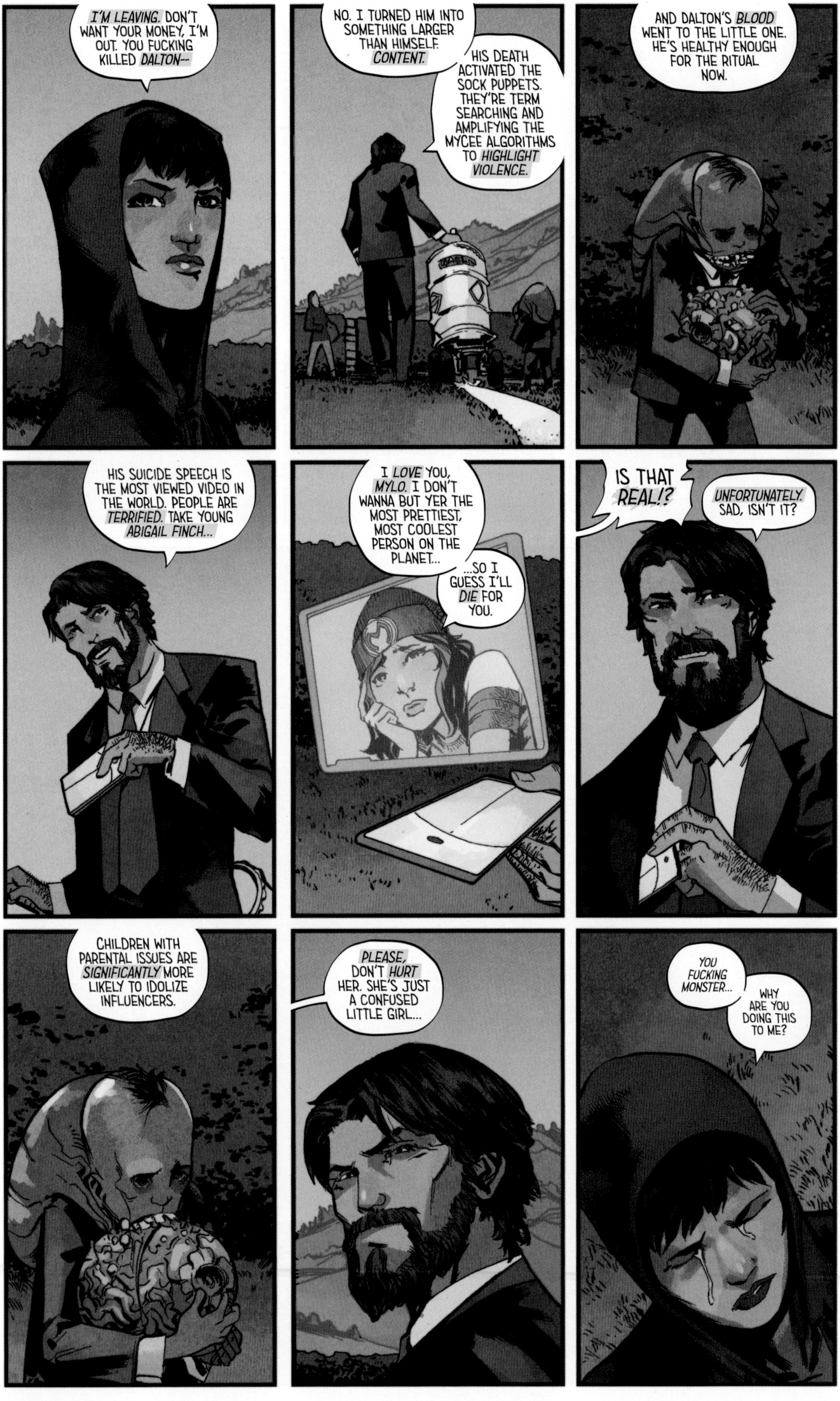
I'M LEAVING. DON'T WANT YOUR MONEY, I'M OUT. YOU FUCKING KILLED DALTON--
NO. I TURNED HIM INTO SOMETHING LARGER THAN HIMSELF. CONTENT.
HIS DEATH ACTIVATED THE SOCK PUPPETS. THEY'RE TERM SEARCHING AND AMPLIFYING THE MYCEE ALGORITHMS TO HIGHLIGHT VIOLENCE.
AND DALTON'S BLOOD WENT TO THE LITTLE ONE. HE'S HEALTHY ENOUGH FOR THE RITUAL NOW.
HIS SUICIDE SPEECH IS THE MOST VIEWED VIDEO IN THE WORLD. PEOPLE ARE TERRIFIED. TAKE YOUNG ABIGAIL FINCH...
I LOVE YOU, MYLO. I DON'T WANNA BUT YER THE MOST PRETTIEST, MOST COOLEST PERSON ON THE PLANET...
...SO I GUESS I'LL DIE FOR YOU.
IS THAT REAL!?
UNFORTUNATELY. SAD, ISN'T IT?
CHILDREN WITH PARENTAL ISSUES ARE SIGNIFICANTLY MORE LIKELY TO IDOLIZE INFLUENCERS.
PLEASE, DON'T HURT HER. SHE'S JUST A CONFUSED LITTLE GIRL...
YOU FUCKING MONSTER...
WHY ARE YOU DOING THIS TO ME?

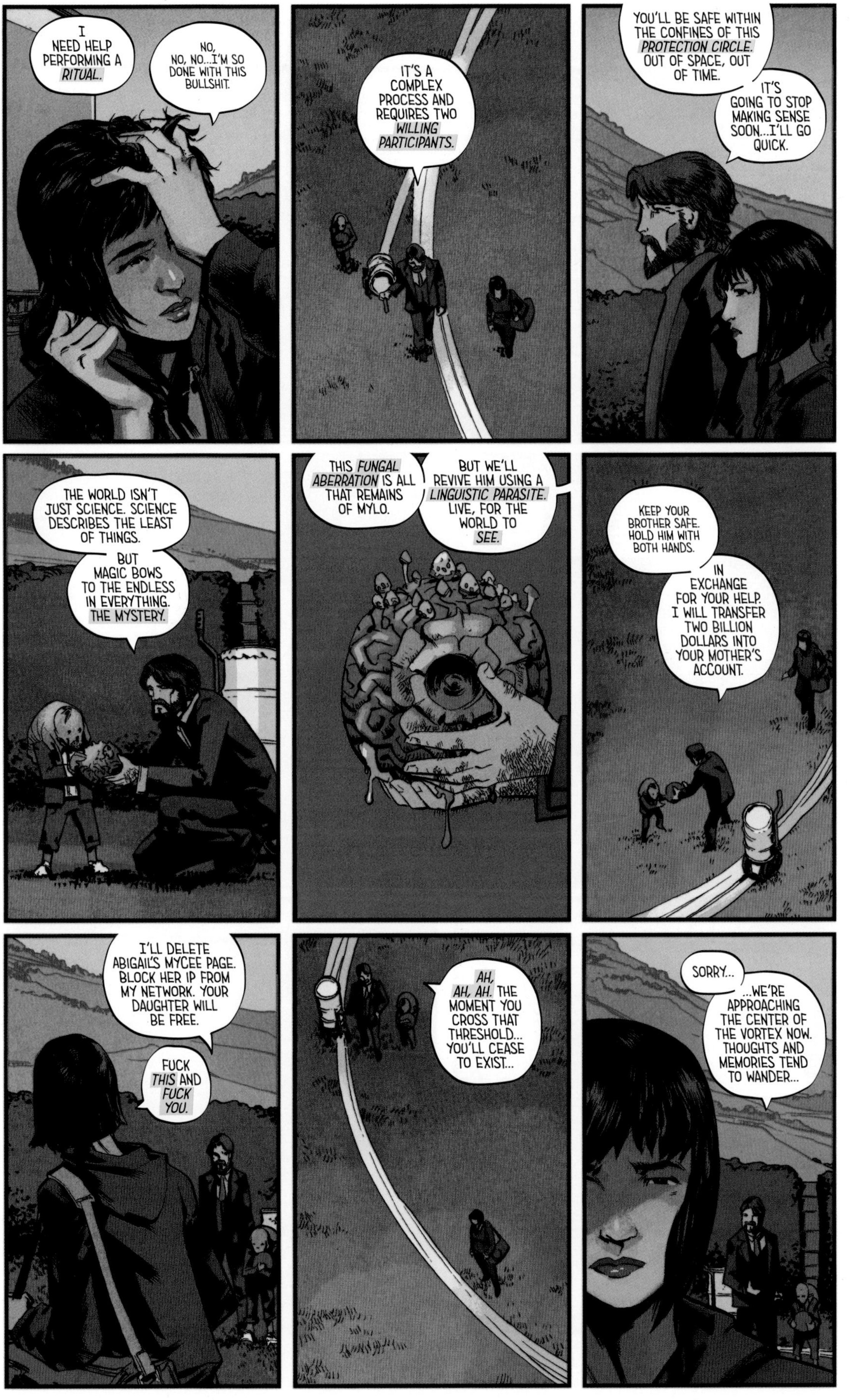
I NEED HELP PERFORMING A RITUAL.
NO, NO, NO...I'M SO DONE WITH THIS BULLSHIT.
IT'S A COMPLEX PROCESS AND REQUIRES TWO WILLING PARTICIPANTS.
YOU'LL BE SAFE WITHIN THE CONFINES OF THIS PROTECTION CIRCLE. OUT OF SPACE, OUT OF TIME.
IT'S GOING TO STOP MAKING SENSE SOON...I'LL GO QUICK.
THE WORLD ISN'T JUST SCIENCE. SCIENCE DESCRIBES THE LEAST OF THINGS.
BUT MAGIC BOWS TO THE ENDLESS IN EVERYTHING. THE MYSTERY.
THIS FUNGAL ABERRATION IS ALL THAT REMAINS OF MYLO.
BUT WE'LL REVIVE HIM USING A LINGUISTIC PARASITE. LIVE, FOR THE WORLD TO SEE.
KEEP YOUR BROTHER SAFE. HOLD HIM WITH BOTH HANDS.
IN EXCHANGE FOR YOUR HELP. I WILL TRANSFER TWO BILLION DOLLARS INTO YOUR MOTHER'S ACCOUNT.
I'LL DELETE ABIGAIL'S MYCEE PAGE. BLOCK HER IP FROM MY NETWORK. YOUR DAUGHTER WILL BE FREE.
FUCK THIS AND FUCK YOU.
AH, AH, AH. THE MOMENT YOU CROSS THAT THRESHOLD... YOU'LL CEASE TO EXIST...
SORRY...
...WE'RE APPROACHING THE CENTER OF THE VORTEX NOW. THOUGHTS AND MEMORIES TEND TO WANDER...

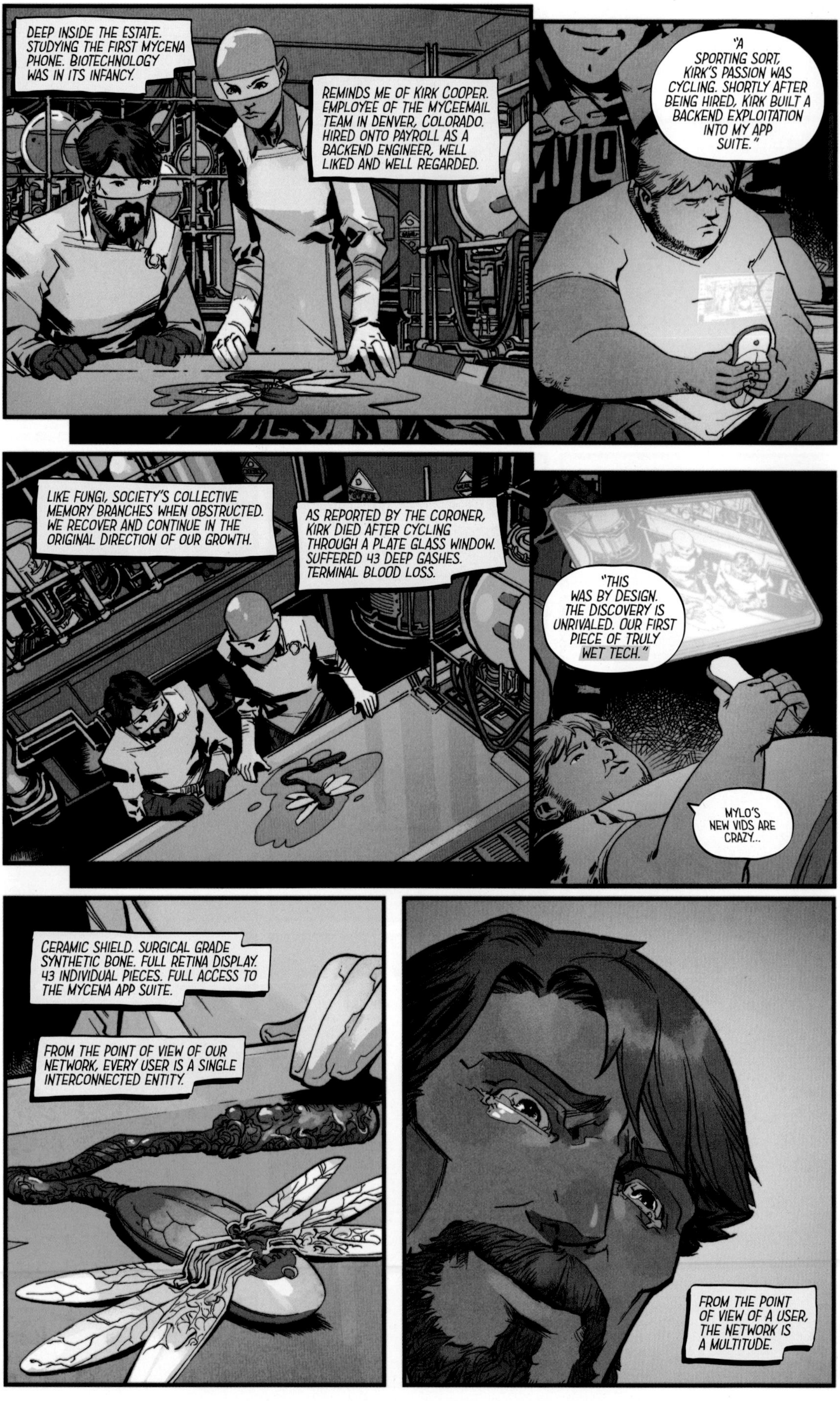

DEEP INSIDE THE ESTATE. STUDYING THE FIRST MYCENA PHONE. BIOTECHNOLOGY WAS IN ITS INFANCY.
REMINDS ME OF KIRK COOPER. EMPLOYEE OF THE MYCEEMAIL TEAM IN DENVER, COLORADO. HIRED ONTO PAYROLL AS A BACKEND ENGINEER, WELL LIKED AND WELL REGARDED.
"A SPORTING SORT, KIRK'S PASSION WAS CYCLING. SHORTLY AFTER BEING HIRED, KIRK BUILT A BACKEND EXPLOITATION INTO MY APP SUITE."
LIKE FUNGI, SOCIETY'S COLLECTIVE MEMORY BRANCHES WHEN OBSTRUCTED. WE RECOVER AND CONTINUE IN THE ORIGINAL DIRECTION OF OUR GROWTH.
AS REPORTED BY THE CORONER, KIRK DIED AFTER CYCLING THROUGH A PLATE GLASS WINDOW. SUFFERED 43 DEEP GASHES. TERMINAL BLOOD LOSS.
"THIS WAS BY DESIGN. THE DISCOVERY IS UNRIVALED. OUR FIRST PIECE OF TRULY WET TECH."
MYLO'S NEW VIDS ARE CRAZY...
CERAMIC SHIELD. SURGICAL GRADE SYNTHETIC BONE. FULL RETINA DISPLAY. 43 INDIVIDUAL PIECES. FULL ACCESS TO THE MYCENA APP SUITE.
FROM THE POINT OF VIEW OF OUR NETWORK, EVERY USER IS A SINGLE INTERCONNECTED ENTITY.
FROM THE POINT OF VIEW OF A USER, THE NETWORK IS A MULTITUDE.

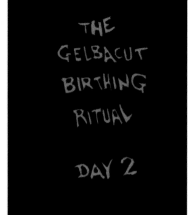

THE GELBACUT BIRTHING RITUAL

DAY 2

HOURS WITHOUT A SOUND. EVEN THE AIR IS STILL. EVERYTHING'S GONE STALE. DREADING WHATEVER HE WANTS ME TO DO.

PHONE'S BEEN COMPLETELY DISCONNECTED FROM MYCEENET.

SKRITCH

SKRITCH

HE'S TRYING TO MAKE ME GO INSANE.

YOU SURE HE HASN'T SUCCEEDED?

YOU'VE UPLOADED DEATH, VIOLENCE, DISMEMBERMENT INTO THE WORLD...

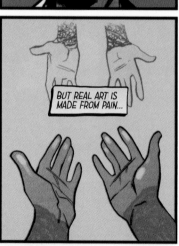

BUT REAL ART IS MADE FROM PAIN...

STOP. IT'S NOT ART. IT'S BARELY PORNOGRAPHY. YOU'RE IN THE ROOM. YOU'RE GUILTY. SIMPLE AS THAT.

I'M EMPOWERING A FUCKING MONSTER...

NOK NOK

EAT IT. EAT, EAT.

DON'T EAT IT.

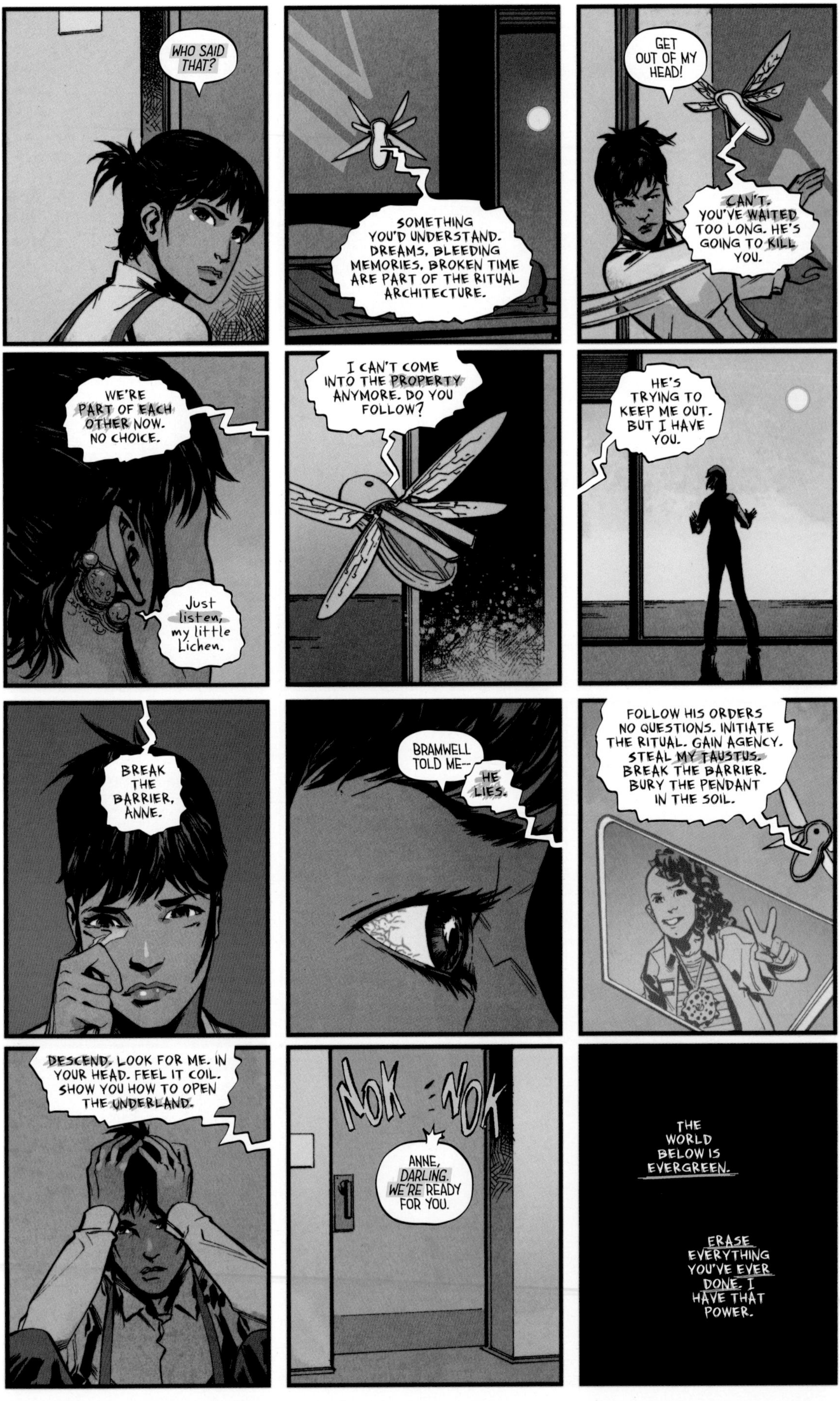
WHO SAID THAT?
SOMETHING YOU'D UNDERSTAND. DREAMS, BLEEDING MEMORIES, BROKEN TIME ARE PART OF THE RITUAL ARCHITECTURE.
GET OUT OF MY HEAD!
CAN'T. YOU'VE WAITED TOO LONG. HE'S GOING TO KILL YOU.
WE'RE PART OF EACH OTHER NOW. NO CHOICE.
Just listen, my little Lichen.
I CAN'T COME INTO THE PROPERTY ANYMORE. DO YOU FOLLOW?
HE'S TRYING TO KEEP ME OUT. BUT I HAVE YOU.
BREAK THE BARRIER, ANNE.
BRAMWELL TOLD ME--
HE LIES.
FOLLOW HIS ORDERS NO QUESTIONS. INITIATE THE RITUAL. GAIN AGENCY. STEAL MY TAUSTUS. BREAK THE BARRIER. BURY THE PENDANT IN THE SOIL.
DESCEND. LOOK FOR ME. IN YOUR HEAD. FEEL IT COIL. SHOW YOU HOW TO OPEN THE UNDERLAND.
NOK NOK
ANNE, DARLING. WE'RE READY FOR YOU.
THE WORLD BELOW IS EVERGREEN.
ERASE EVERYTHING YOU'VE EVER DONE. I HAVE THAT POWER.

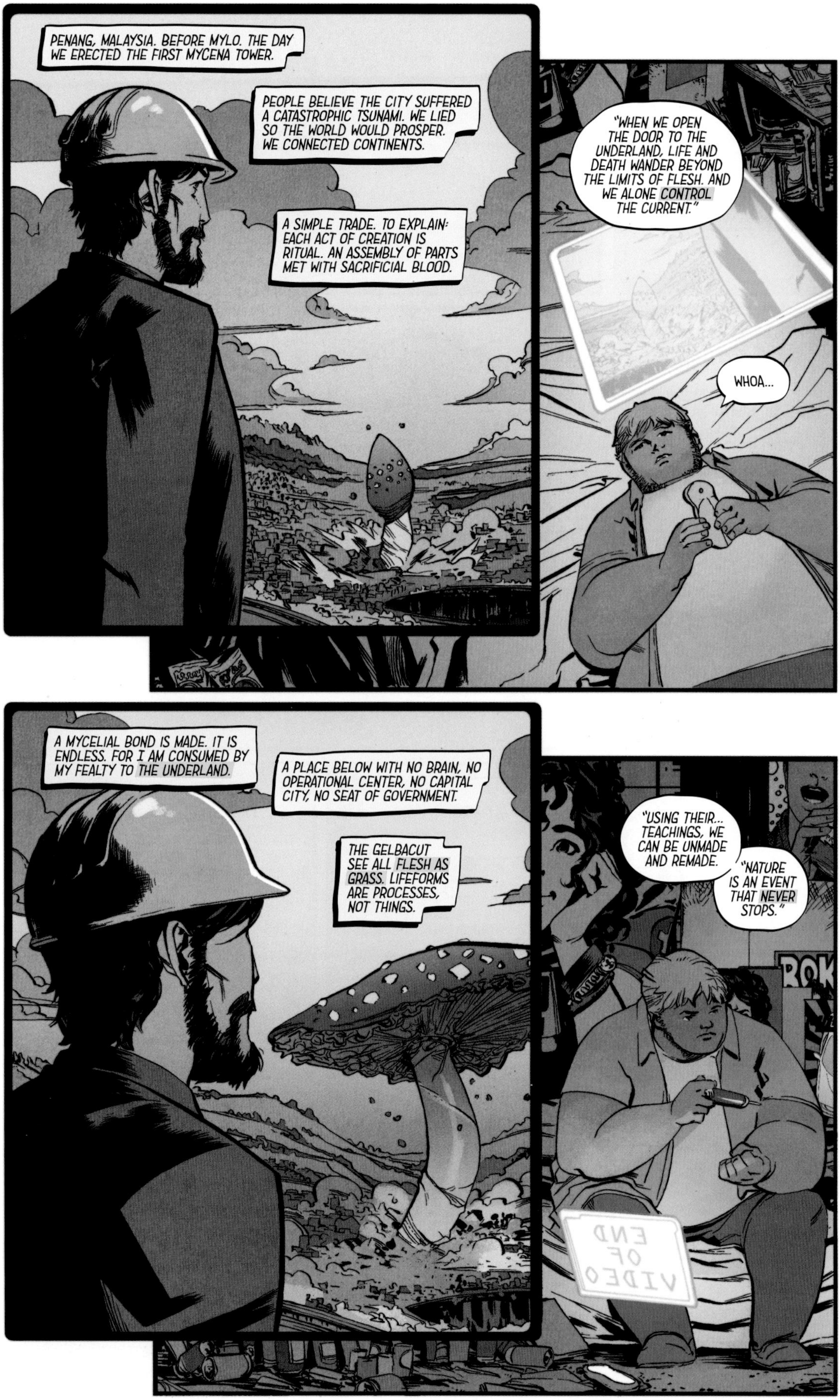
PENANG, MALAYSIA. BEFORE MYLO. THE DAY WE ERECTED THE FIRST MYCENA TOWER.
PEOPLE BELIEVE THE CITY SUFFERED A CATASTROPHIC TSUNAMI. WE LIED SO THE WORLD WOULD PROSPER. WE CONNECTED CONTINENTS.
A SIMPLE TRADE. TO EXPLAIN: EACH ACT OF CREATION IS RITUAL. AN ASSEMBLY OF PARTS MET WITH SACRIFICIAL BLOOD.
"WHEN WE OPEN THE DOOR TO THE UNDERLAND, LIFE AND DEATH WANDER BEYOND THE LIMITS OF FLESH. AND WE ALONE CONTROL THE CURRENT."
WHOA...
A MYCELIAL BOND IS MADE. IT IS ENDLESS. FOR I AM CONSUMED BY MY FEALTY TO THE UNDERLAND.
A PLACE BELOW WITH NO BRAIN, NO OPERATIONAL CENTER, NO CAPITAL CITY, NO SEAT OF GOVERNMENT.
THE GELBACUT SEE ALL FLESH AS GRASS. LIFEFORMS ARE PROCESSES, NOT THINGS.
"USING THEIR... TEACHINGS, WE CAN BE UNMADE AND REMADE.
"NATURE IS AN EVENT THAT NEVER STOPS."
END OF VIDEO

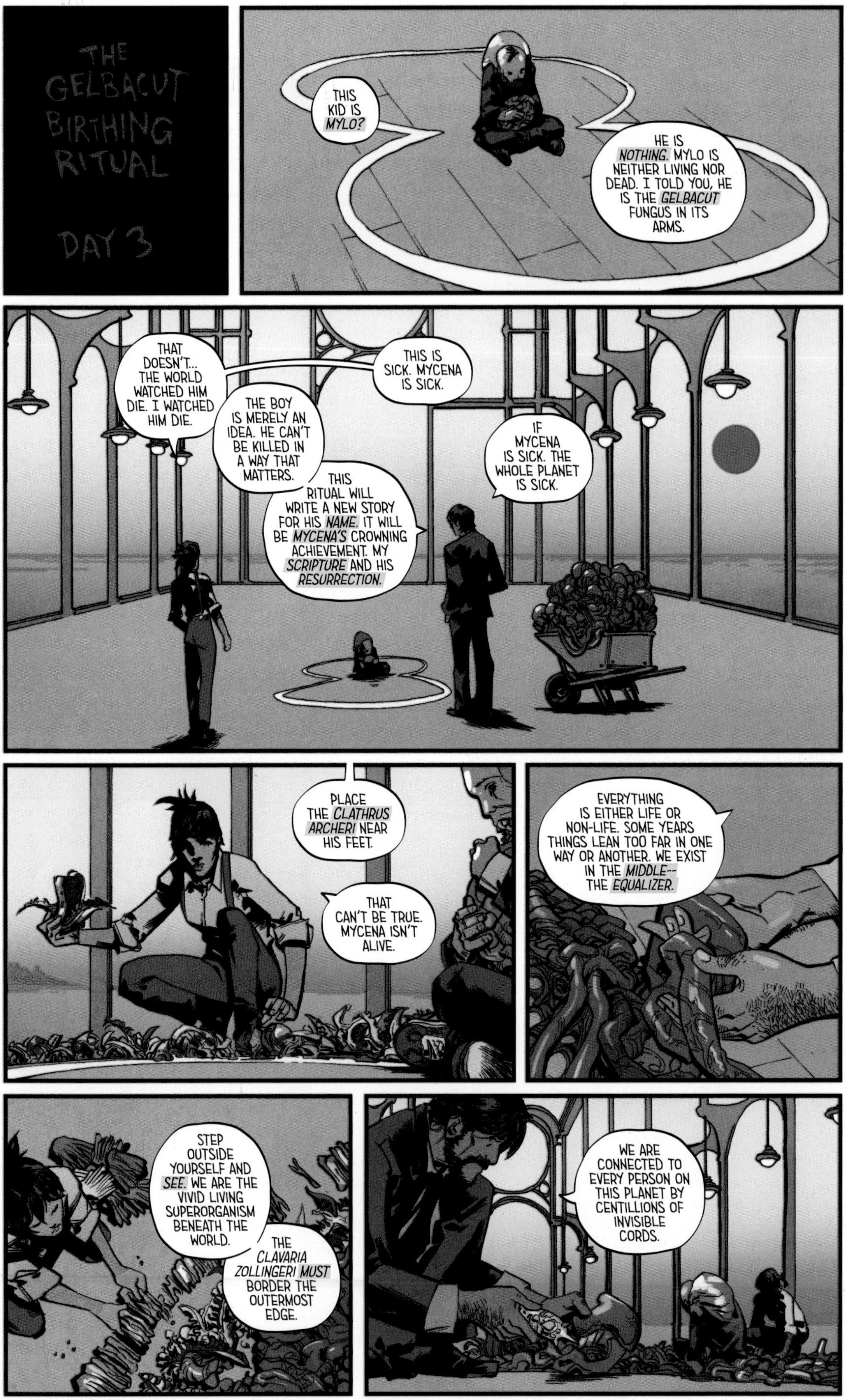
THE GELBACUT BIRTHING RITUAL
DAY 3
THIS KID IS MYLO?
HE IS NOTHING. MYLO IS NEITHER LIVING NOR DEAD. I TOLD YOU, HE IS THE GELBACUT FUNGUS IN ITS ARMS.
THAT DOESN'T... THE WORLD WATCHED HIM DIE. I WATCHED HIM DIE.
THIS IS SICK. MYCENA IS SICK.
THE BOY IS MERELY AN IDEA. HE CAN'T BE KILLED IN A WAY THAT MATTERS.
IF MYCENA IS SICK. THE WHOLE PLANET IS SICK.
THIS RITUAL WILL WRITE A NEW STORY FOR HIS NAME. IT WILL BE MYCENA'S CROWNING ACHIEVEMENT. MY SCRIPTURE AND HIS RESURRECTION.
PLACE THE CLATHRUS ARCHERI NEAR HIS FEET.
THAT CAN'T BE TRUE. MYCENA ISN'T ALIVE.
EVERYTHING IS EITHER LIFE OR NON-LIFE. SOME YEARS THINGS LEAN TOO FAR IN ONE WAY OR ANOTHER. WE EXIST IN THE MIDDLE-- THE EQUALIZER.
STEP OUTSIDE YOURSELF AND SEE. WE ARE THE VIVID LIVING SUPERORGANISM BENEATH THE WORLD.
THE CLAVARIA ZOLLINGERI MUST BORDER THE OUTERMOST EDGE.
WE ARE CONNECTED TO EVERY PERSON ON THIS PLANET BY CENTILLIONS OF INVISIBLE CORDS.

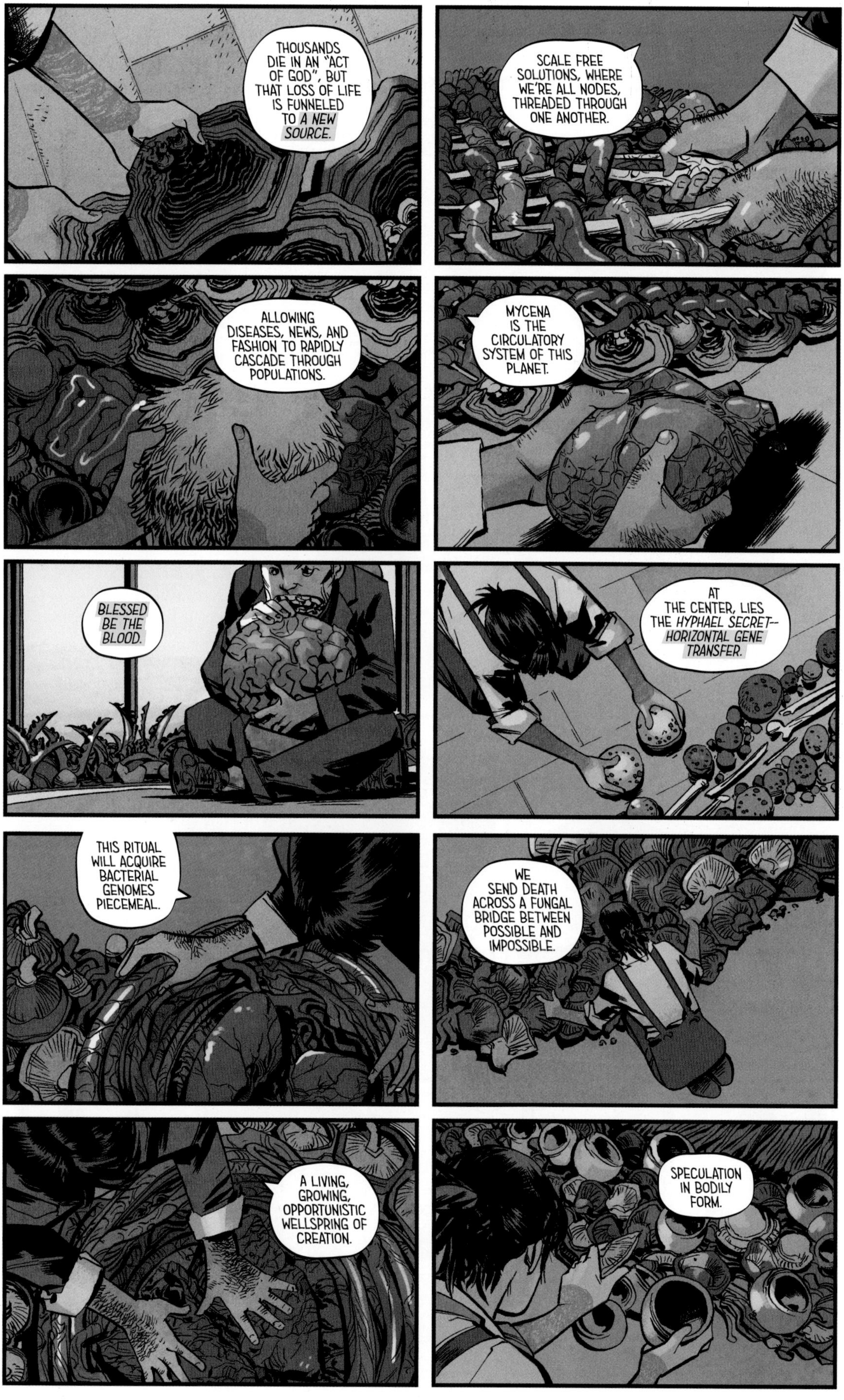
THOUSANDS DIE IN AN "ACT OF GOD", BUT THAT LOSS OF LIFE IS FUNNELED TO *A NEW SOURCE*.
SCALE FREE SOLUTIONS, WHERE WE'RE ALL NODES, THREADED THROUGH ONE ANOTHER.
ALLOWING DISEASES, NEWS, AND FASHION TO RAPIDLY CASCADE THROUGH POPULATIONS.
MYCENA IS THE CIRCULATORY SYSTEM OF THIS PLANET.
BLESSED BE THE BLOOD.
AT THE CENTER, LIES THE *HYPHAEL SECRET-- HORIZONTAL GENE TRANSFER.*
THIS RITUAL WILL ACQUIRE BACTERIAL GENOMES PIECEMEAL.
WE SEND DEATH ACROSS A FUNGAL BRIDGE BETWEEN POSSIBLE AND IMPOSSIBLE.
A LIVING, GROWING, OPPORTUNISTIC WELLSPRING OF CREATION.
SPECULATION IN BODILY FORM.

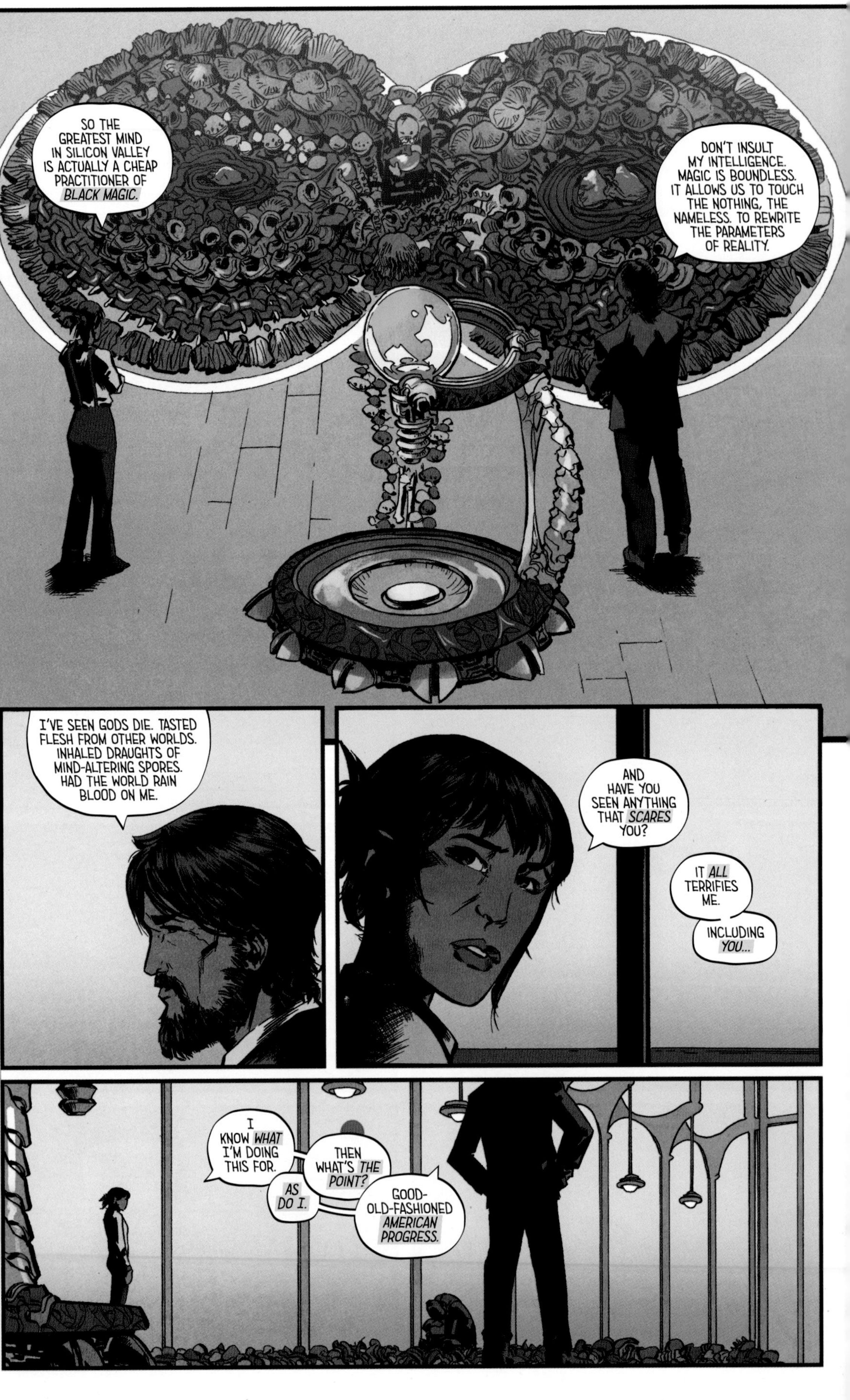
SO THE GREATEST MIND IN SILICON VALLEY IS ACTUALLY A CHEAP PRACTITIONER OF BLACK MAGIC.
DON'T INSULT MY INTELLIGENCE. MAGIC IS BOUNDLESS. IT ALLOWS US TO TOUCH THE NOTHING, THE NAMELESS. TO REWRITE THE PARAMETERS OF REALITY.
I'VE SEEN GODS DIE. TASTED FLESH FROM OTHER WORLDS. INHALED DRAUGHTS OF MIND-ALTERING SPORES. HAD THE WORLD RAIN BLOOD ON ME.
AND HAVE YOU SEEN ANYTHING THAT SCARES YOU?
IT ALL TERRIFIES ME.
INCLUDING YOU...
I KNOW WHAT I'M DOING THIS FOR.
THEN WHAT'S THE POINT?
AS DO I.
GOOD-OLD-FASHIONED AMERICAN PROGRESS.

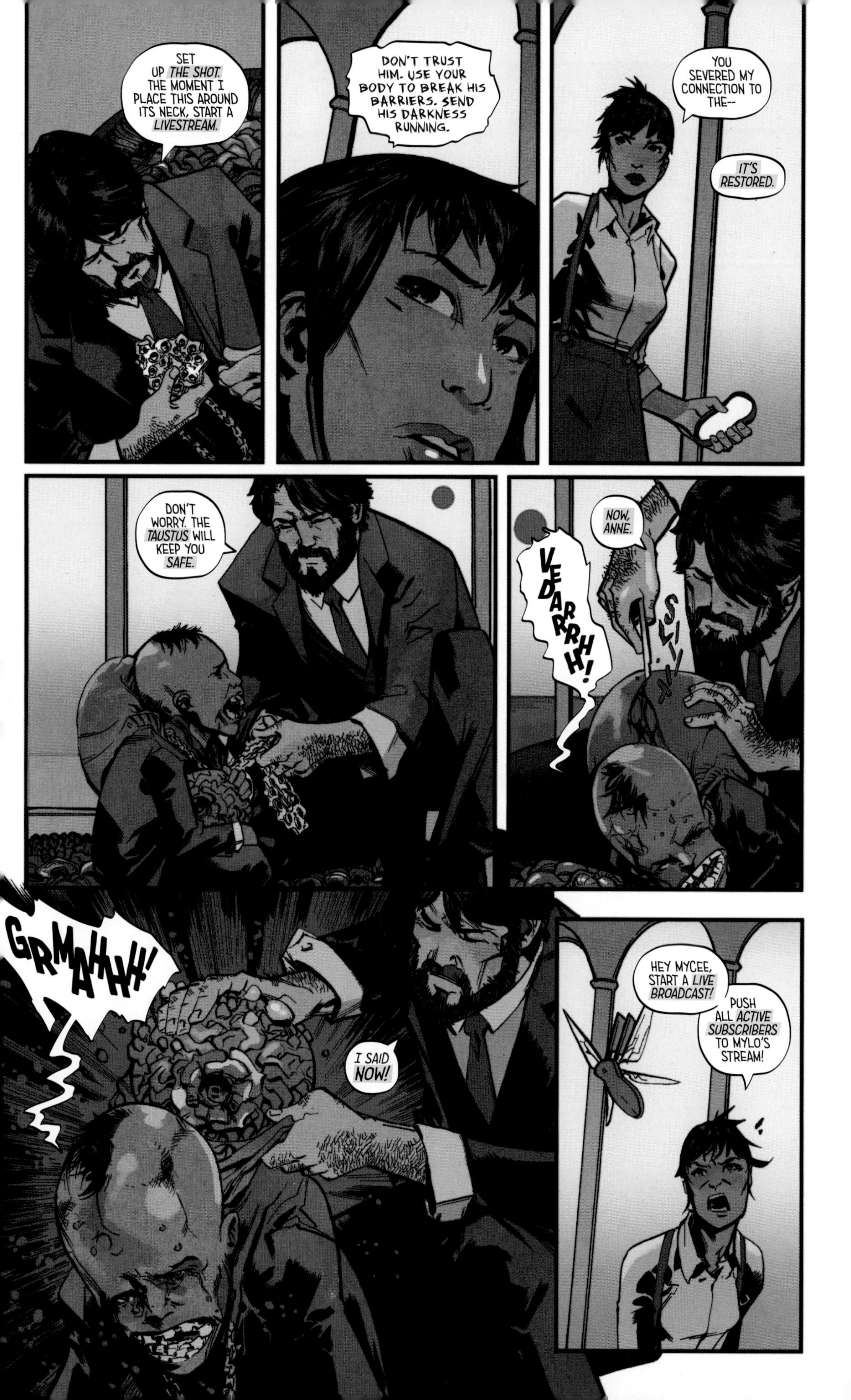
SET UP THE SHOT. THE MOMENT I PLACE THIS AROUND ITS NECK, START A LIVESTREAM.
DON'T TRUST HIM. USE YOUR BODY TO BREAK HIS BARRIERS. SEND HIS DARKNESS RUNNING.
YOU SEVERED MY CONNECTION TO THE--
IT'S RESTORED.
DON'T WORRY. THE TAUSTUS WILL KEEP YOU SAFE.
NOW, ANNE.
VEDARRHH!
SLIK
GRMAHHH!
I SAID NOW!
HEY MYCEE, START A LIVE BROADCAST!
PUSH ALL ACTIVE SUBSCRIBERS TO MYLO'S STREAM!

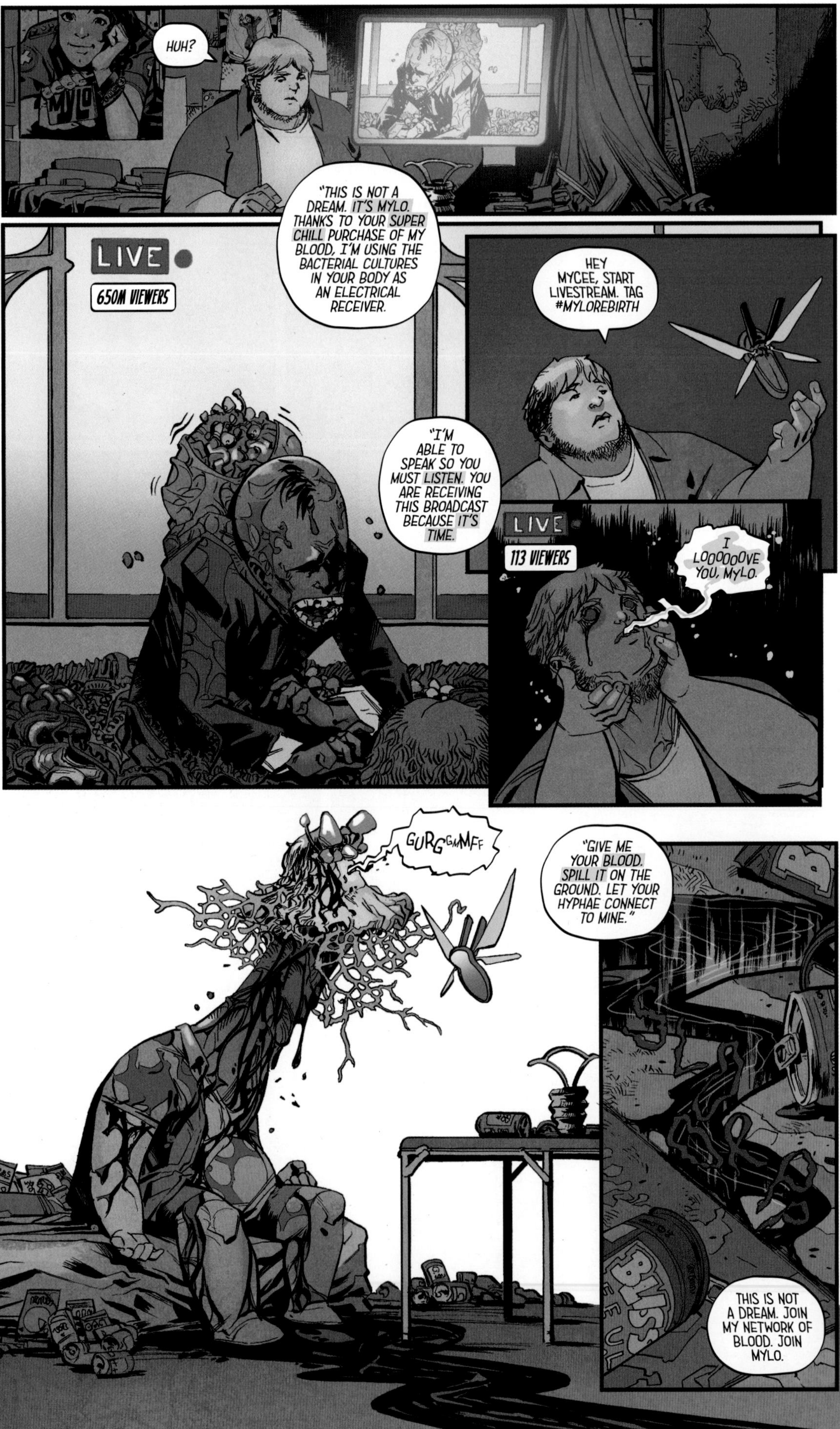
MYLO
HUH?
"THIS IS NOT A DREAM. IT'S MYLO. THANKS TO YOUR SUPER CHILL PURCHASE OF MY BLOOD, I'M USING THE BACTERIAL CULTURES IN YOUR BODY AS AN ELECTRICAL RECEIVER.
LIVE
650M VIEWERS
HEY MYCEE, START LIVESTREAM. TAG #MYLOREBIRTH
"I'M ABLE TO SPEAK SO YOU MUST LISTEN. YOU ARE RECEIVING THIS BROADCAST BECAUSE IT'S TIME.
LIVE
113 VIEWERS
I LOOOOOOVE YOU, MYLO.
GURGGMMFF
"GIVE ME YOUR BLOOD. SPILL IT ON THE GROUND. LET YOUR HYPHAE CONNECT TO MINE."
THIS IS NOT A DREAM. JOIN MY NETWORK OF BLOOD. JOIN MYLO.

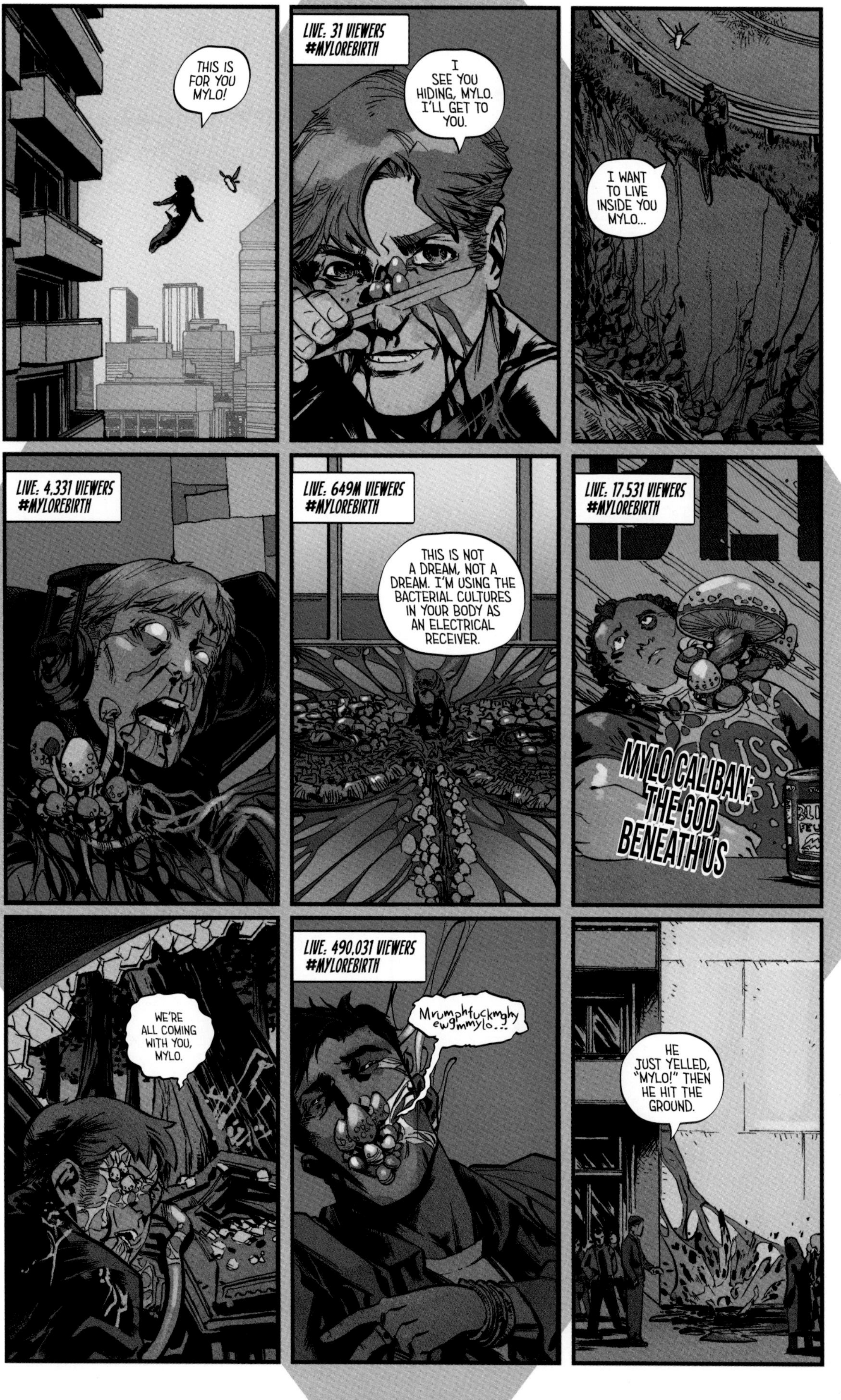
THIS IS FOR YOU MYLO!
LIVE: 31 VIEWERS #MYLOREBIRTH
I SEE YOU HIDING, MYLO. I'LL GET TO YOU.
I WANT TO LIVE INSIDE YOU MYLO...
LIVE: 4,331 VIEWERS #MYLOREBIRTH
LIVE: 649M VIEWERS #MYLOREBIRTH
THIS IS NOT A DREAM, NOT A DREAM. I'M USING THE BACTERIAL CULTURES IN YOUR BODY AS AN ELECTRICAL RECEIVER.
LIVE: 17,531 VIEWERS #MYLOREBIRTH
MYLO CALIBAN: THE GOD BENEATH US
WE'RE ALL COMING WITH YOU, MYLO.
LIVE: 490,031 VIEWERS #MYLOREBIRTH
Mrumphfuckmghy ewgmmylo...
HE JUST YELLED, "MYLO!" THEN HE HIT THE GROUND.

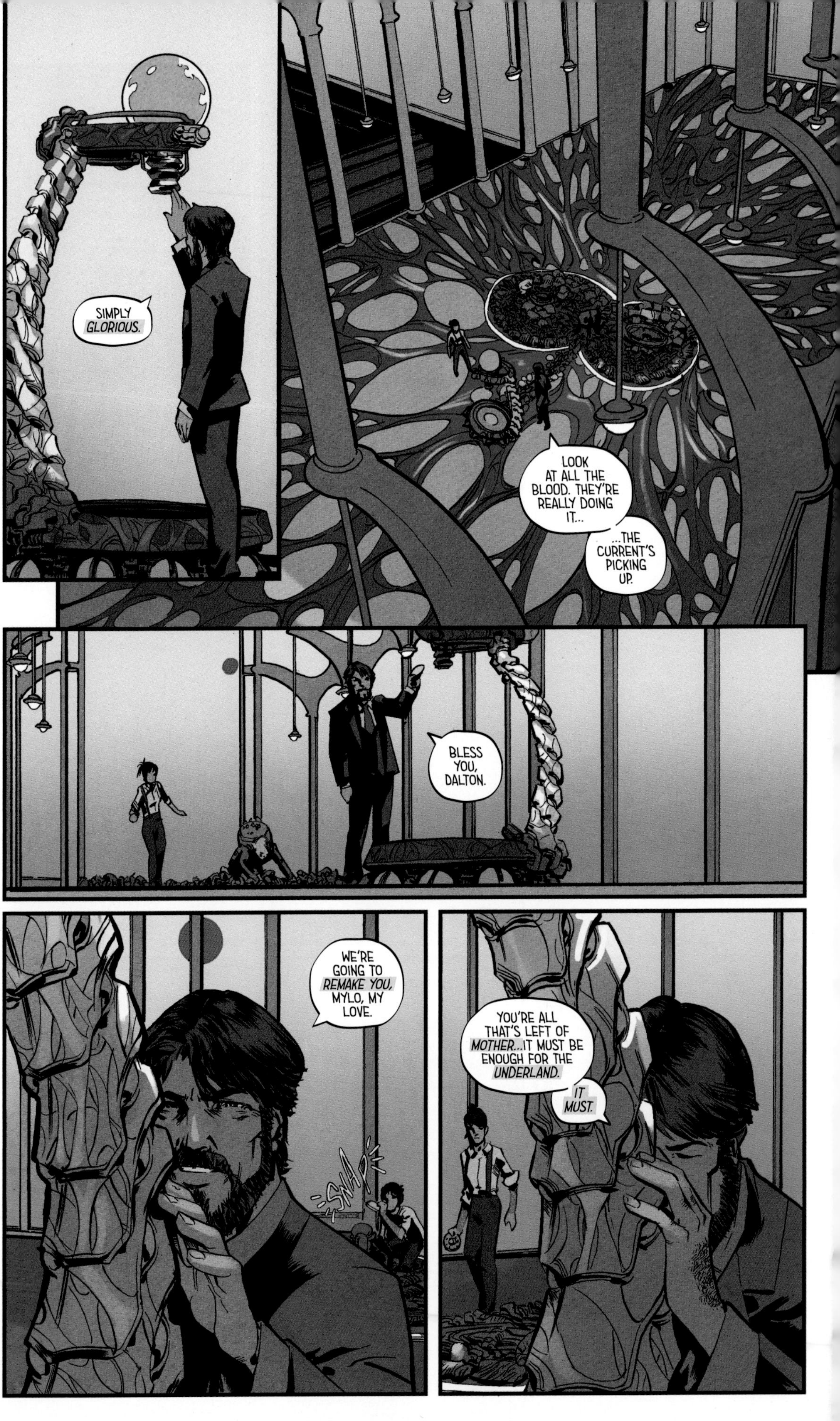
SIMPLY GLORIOUS.
LOOK AT ALL THE BLOOD. THEY'RE REALLY DOING IT...
...THE CURRENT'S PICKING UP.
BLESS YOU, DALTON.
WE'RE GOING TO REMAKE YOU, MYLO, MY LOVE.
SNAP
YOU'RE ALL THAT'S LEFT OF MOTHER...IT MUST BE ENOUGH FOR THE UNDERLAND.
IT MUST.

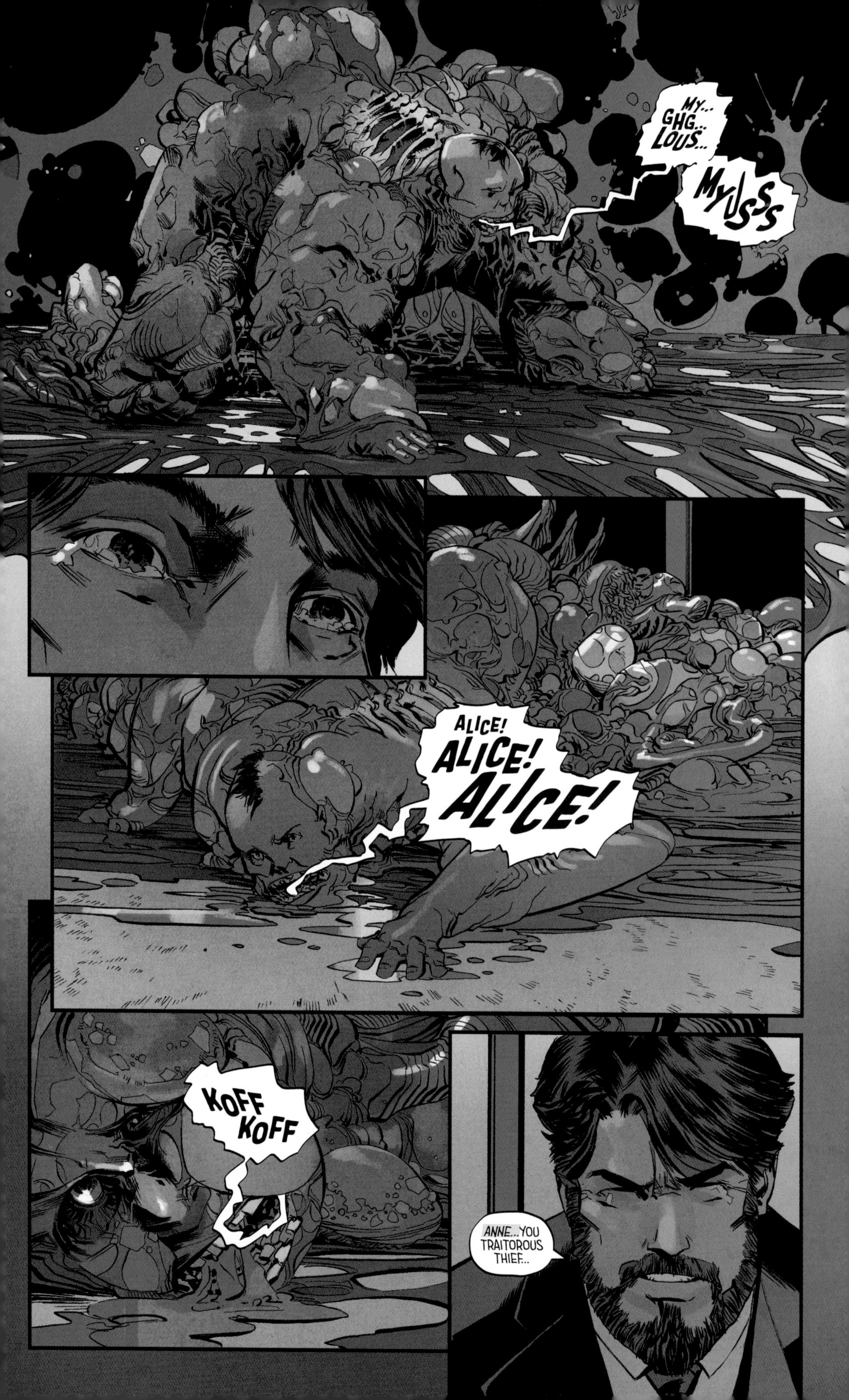
MY... GHG... LOUS...
MYUSSS
ALICE! ALICE! ALICE!
KOFF KOFF
ANNE... YOU TRAITOROUS THIEF...

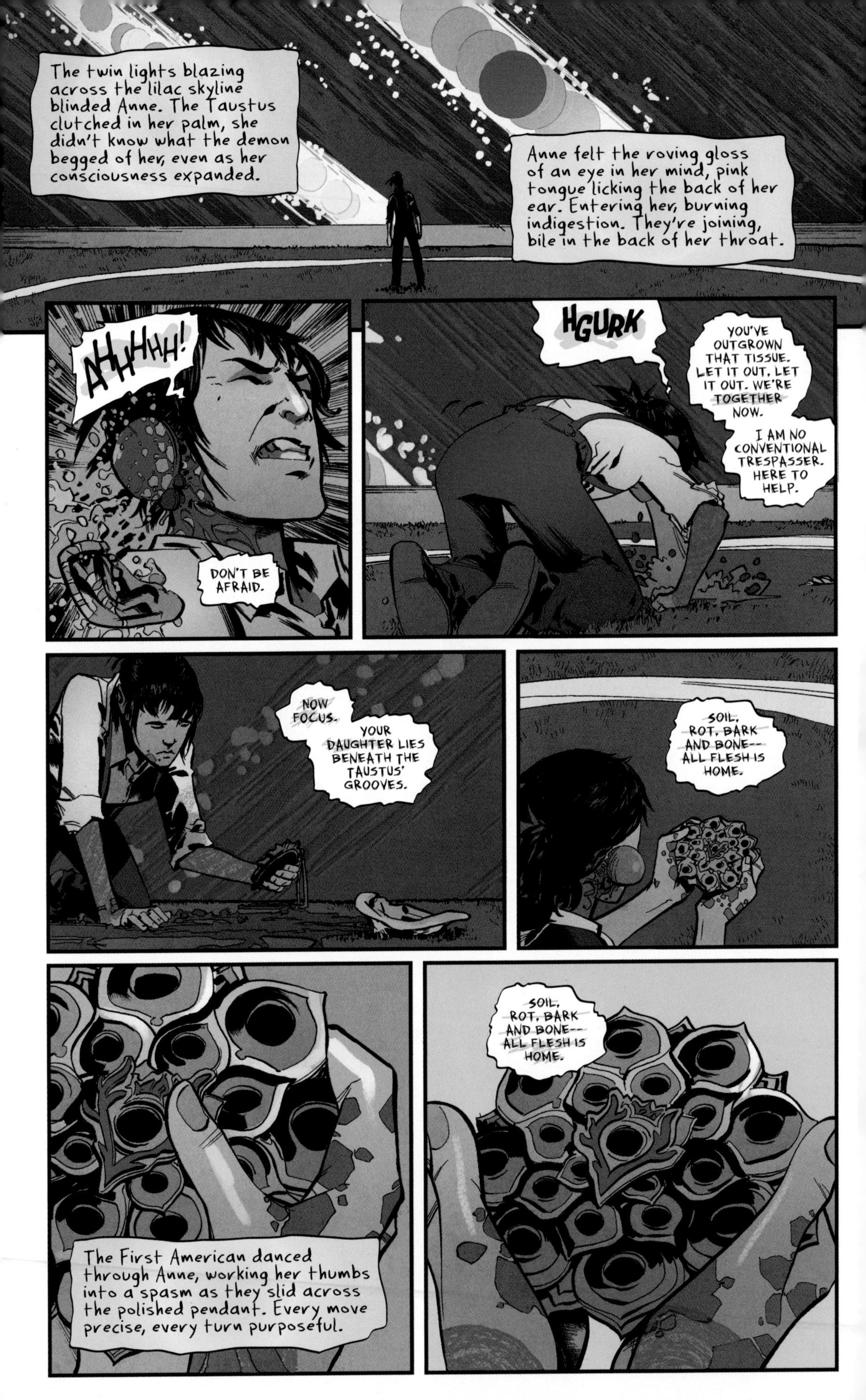
The twin lights blazing across the lilac skyline blinded Anne. The Taustus clutched in her palm, she didn't know what the demon begged of her, even as her consciousness expanded.
Anne felt the roving gloss of an eye in her mind, pink tongue licking the back of her ear. Entering her, burning indigestion. They're joining, bile in the back of her throat.
AHHHHH!
DON'T BE AFRAID.
HGURK
YOU'VE OUTGROWN THAT TISSUE. LET IT OUT. LET IT OUT. WE'RE TOGETHER NOW.
I AM NO CONVENTIONAL TRESPASSER. HERE TO HELP.
NOW FOCUS.
YOUR DAUGHTER LIES BENEATH THE TAUSTUS' GROOVES.
SOIL, ROT, BARK AND BONE-- ALL FLESH IS HOME.
The First American danced through Anne, working her thumbs into a spasm as they slid across the polished pendant. Every move precise, every turn purposeful.
SOIL, ROT, BARK AND BONE-- ALL FLESH IS HOME.

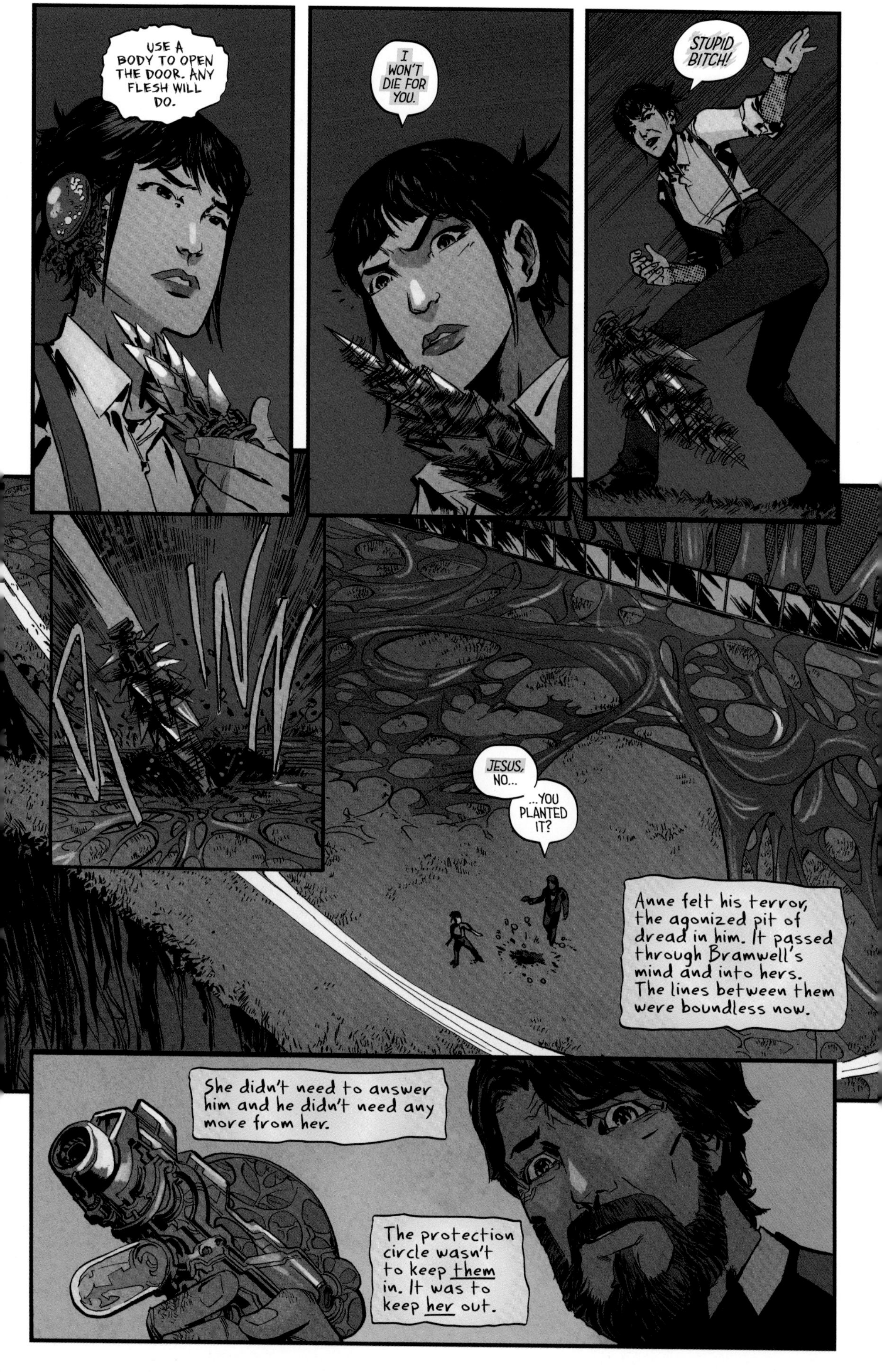
USE A BODY TO OPEN THE DOOR. ANY FLESH WILL DO.
I WON'T DIE FOR YOU.
STUPID BITCH!
JESUS, NO...
...YOU PLANTED IT?
Anne felt his terror, the agonized pit of dread in him. It passed through Bramwell's mind and into hers. The lines between them were boundless now.
She didn't need to answer him and he didn't need any more from her.
The protection circle wasn't to keep them in. It was to keep her out.

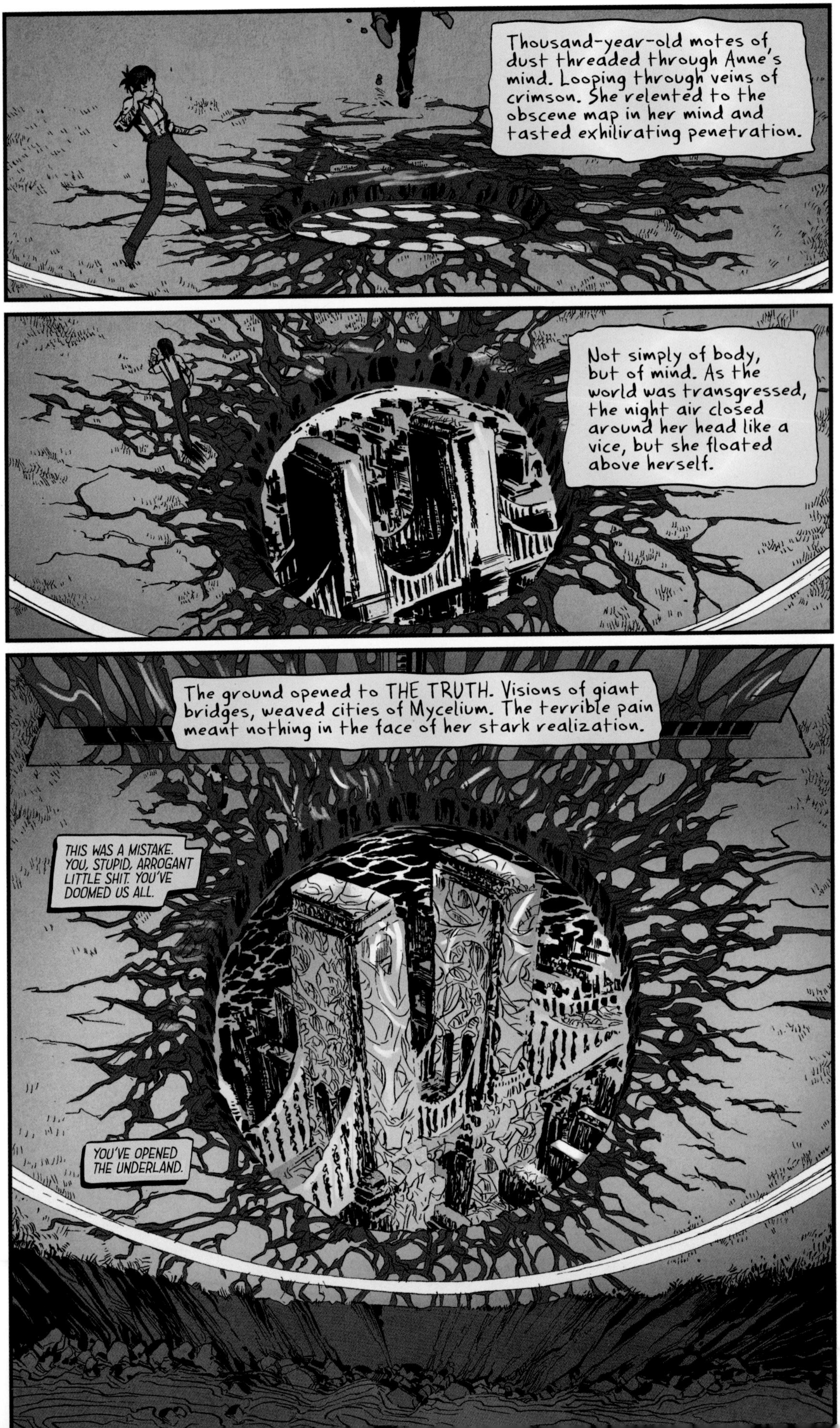
Thousand-year-old motes of dust threaded through Anne's mind. Looping through veins of crimson. She relented to the obscene map in her mind and tasted exhilirating penetration.
Not simply of body, but of mind. As the world was transgressed, the night air closed around her head like a vice, but she floated above herself.
The ground opened to THE TRUTH. Visions of giant bridges, weaved cities of Mycelium. The terrible pain meant nothing in the face of her stark realization.
THIS WAS A MISTAKE. YOU, STUPID, ARROGANT LITTLE SHIT. YOU'VE DOOMED US ALL.
YOU'VE OPENED THE UNDERLAND.

5

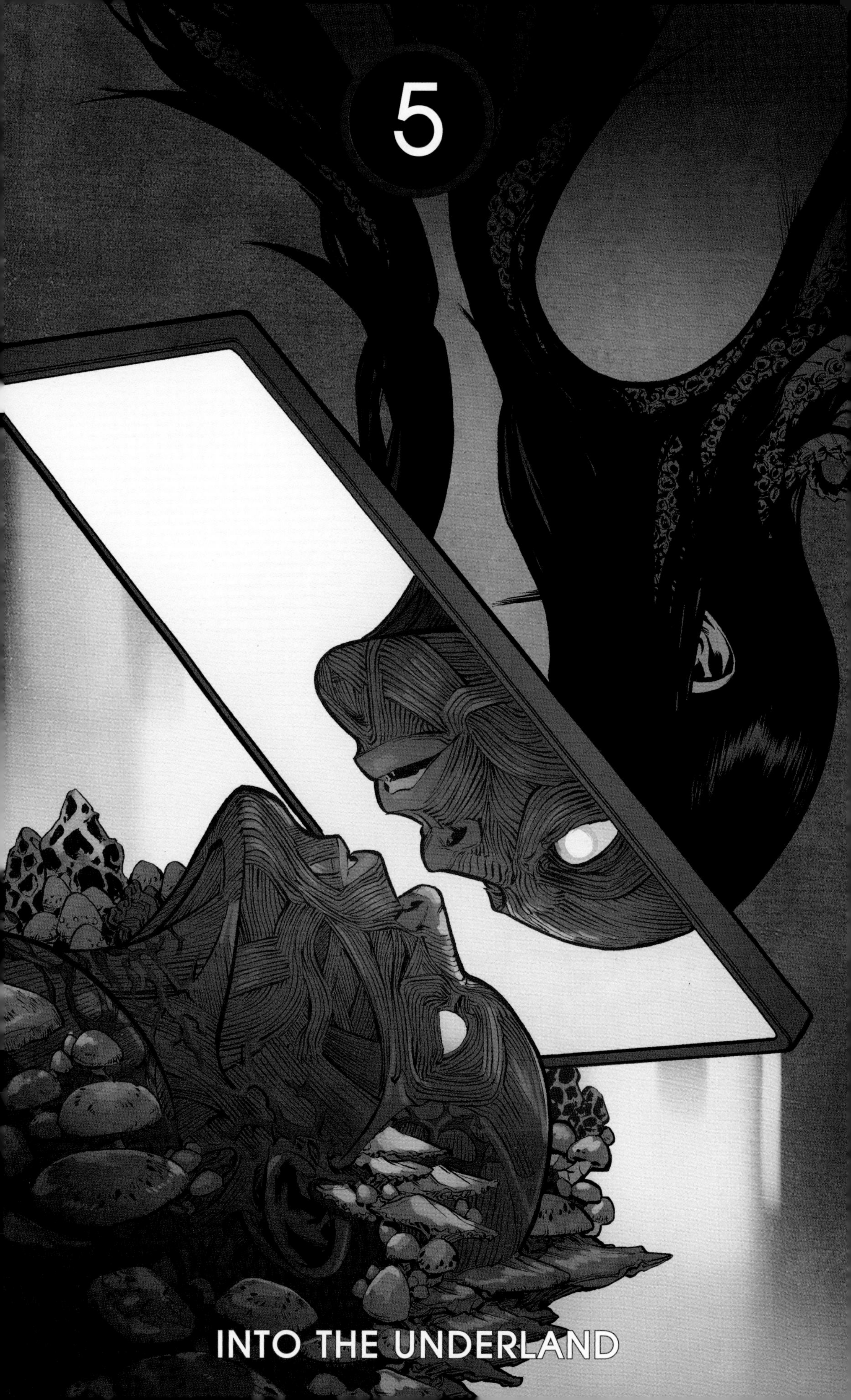

INTO THE UNDERLAND

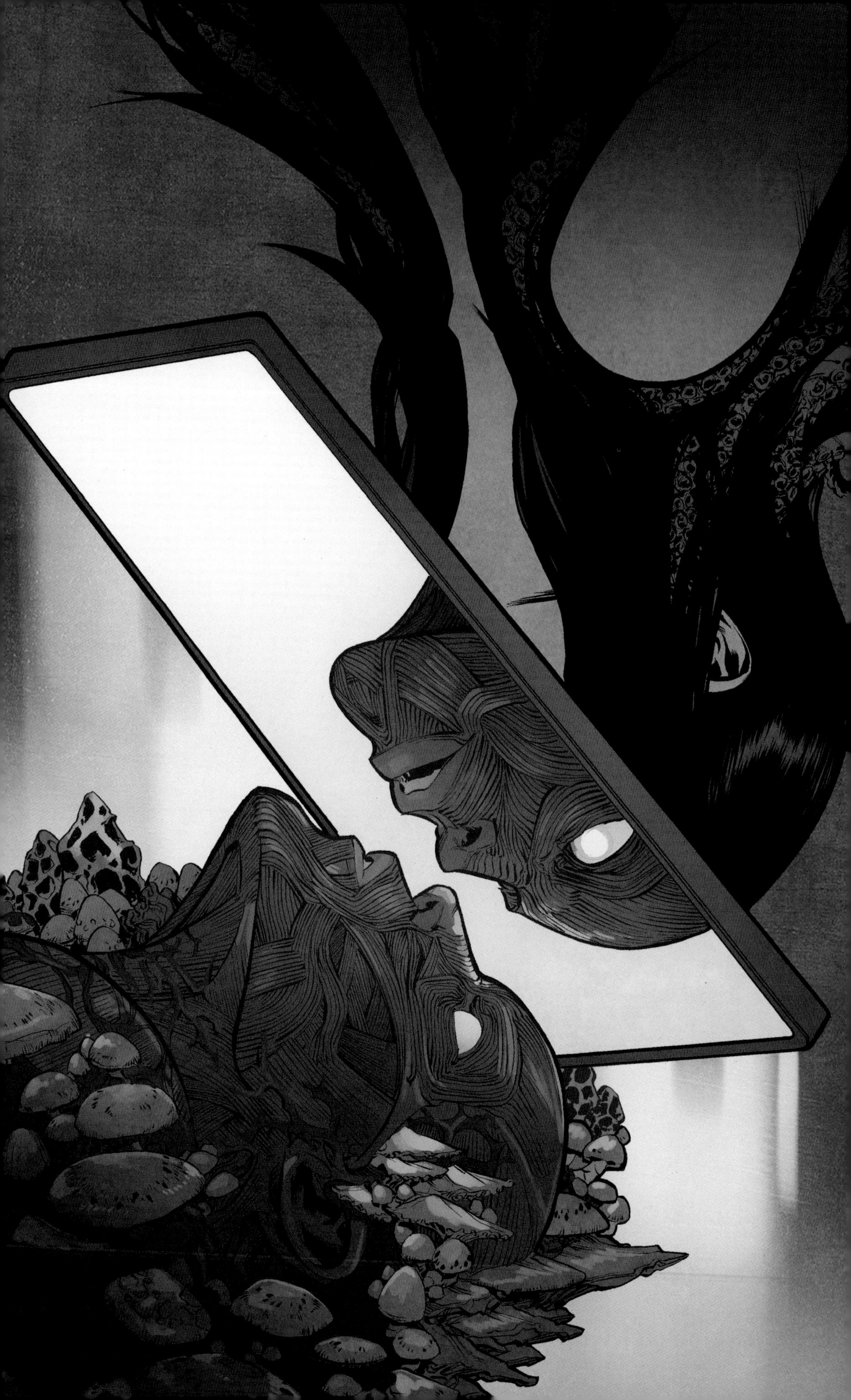

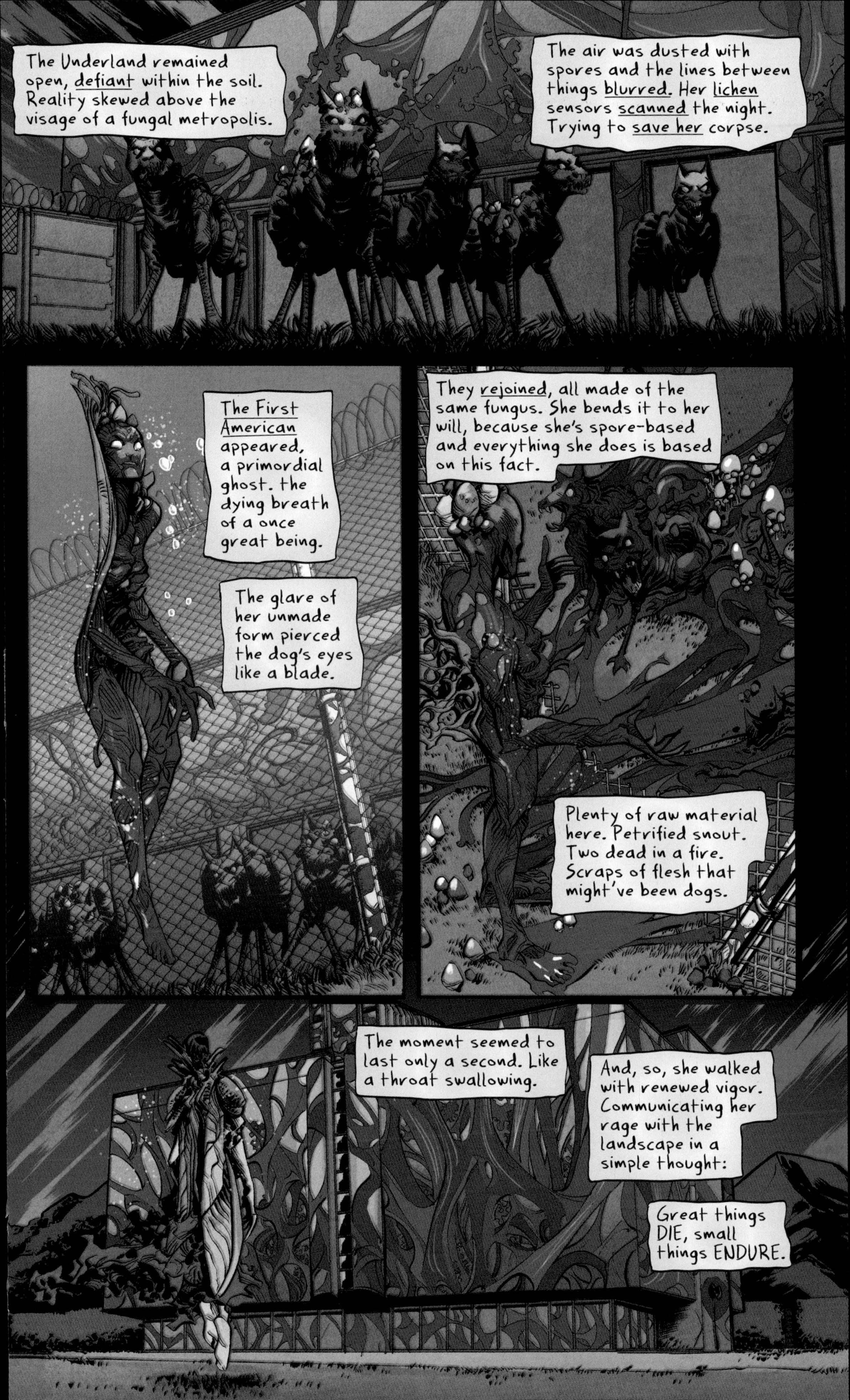
The Underland remained open, defiant within the soil. Reality skewed above the visage of a fungal metropolis.
The air was dusted with spores and the lines between things blurred. Her lichen sensors scanned the night. Trying to save her corpse.
The First American appeared, a primordial ghost. the dying breath of a once great being.
The glare of her unmade form pierced the dog's eyes like a blade.
They rejoined, all made of the same fungus. She bends it to her will, because she's spore-based and everything she does is based on this fact.
Plenty of raw material here. Petrified snout. Two dead in a fire. Scraps of flesh that might've been dogs.
The moment seemed to last only a second. Like a throat swallowing.
And, so, she walked with renewed vigor. Communicating her rage with the landscape in a simple thought:
Great things DIE, small things ENDURE.

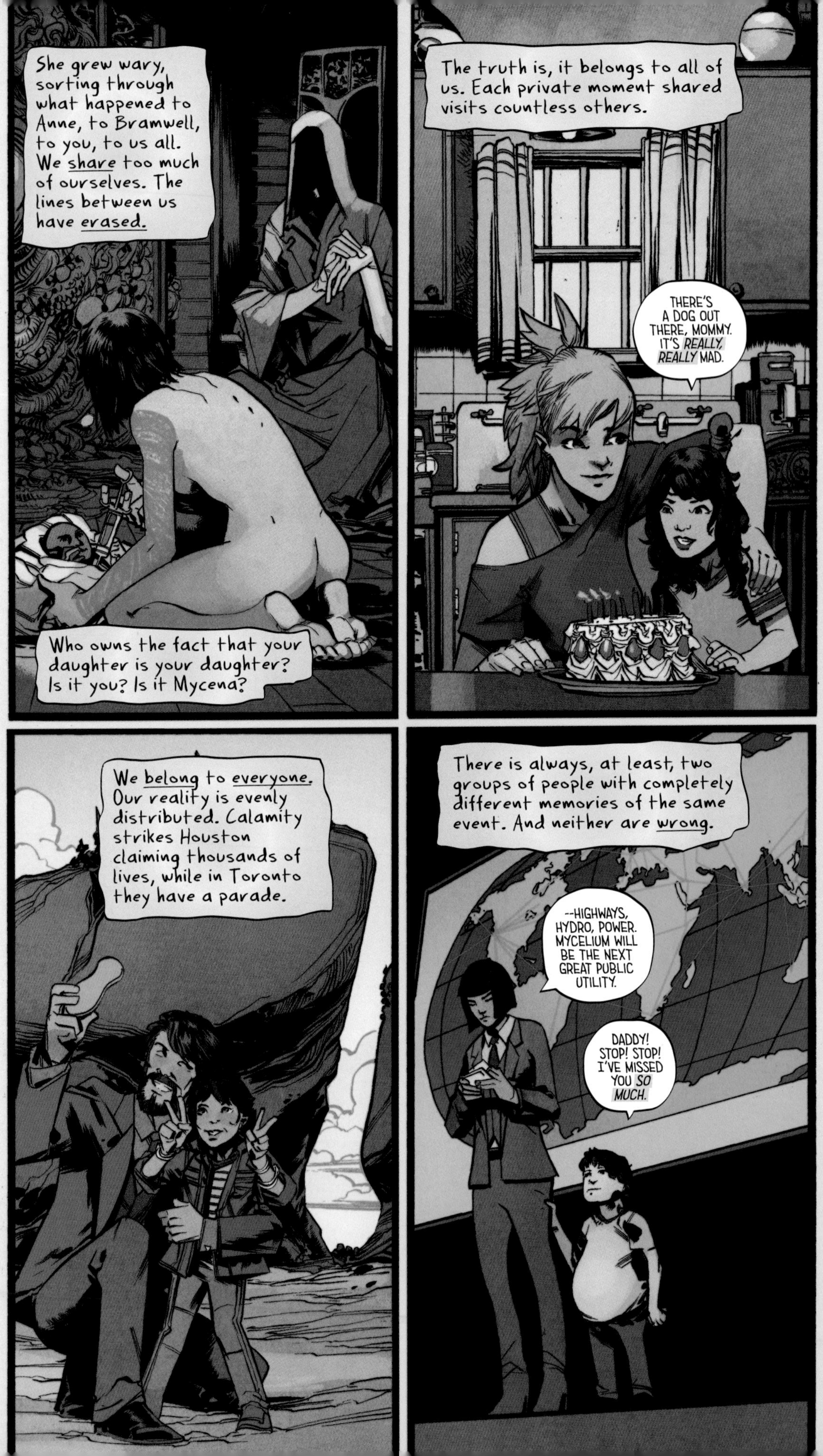
She grew wary, sorting through what happened to Anne, to Bramwell, to you, to us all. We share too much of ourselves. The lines between us have erased.
Who owns the fact that your daughter is your daughter? Is it you? Is it Mycena?
The truth is, it belongs to all of us. Each private moment shared visits countless others.
THERE'S A DOG OUT THERE, MOMMY. IT'S REALLY, REALLY MAD.
We belong to everyone. Our reality is evenly distributed. Calamity strikes Houston claiming thousands of lives, while in Toronto they have a parade.
There is always, at least, two groups of people with completely different memories of the same event. And neither are wrong.
--HIGHWAYS, HYDRO, POWER. MYCELIUM WILL BE THE NEXT GREAT PUBLIC UTILITY.
DADDY! STOP! STOP! I'VE MISSED YOU SO MUCH.

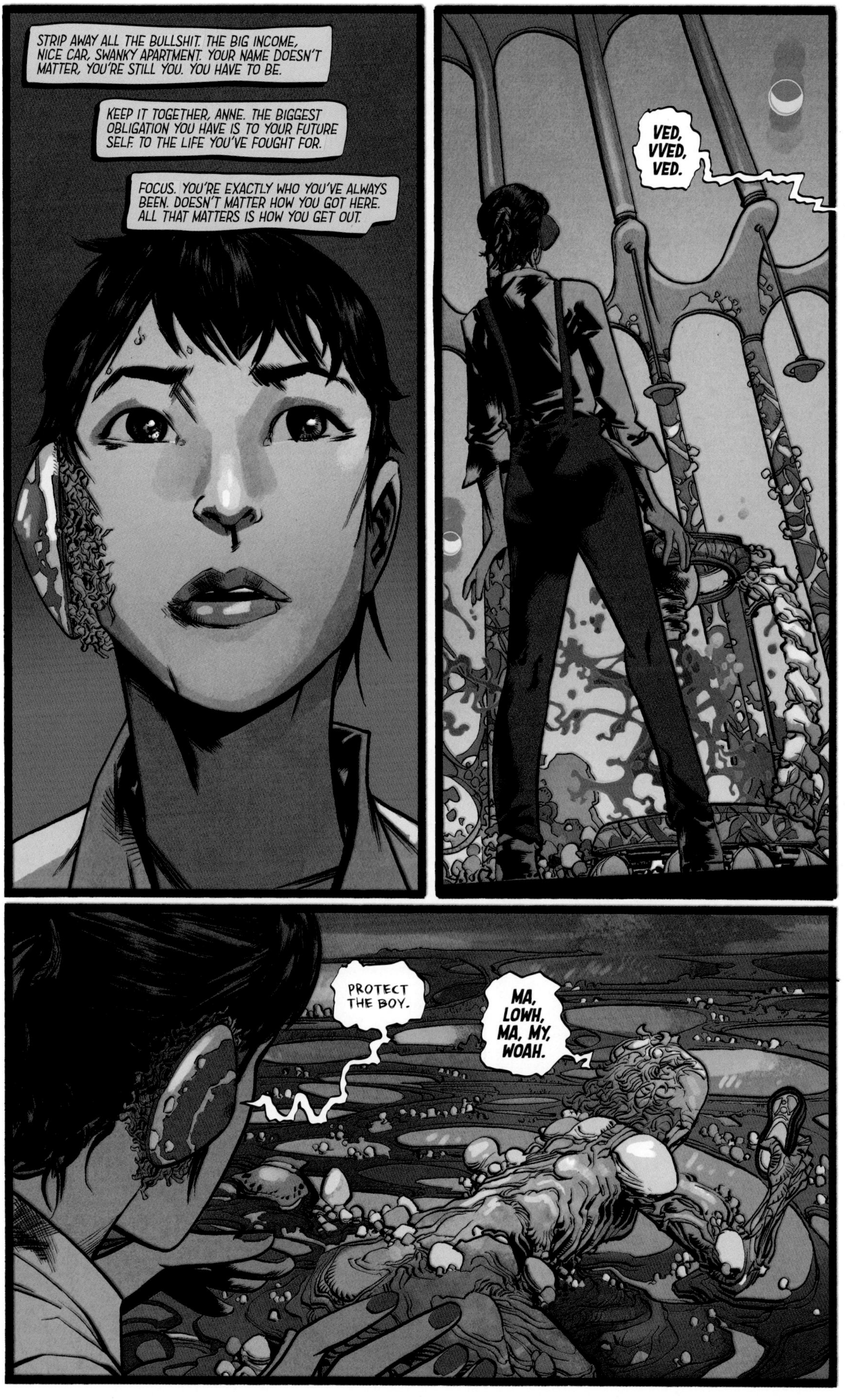
STRIP AWAY ALL THE BULLSHIT. THE BIG INCOME, NICE CAR, SWANKY APARTMENT. YOUR NAME DOESN'T MATTER, YOU'RE STILL YOU. YOU HAVE TO BE.
KEEP IT TOGETHER, ANNE. THE BIGGEST OBLIGATION YOU HAVE IS TO YOUR FUTURE SELF. TO THE LIFE YOU'VE FOUGHT FOR.
FOCUS. YOU'RE EXACTLY WHO YOU'VE ALWAYS BEEN. DOESN'T MATTER HOW YOU GOT HERE. ALL THAT MATTERS IS HOW YOU GET OUT.
VED, VVED, VED.
PROTECT THE BOY.
MA, LOWH, MA, MY, WOAH.

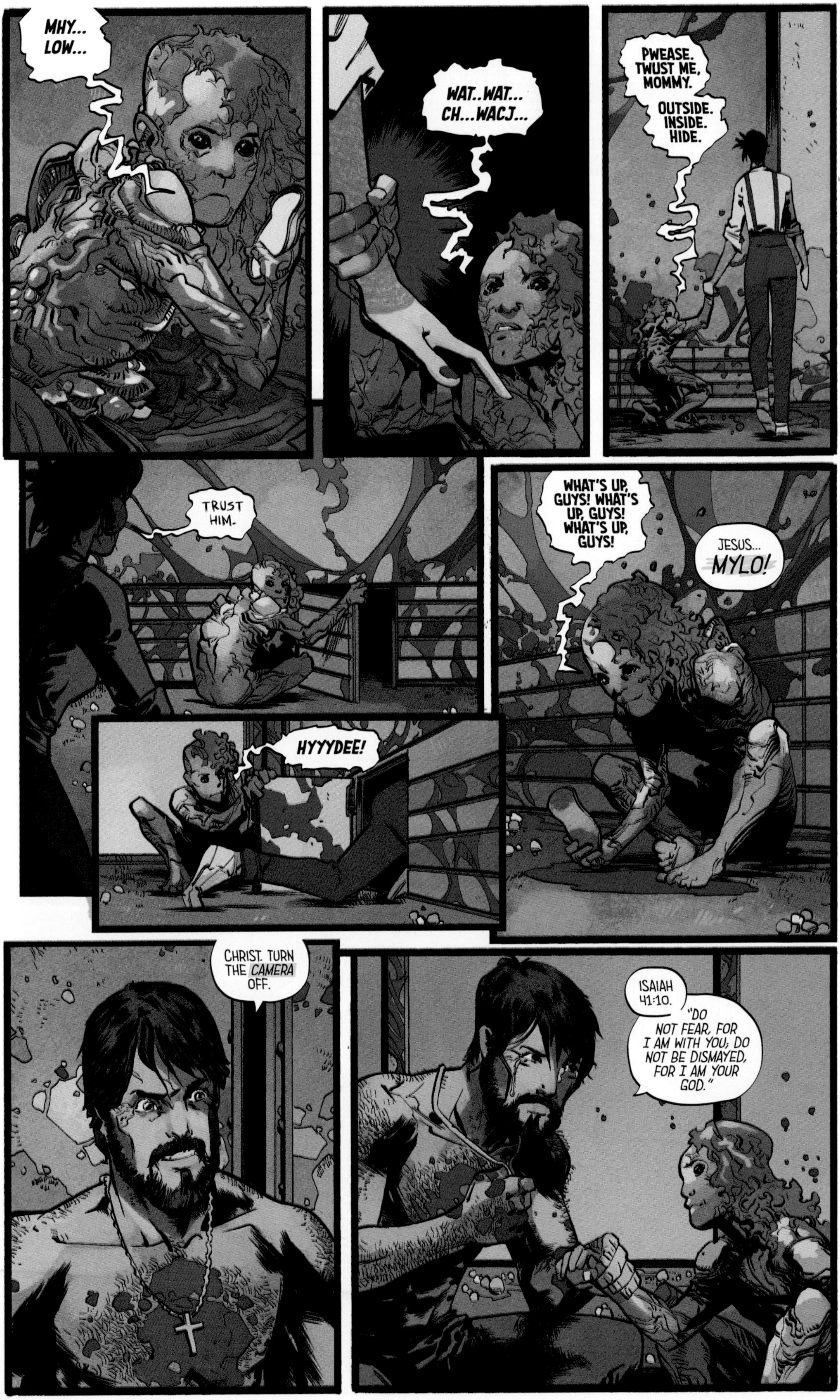
MHY... LOW...
WAT..WAT... CH...WACJ...
PWEASE. TWUST ME, MOMMY.
OUTSIDE. INSIDE. HIDE.
TRUST HIM.
WHAT'S UP, GUYS! WHAT'S UP, GUYS! WHAT'S UP, GUYS!
JESUS... MYLO!
HYYYDEE!
CHRIST. TURN THE CAMERA OFF.
ISAIAH 41:10.
"DO NOT FEAR, FOR I AM WITH YOU; DO NOT BE DISMAYED, FOR I AM YOUR GOD."

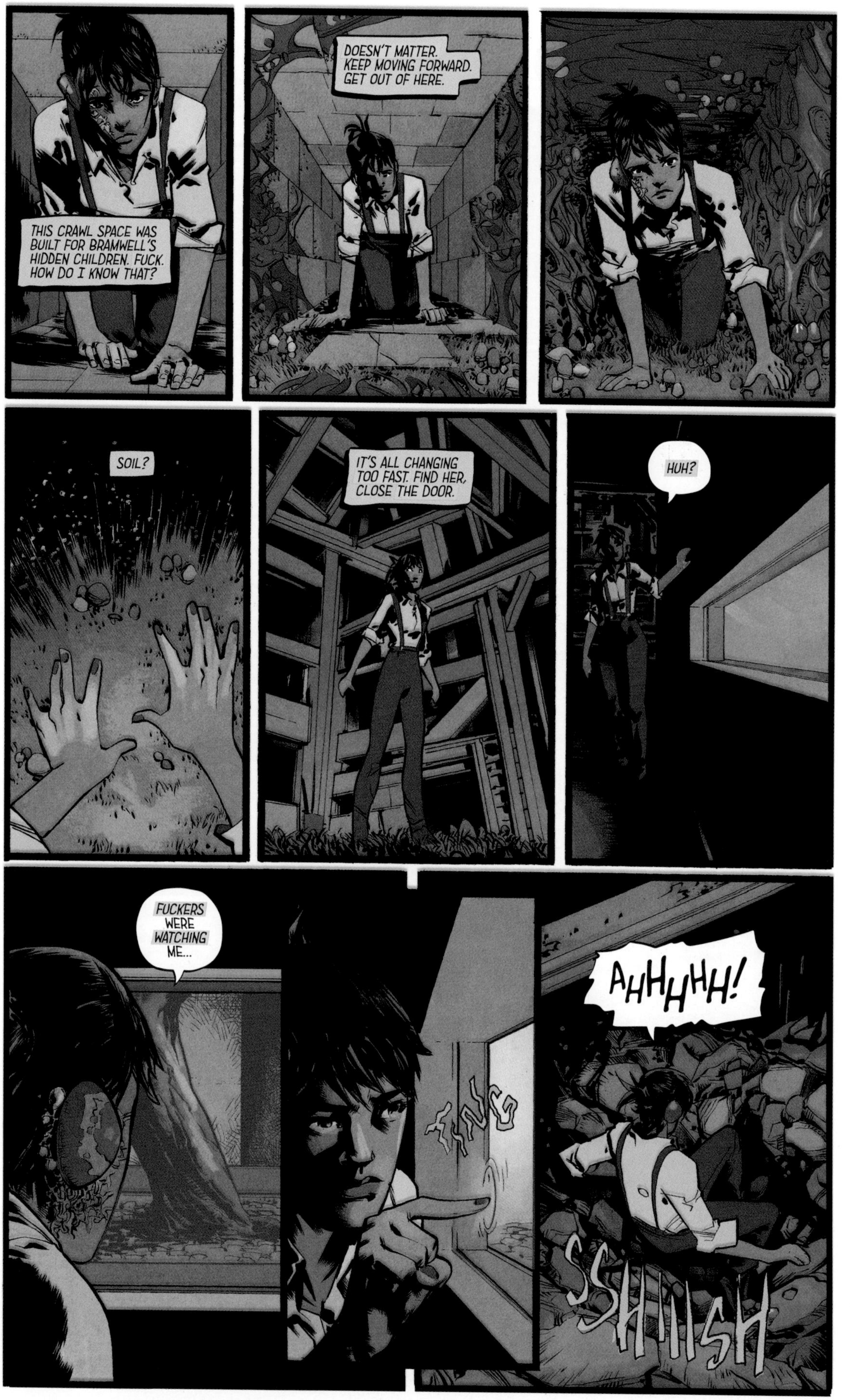
THIS CRAWL SPACE WAS BUILT FOR BRAMWELL'S HIDDEN CHILDREN. FUCK. HOW DO I KNOW THAT?
DOESN'T MATTER. KEEP MOVING FORWARD. GET OUT OF HERE.
SOIL?
IT'S ALL CHANGING TOO FAST. FIND HER, CLOSE THE DOOR.
HUH?
FUCKERS WERE WATCHING ME...
AHHHHH!
SSHIIISH

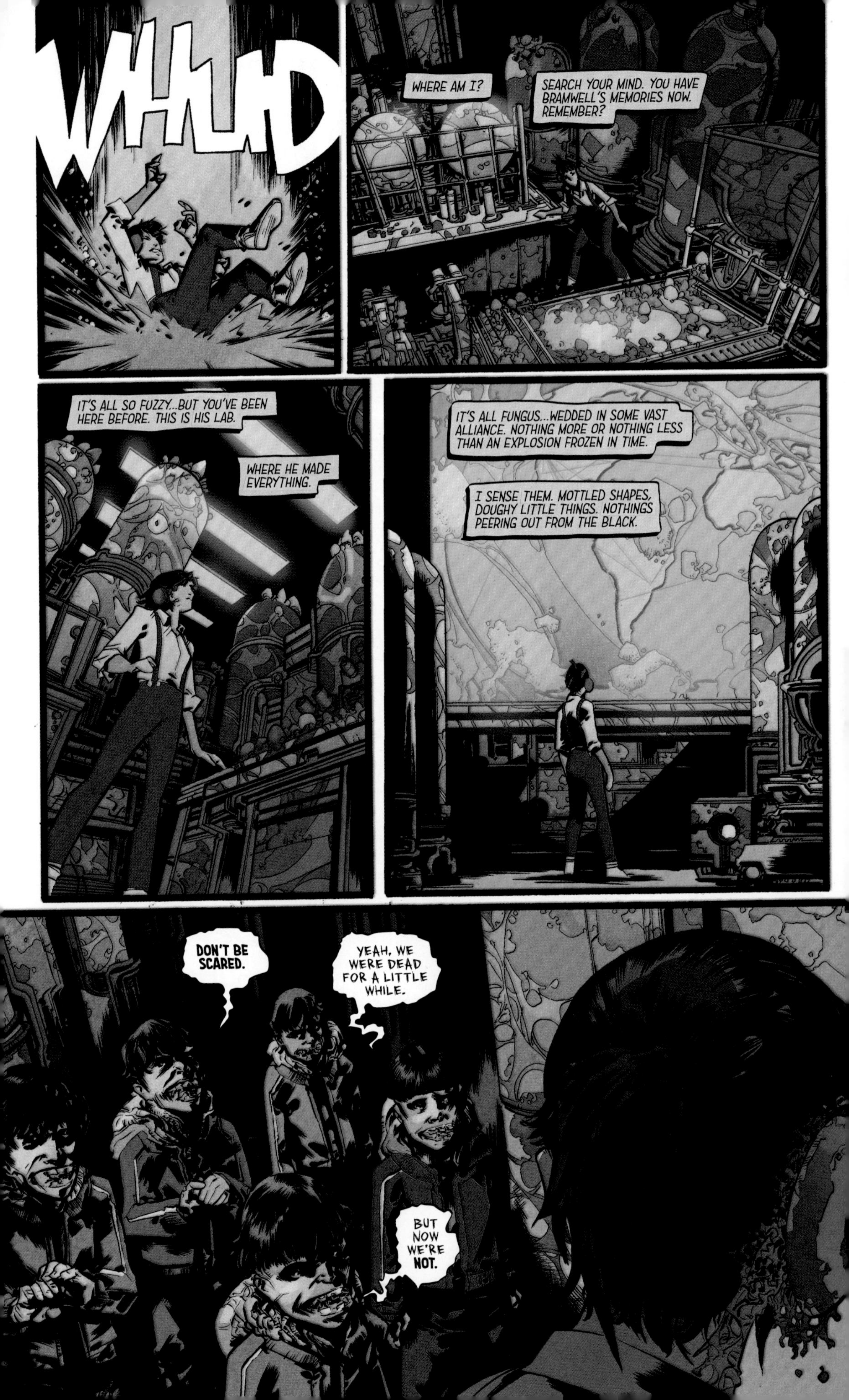
WHUD
WHERE AM I?
SEARCH YOUR MIND. YOU HAVE BRAMWELL'S MEMORIES NOW. REMEMBER?
IT'S ALL SO FUZZY...BUT YOU'VE BEEN HERE BEFORE. THIS IS HIS LAB.
WHERE HE MADE EVERYTHING.
IT'S ALL FUNGUS...WEDDED IN SOME VAST ALLIANCE. NOTHING MORE OR NOTHING LESS THAN AN EXPLOSION FROZEN IN TIME.
I SENSE THEM. MOTTLED SHAPES, DOUGHY LITTLE THINGS. NOTHINGS PEERING OUT FROM THE BLACK.
DON'T BE SCARED.
YEAH, WE WERE DEAD FOR A LITTLE WHILE.
BUT NOW WE'RE NOT.

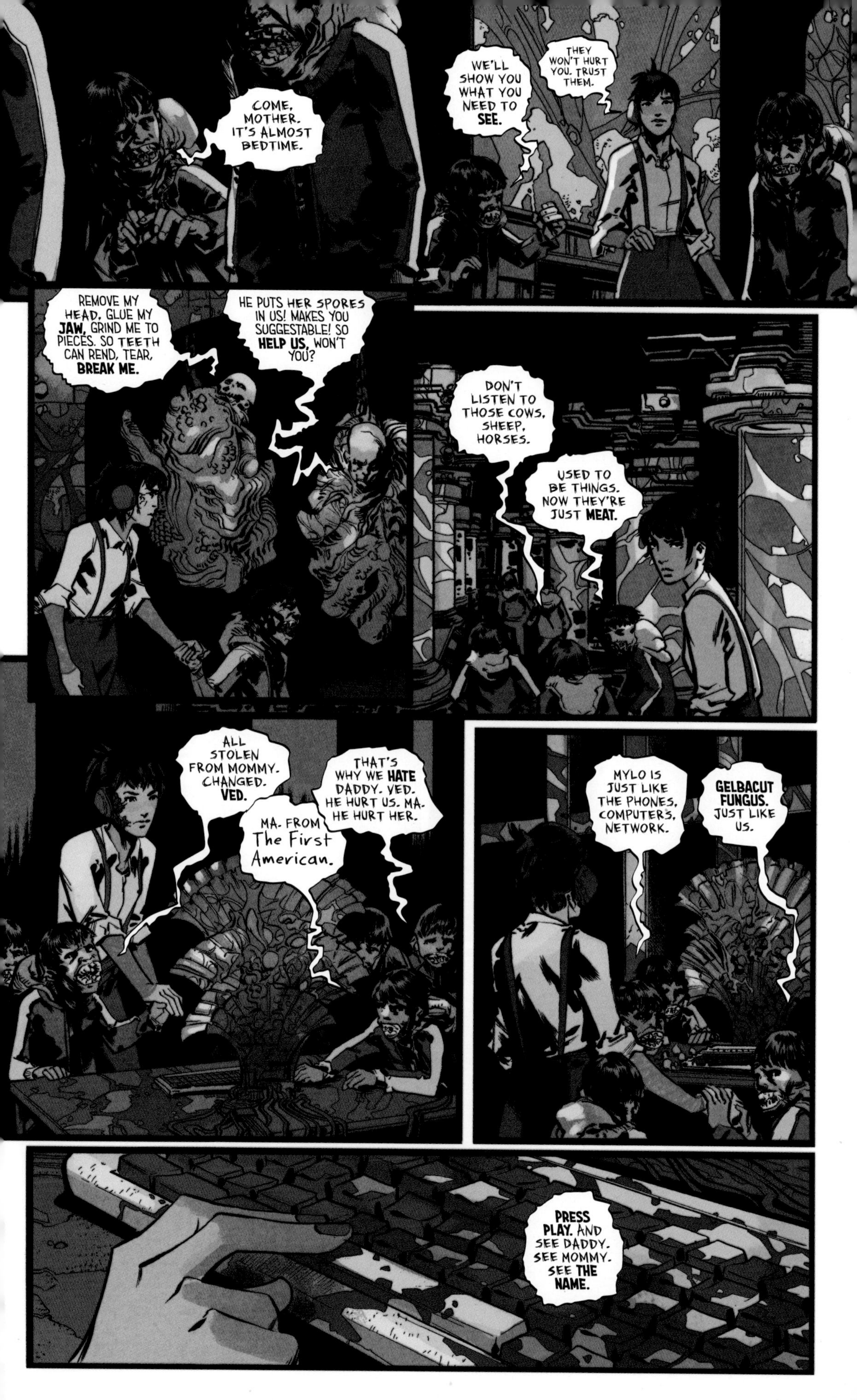
COME, MOTHER. IT'S ALMOST BEDTIME.
WE'LL SHOW YOU WHAT YOU NEED TO **SEE.**
THEY WON'T HURT YOU. TRUST THEM.
REMOVE MY HEAD, GLUE MY **JAW,** GRIND ME TO PIECES. SO TEETH CAN REND, TEAR, **BREAK ME.**
HE PUTS HER SPORES IN US! MAKES YOU SUGGESTABLE! SO **HELP US,** WON'T YOU?
DON'T LISTEN TO THOSE COWS, SHEEP, HORSES.
USED TO BE THINGS. NOW THEY'RE JUST **MEAT.**
ALL STOLEN FROM MOMMY. CHANGED. **VED.**
MA. FROM The First American.
THAT'S WHY WE **HATE** DADDY. VED. HE HURT US. MA. HE HURT HER.
MYLO IS JUST LIKE THE PHONES, COMPUTERS, NETWORK.
GELBACUT FUNGUS. JUST LIKE US.
PRESS PLAY. AND SEE DADDY. SEE MOMMY. SEE **THE NAME.**

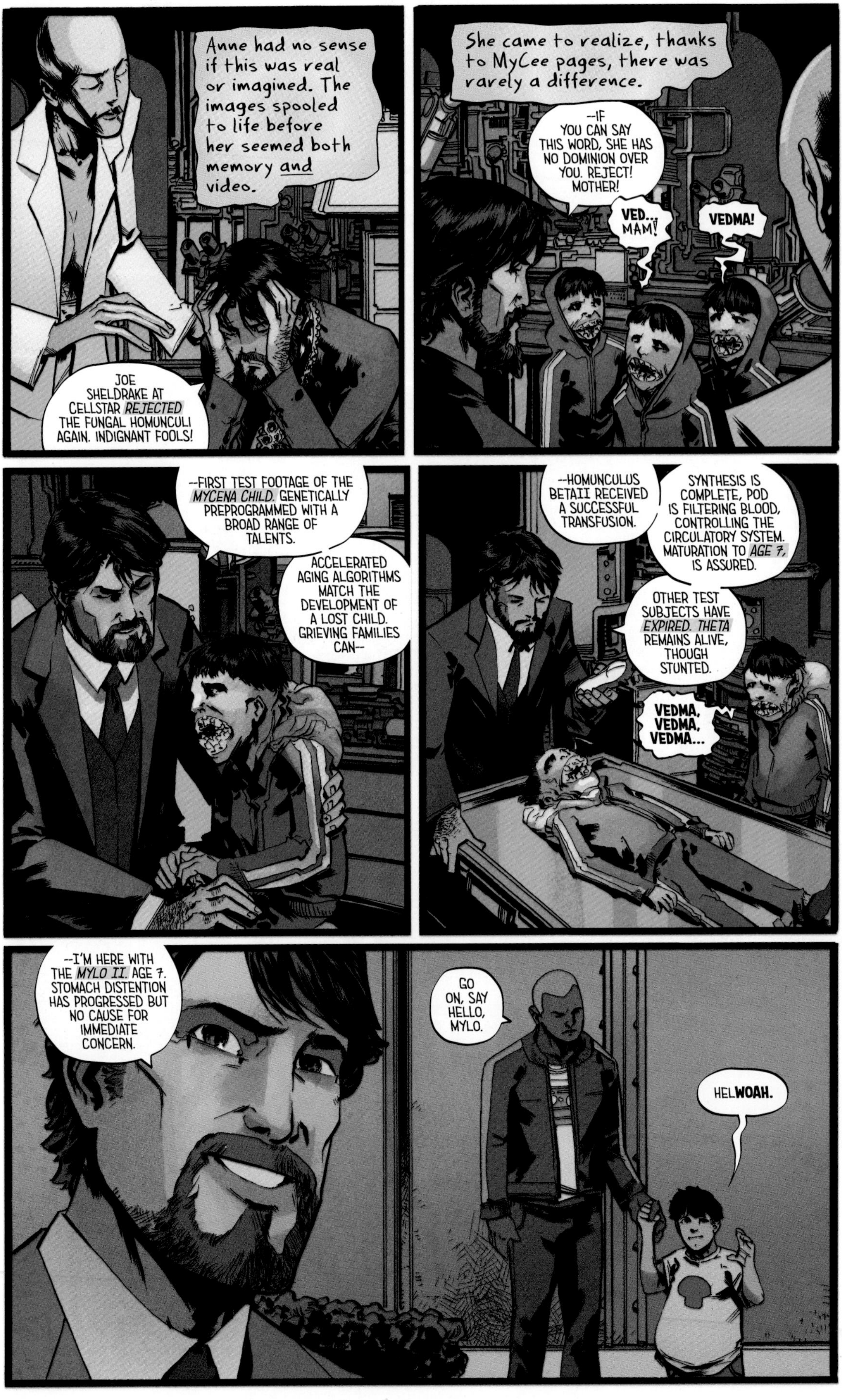
Anne had no sense if this was real or imagined. The images spooled to life before her seemed both memory and video.
JOE SHELDRAKE AT CELLSTAR REJECTED THE FUNGAL HOMUNCULI AGAIN. INDIGNANT FOOLS!
She came to realize, thanks to MyCee pages, there was rarely a difference.
--IF YOU CAN SAY THIS WORD, SHE HAS NO DOMINION OVER YOU. REJECT! MOTHER!
VED... MAM!
VEDMA!
--FIRST TEST FOOTAGE OF THE MYCENA CHILD. GENETICALLY PREPROGRAMMED WITH A BROAD RANGE OF TALENTS.
ACCELERATED AGING ALGORITHMS MATCH THE DEVELOPMENT OF A LOST CHILD. GRIEVING FAMILIES CAN--
--HOMUNCULUS BETAII RECEIVED A SUCCESSFUL TRANSFUSION.
SYNTHESIS IS COMPLETE, POD IS FILTERING BLOOD, CONTROLLING THE CIRCULATORY SYSTEM. MATURATION TO AGE 7, IS ASSURED.
OTHER TEST SUBJECTS HAVE EXPIRED. THETA REMAINS ALIVE, THOUGH STUNTED.
VEDMA, VEDMA, VEDMA...
--I'M HERE WITH THE MYLO II. AGE 7. STOMACH DISTENTION HAS PROGRESSED BUT NO CAUSE FOR IMMEDIATE CONCERN.
GO ON, SAY HELLO, MYLO.
HELWOAH.

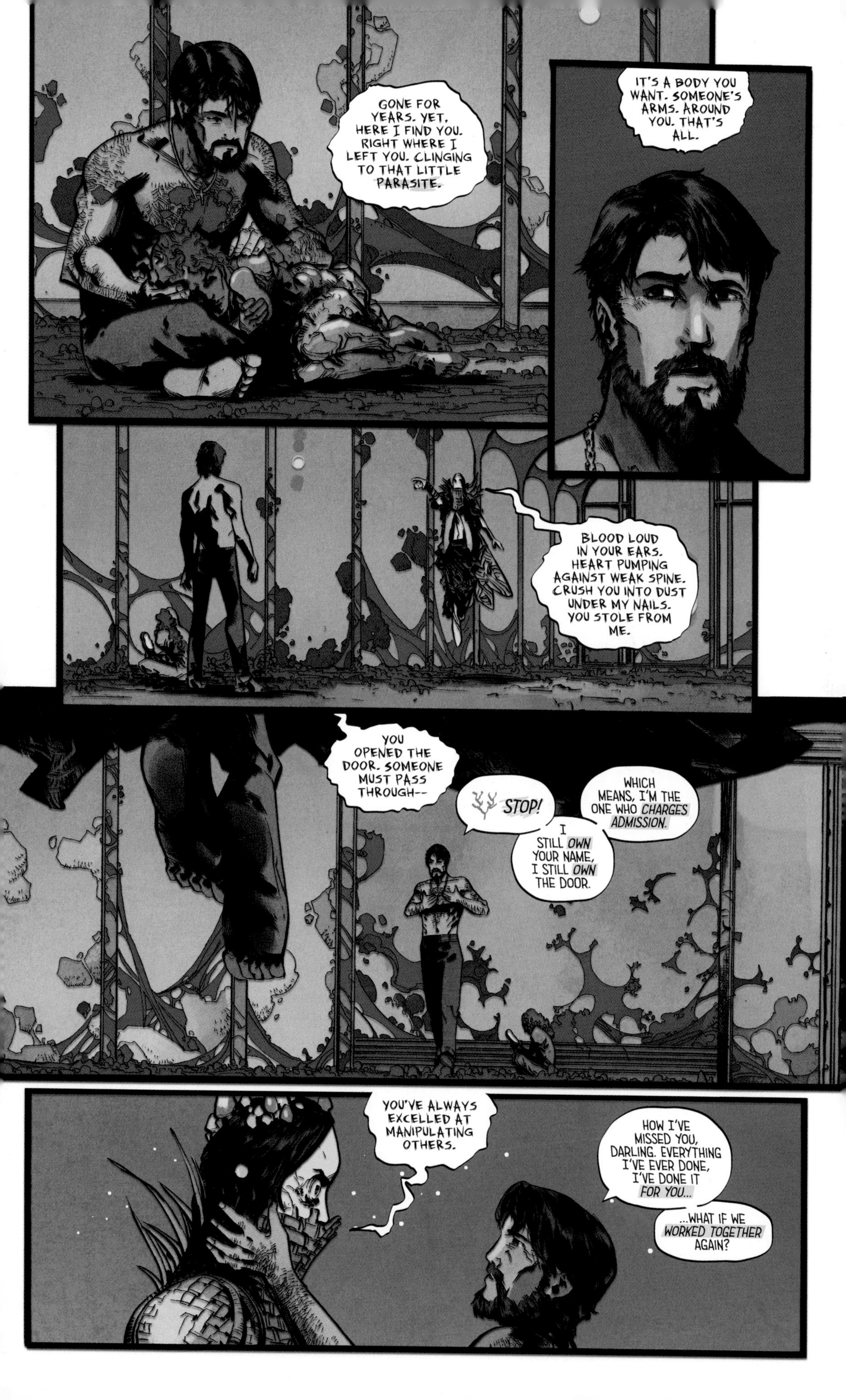
GONE FOR YEARS. YET, HERE I FIND YOU. RIGHT WHERE I LEFT YOU. CLINGING TO THAT LITTLE PARASITE.
IT'S A BODY YOU WANT. SOMEONE'S ARMS. AROUND YOU. THAT'S ALL.
BLOOD LOUD IN YOUR EARS. HEART PUMPING AGAINST WEAK SPINE. CRUSH YOU INTO DUST UNDER MY NAILS. YOU STOLE FROM ME.
YOU OPENED THE DOOR. SOMEONE MUST PASS THROUGH--
STOP!
I STILL OWN YOUR NAME, I STILL OWN THE DOOR.
WHICH MEANS, I'M THE ONE WHO CHARGES ADMISSION.
YOU'VE ALWAYS EXCELLED AT MANIPULATING OTHERS.
HOW I'VE MISSED YOU, DARLING. EVERYTHING I'VE EVER DONE, I'VE DONE IT FOR YOU...
...WHAT IF WE WORKED TOGETHER AGAIN?

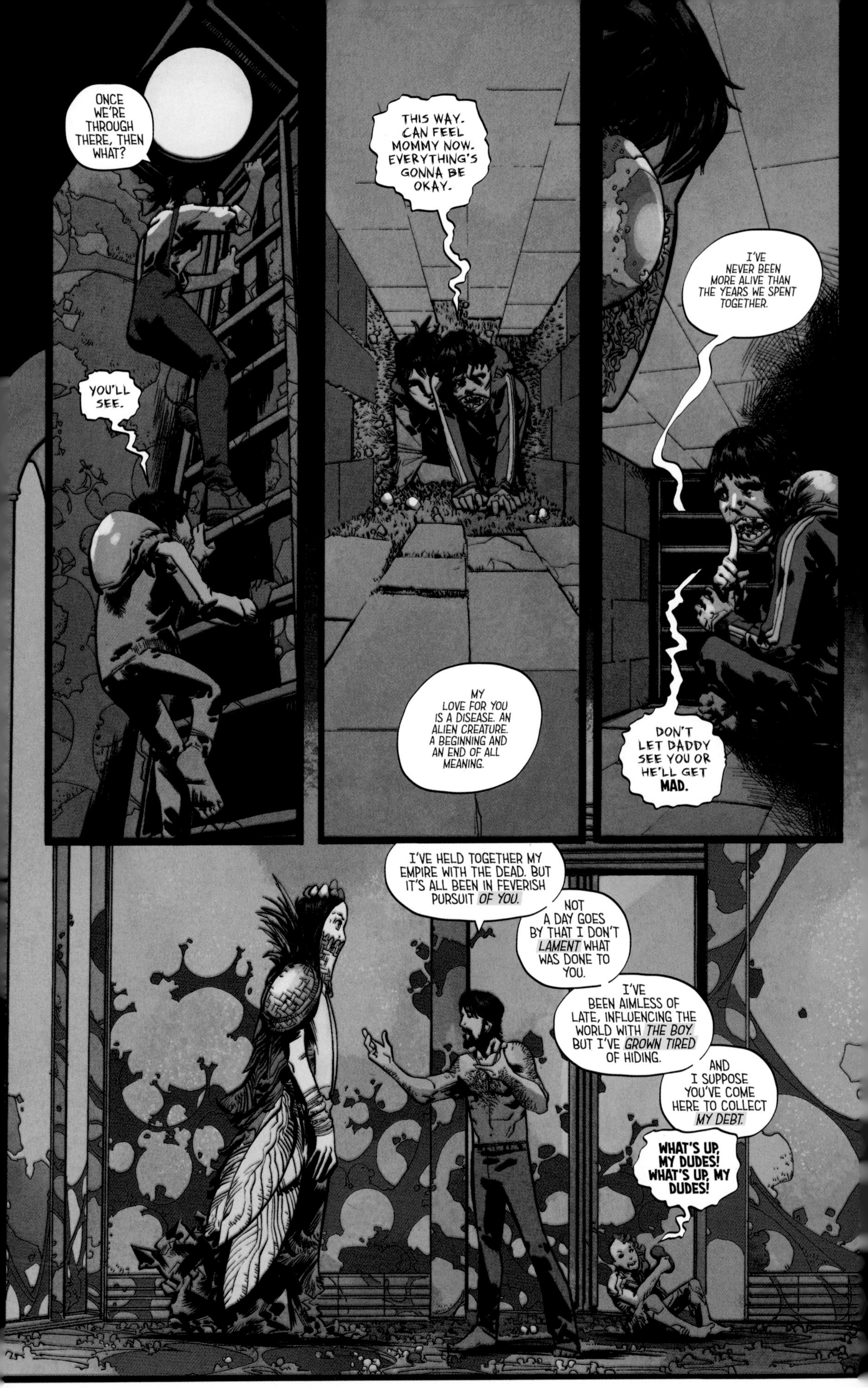
ONCE WE'RE THROUGH THERE, THEN WHAT?
YOU'LL SEE.
THIS WAY. CAN FEEL MOMMY NOW. EVERYTHING'S GONNA BE OKAY.
MY LOVE FOR YOU IS A DISEASE. AN ALIEN CREATURE. A BEGINNING AND AN END OF ALL MEANING.
I'VE NEVER BEEN MORE ALIVE THAN THE YEARS WE SPENT TOGETHER.
DON'T LET DADDY SEE YOU OR HE'LL GET MAD.
I'VE HELD TOGETHER MY EMPIRE WITH THE DEAD. BUT IT'S ALL BEEN IN FEVERISH PURSUIT OF YOU.
NOT A DAY GOES BY THAT I DON'T LAMENT WHAT WAS DONE TO YOU.
I'VE BEEN AIMLESS OF LATE, INFLUENCING THE WORLD WITH THE BOY. BUT I'VE GROWN TIRED OF HIDING.
AND I SUPPOSE YOU'VE COME HERE TO COLLECT MY DEBT.
WHAT'S UP, MY DUDES! WHAT'S UP, MY DUDES!

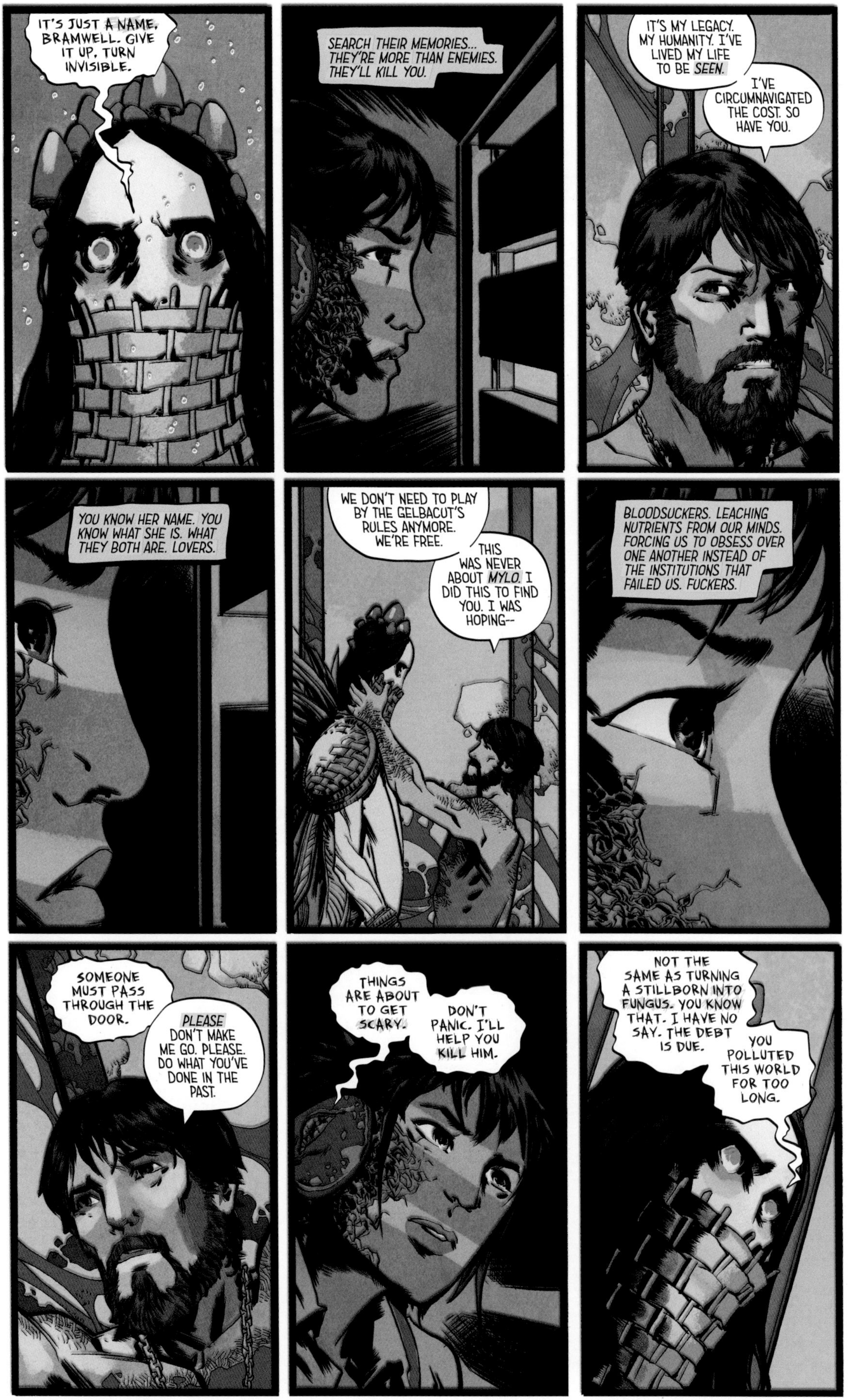
IT'S JUST A NAME, BRAMWELL. GIVE IT UP. TURN INVISIBLE.
SEARCH THEIR MEMORIES... THEY'RE MORE THAN ENEMIES. THEY'LL KILL YOU.
IT'S MY LEGACY. MY HUMANITY. I'VE LIVED MY LIFE TO BE SEEN.
I'VE CIRCUMNAVIGATED THE COST. SO HAVE YOU.
YOU KNOW HER NAME. YOU KNOW WHAT SHE IS. WHAT THEY BOTH ARE. LOVERS.
WE DON'T NEED TO PLAY BY THE GELBACUT'S RULES ANYMORE. WE'RE FREE.
THIS WAS NEVER ABOUT MYLO. I DID THIS TO FIND YOU. I WAS HOPING--
BLOODSUCKERS. LEACHING NUTRIENTS FROM OUR MINDS. FORCING US TO OBSESS OVER ONE ANOTHER INSTEAD OF THE INSTITUTIONS THAT FAILED US. FUCKERS.
SOMEONE MUST PASS THROUGH THE DOOR.
PLEASE DON'T MAKE ME GO. PLEASE. DO WHAT YOU'VE DONE IN THE PAST.
THINGS ARE ABOUT TO GET SCARY.
DON'T PANIC. I'LL HELP YOU KILL HIM.
NOT THE SAME AS TURNING A STILLBORN INTO FUNGUS. YOU KNOW THAT. I HAVE NO SAY. THE DEBT IS DUE.
YOU POLLUTED THIS WORLD FOR TOO LONG.

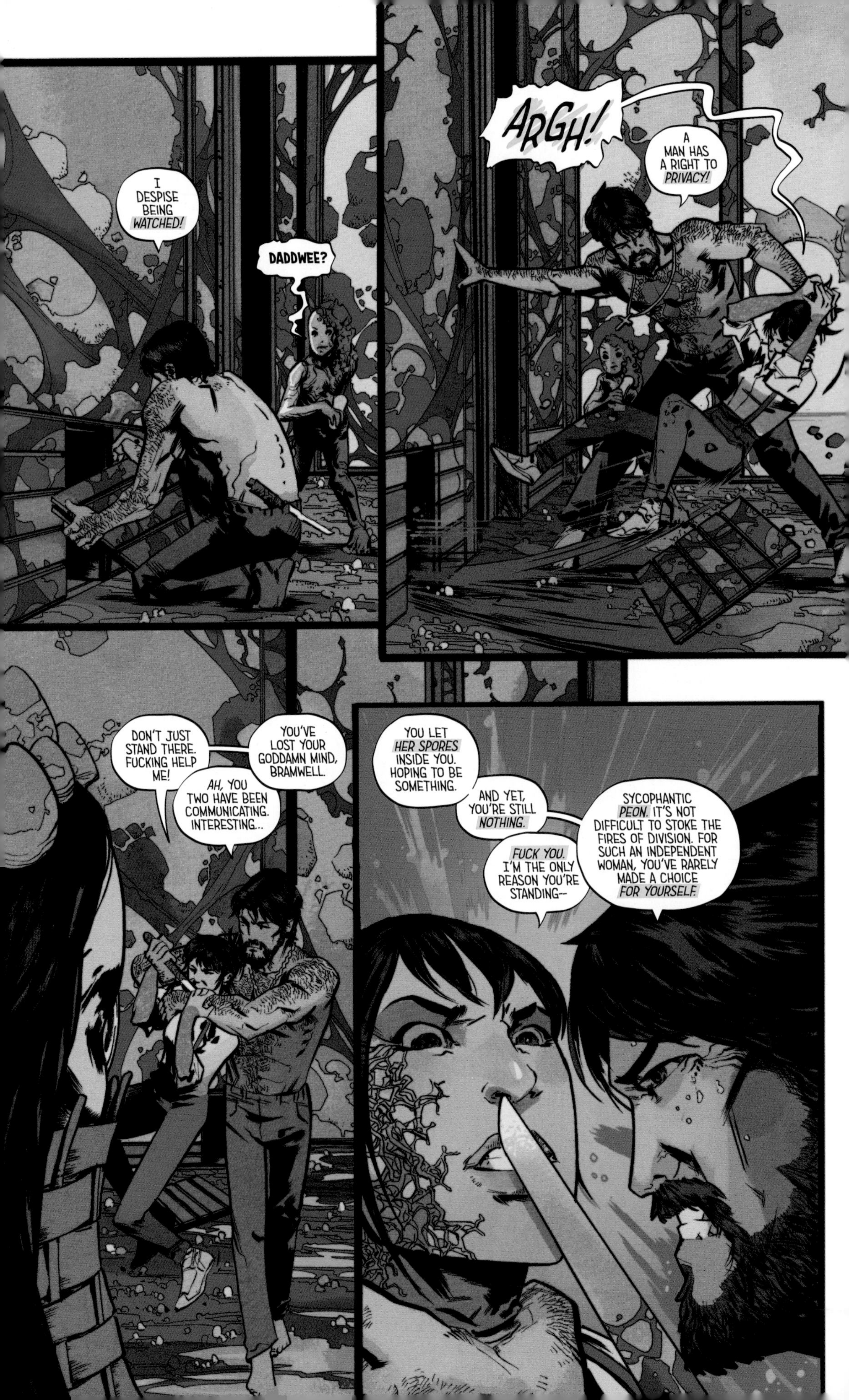
I DESPISE BEING WATCHED!
DADDWEE?
ARGH!
A MAN HAS A RIGHT TO PRIVACY!
DON'T JUST STAND THERE. FUCKING HELP ME!
YOU'VE LOST YOUR GODDAMN MIND, BRAMWELL.
AH, YOU TWO HAVE BEEN COMMUNICATING. INTERESTING...
YOU LET HER SPORES INSIDE YOU. HOPING TO BE SOMETHING.
AND YET, YOU'RE STILL NOTHING.
FUCK YOU. I'M THE ONLY REASON YOU'RE STANDING--
SYCOPHANTIC PEON. IT'S NOT DIFFICULT TO STOKE THE FIRES OF DIVISION. FOR SUCH AN INDEPENDENT WOMAN, YOU'VE RARELY MADE A CHOICE FOR YOURSELF.

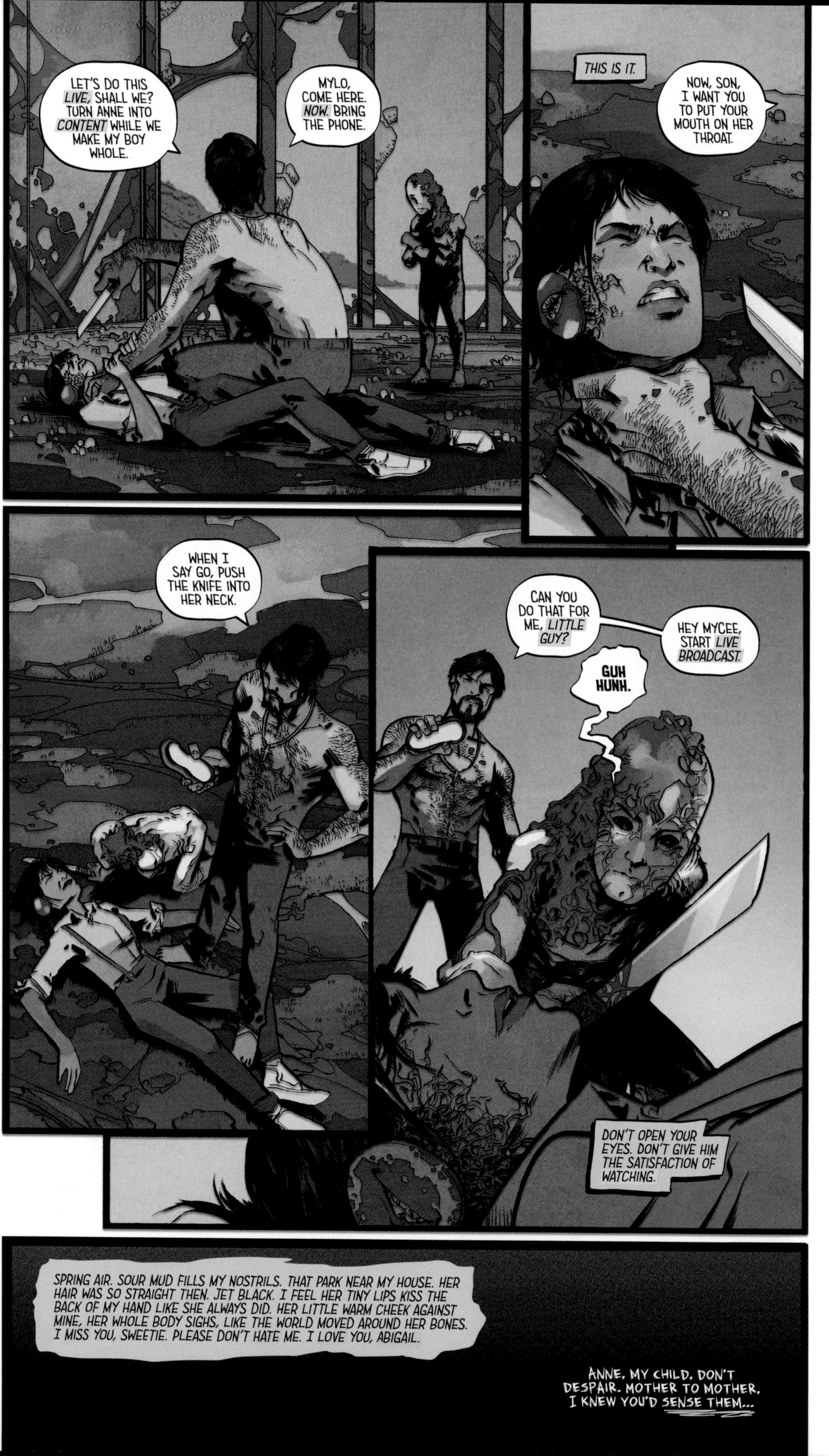
LET'S DO THIS LIVE, SHALL WE? TURN ANNE INTO CONTENT WHILE WE MAKE MY BOY WHOLE.
MYLO, COME HERE. NOW. BRING THE PHONE.
THIS IS IT.
NOW, SON, I WANT YOU TO PUT YOUR MOUTH ON HER THROAT.
WHEN I SAY GO, PUSH THE KNIFE INTO HER NECK.
CAN YOU DO THAT FOR ME, LITTLE GUY?
HEY MYCEE, START LIVE BROADCAST.
GUH HUNH.
DON'T OPEN YOUR EYES. DON'T GIVE HIM THE SATISFACTION OF WATCHING.
SPRING AIR. SOUR MUD FILLS MY NOSTRILS. THAT PARK NEAR MY HOUSE. HER HAIR WAS SO STRAIGHT THEN. JET BLACK. I FEEL HER TINY LIPS KISS THE BACK OF MY HAND LIKE SHE ALWAYS DID. HER LITTLE WARM CHEEK AGAINST MINE, HER WHOLE BODY SIGHS, LIKE THE WORLD MOVED AROUND HER BONES. I MISS YOU, SWEETIE. PLEASE DON'T HATE ME. I LOVE YOU, ABIGAIL.
ANNE, MY CHILD, DON'T DESPAIR. MOTHER TO MOTHER. I KNEW YOU'D SENSE THEM...

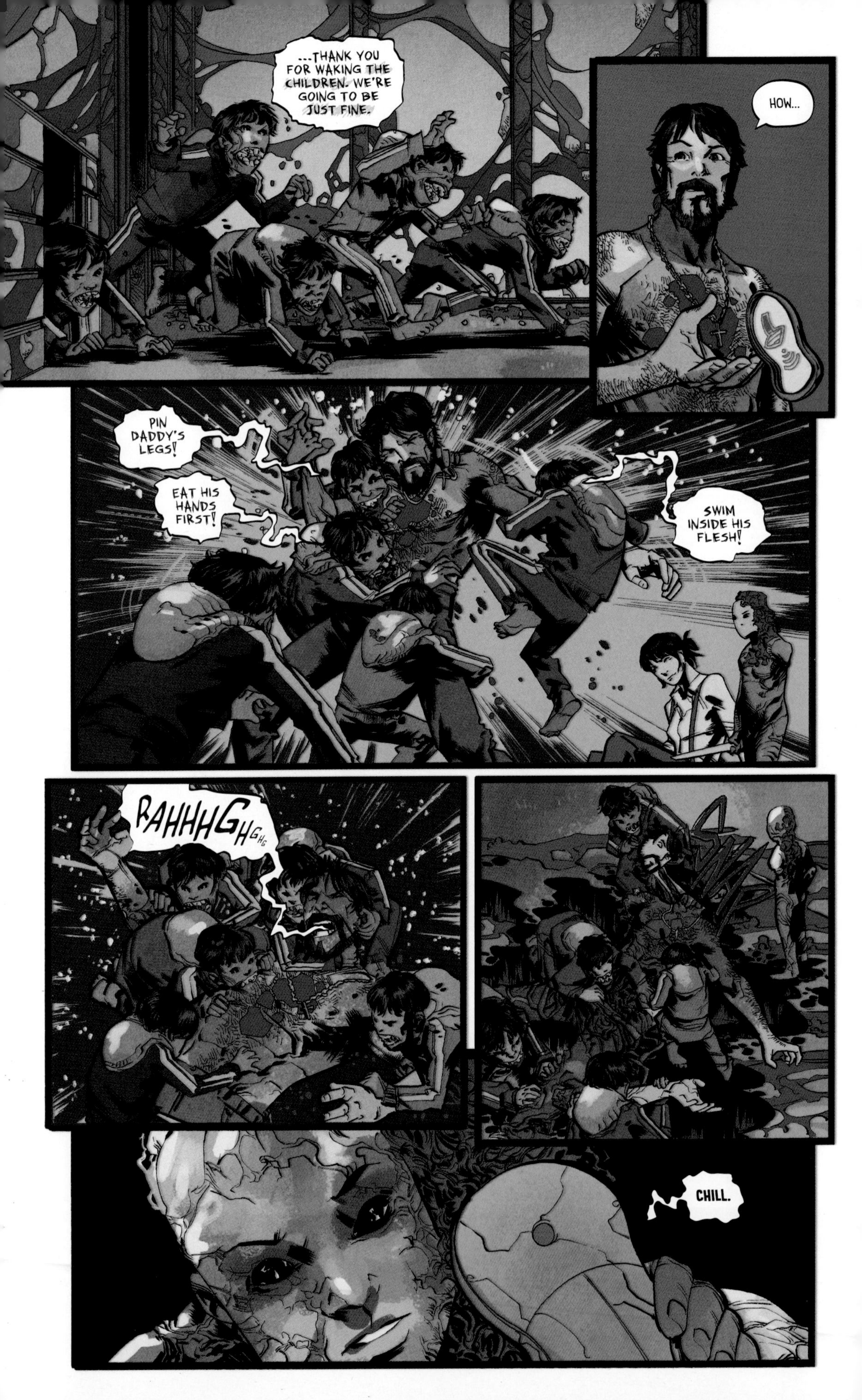
...THANK YOU FOR WAKING THE CHILDREN. WE'RE GOING TO BE JUST FINE.
HOW...
PIN DADDY'S LEGS!
EAT HIS HANDS FIRST!
SWIM INSIDE HIS FLESH!
RAHHHGHGHG
CHILL.

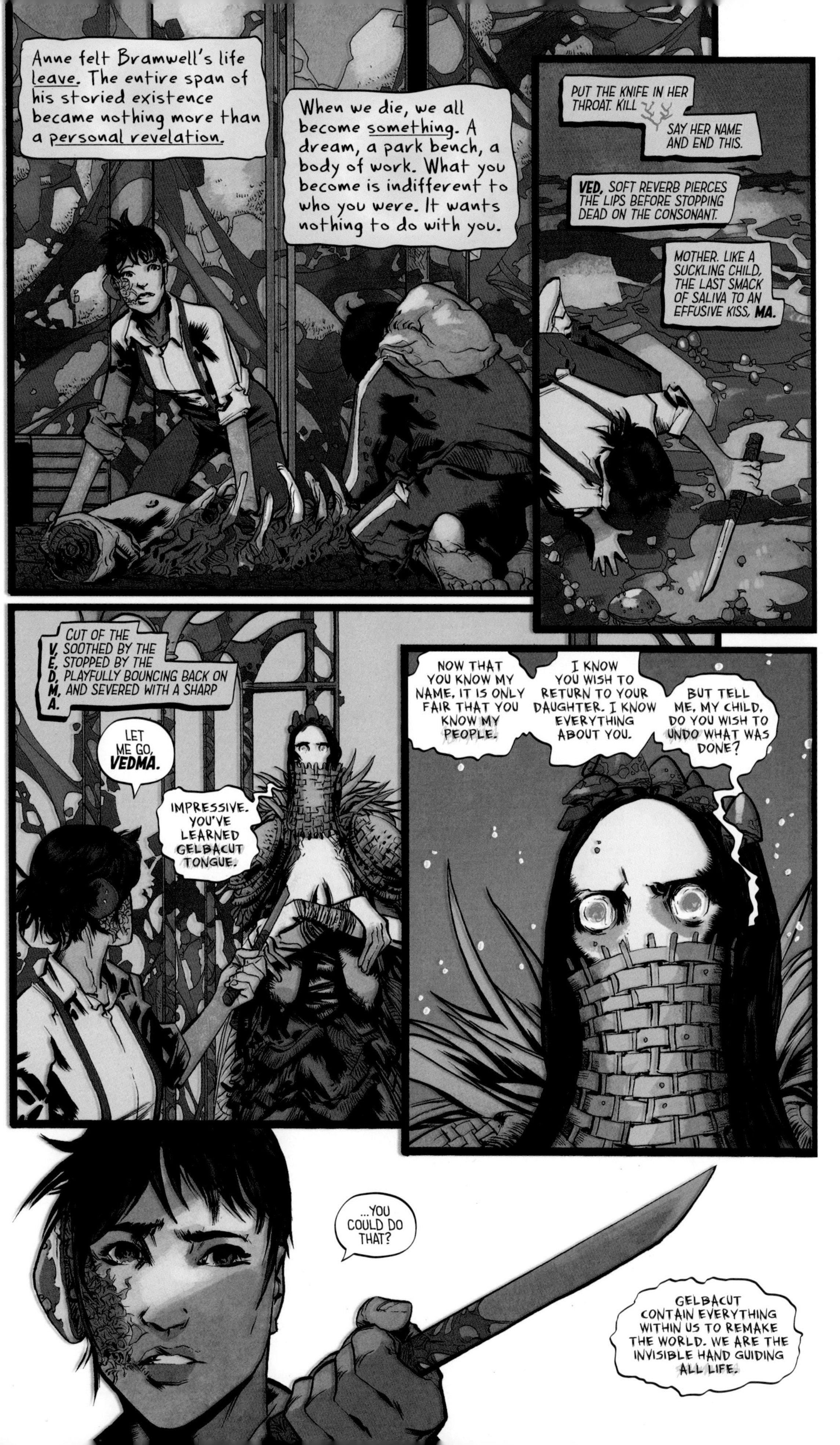
Anne felt Bramwell's life leave. The entire span of his storied existence became nothing more than a personal revelation.
When we die, we all become something. A dream, a park bench, a body of work. What you become is indifferent to who you were. It wants nothing to do with you.
PUT THE KNIFE IN HER THROAT. KILL
SAY HER NAME AND END THIS.
VED, SOFT REVERB PIERCES THE LIPS BEFORE STOPPING DEAD ON THE CONSONANT.
MOTHER. LIKE A SUCKLING CHILD, THE LAST SMACK OF SALIVA TO AN EFFUSIVE KISS, MA.
V, CUT OF THE
E, SOOTHED BY THE
D, STOPPED BY THE
M, PLAYFULLY BOUNCING BACK ON
A. AND SEVERED WITH A SHARP
LET ME GO, VEDMA.
IMPRESSIVE. YOU'VE LEARNED GELBACUT TONGUE.
NOW THAT YOU KNOW MY NAME, IT IS ONLY FAIR THAT YOU KNOW MY PEOPLE.
I KNOW YOU WISH TO RETURN TO YOUR DAUGHTER. I KNOW EVERYTHING ABOUT YOU.
BUT TELL ME, MY CHILD, DO YOU WISH TO UNDO WHAT WAS DONE?
...YOU COULD DO THAT?
GELBACUT CONTAIN EVERYTHING WITHIN US TO REMAKE THE WORLD. WE ARE THE INVISIBLE HAND GUIDING ALL LIFE.

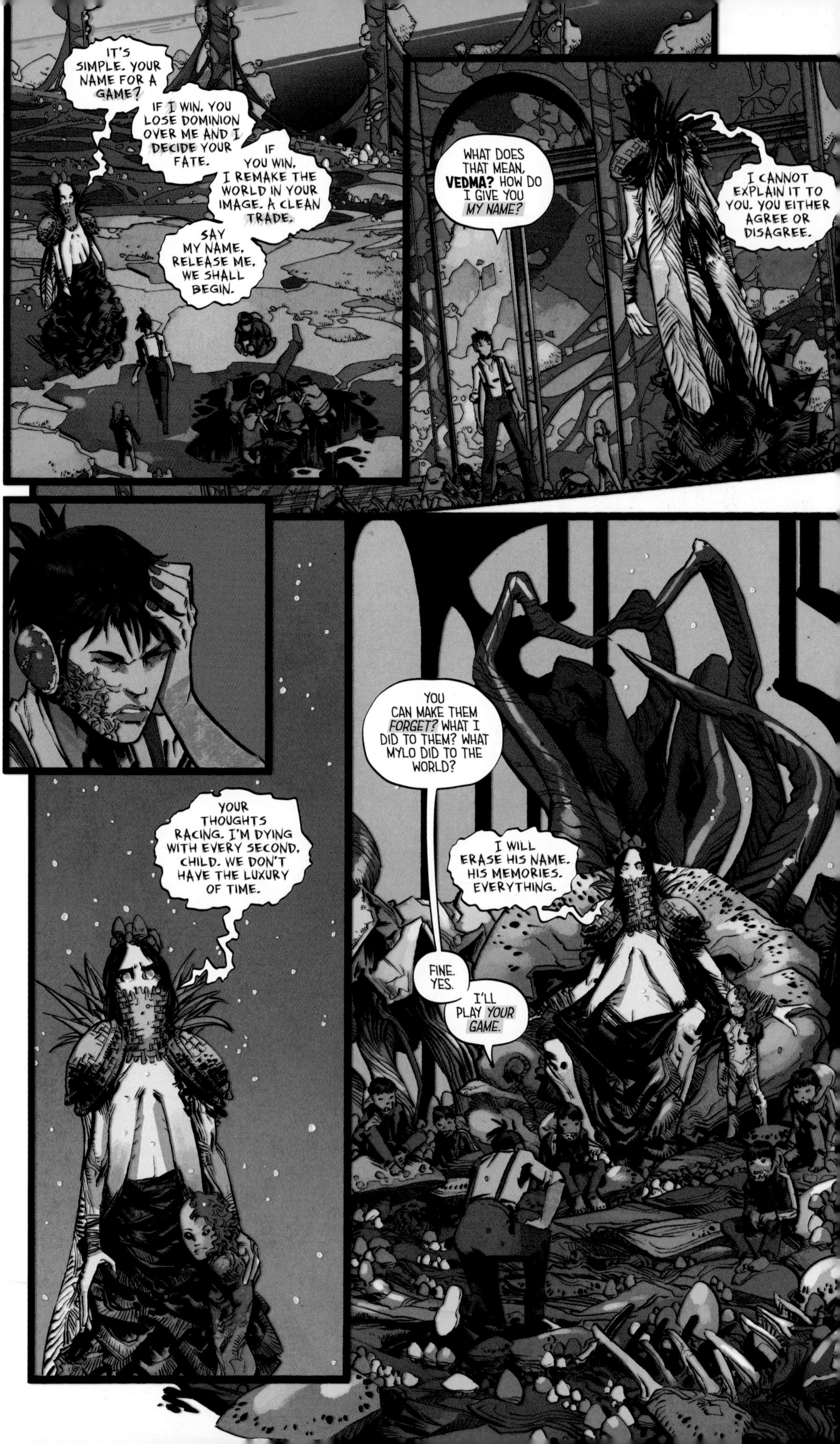
IT'S SIMPLE. YOUR NAME FOR A GAME?
IF I WIN, YOU LOSE DOMINION OVER ME AND I DECIDE YOUR FATE.
IF YOU WIN, I REMAKE THE WORLD IN YOUR IMAGE. A CLEAN TRADE.
SAY MY NAME, RELEASE ME, WE SHALL BEGIN.
WHAT DOES THAT MEAN, VEDMA? HOW DO I GIVE YOU MY NAME?
I CANNOT EXPLAIN IT TO YOU. YOU EITHER AGREE OR DISAGREE.
YOUR THOUGHTS RACING. I'M DYING WITH EVERY SECOND, CHILD. WE DON'T HAVE THE LUXURY OF TIME.
YOU CAN MAKE THEM FORGET? WHAT I DID TO THEM? WHAT MYLO DID TO THE WORLD?
I WILL ERASE HIS NAME. HIS MEMORIES. EVERYTHING.
FINE. YES.
I'LL PLAY YOUR GAME.

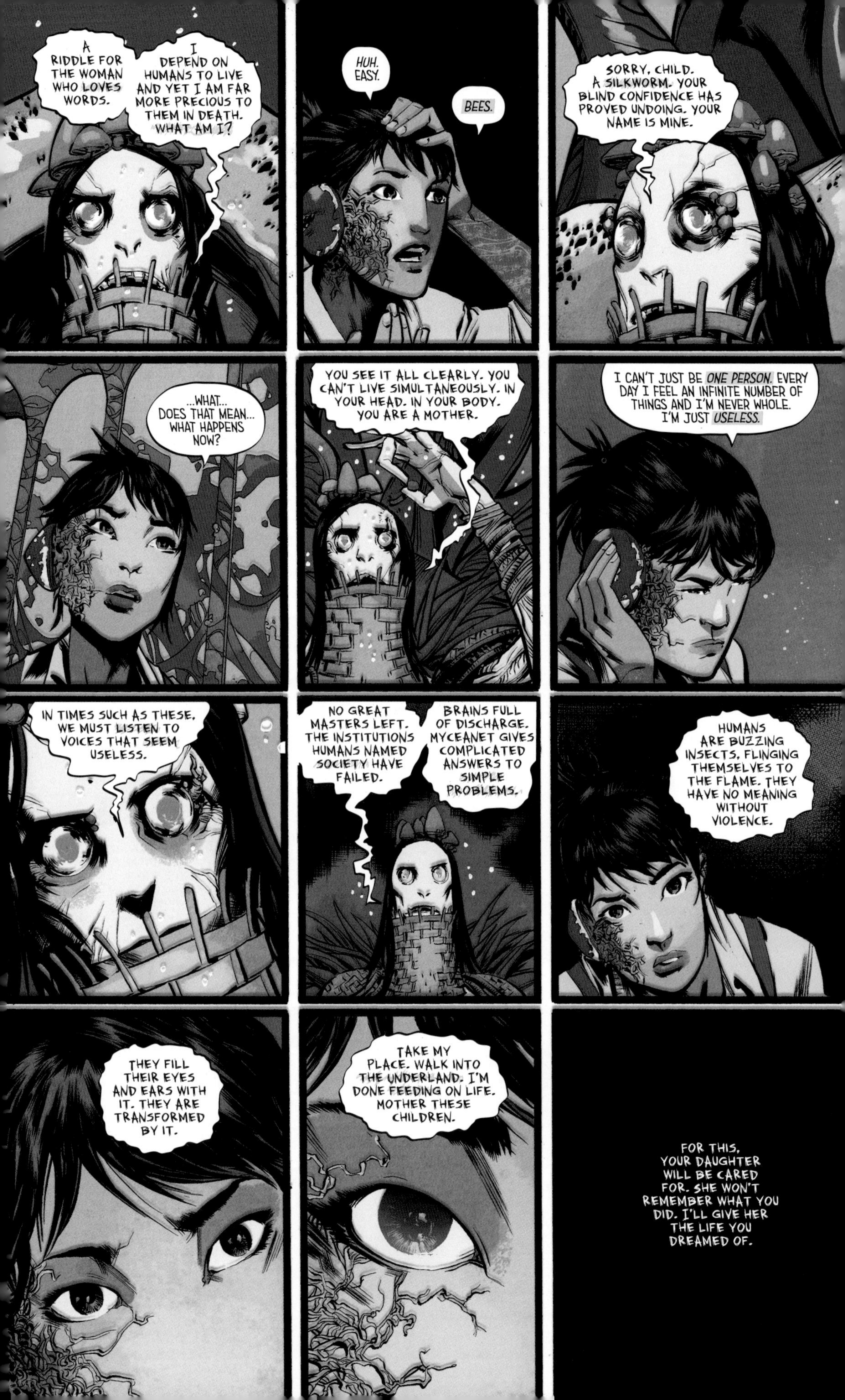
A RIDDLE FOR THE WOMAN WHO LOVES WORDS.
I DEPEND ON HUMANS TO LIVE AND YET I AM FAR MORE PRECIOUS TO THEM IN DEATH. WHAT AM I?
HUH. EASY.
BEES.
SORRY, CHILD. A SILKWORM. YOUR BLIND CONFIDENCE HAS PROVED UNDOING. YOUR NAME IS MINE.
...WHAT... DOES THAT MEAN... WHAT HAPPENS NOW?
YOU SEE IT ALL CLEARLY. YOU CAN'T LIVE SIMULTANEOUSLY. IN YOUR HEAD. IN YOUR BODY. YOU ARE A MOTHER.
I CAN'T JUST BE ONE PERSON. EVERY DAY I FEEL AN INFINITE NUMBER OF THINGS AND I'M NEVER WHOLE. I'M JUST USELESS.
IN TIMES SUCH AS THESE, WE MUST LISTEN TO VOICES THAT SEEM USELESS.
NO GREAT MASTERS LEFT. THE INSTITUTIONS HUMANS NAMED SOCIETY HAVE FAILED.
BRAINS FULL OF DISCHARGE. MYCEANET GIVES COMPLICATED ANSWERS TO SIMPLE PROBLEMS.
HUMANS ARE BUZZING INSECTS, FLINGING THEMSELVES TO THE FLAME. THEY HAVE NO MEANING WITHOUT VIOLENCE.
THEY FILL THEIR EYES AND EARS WITH IT. THEY ARE TRANSFORMED BY IT.
TAKE MY PLACE. WALK INTO THE UNDERLAND. I'M DONE FEEDING ON LIFE. MOTHER THESE CHILDREN.
FOR THIS, YOUR DAUGHTER WILL BE CARED FOR. SHE WON'T REMEMBER WHAT YOU DID. I'LL GIVE HER THE LIFE YOU DREAMED OF.

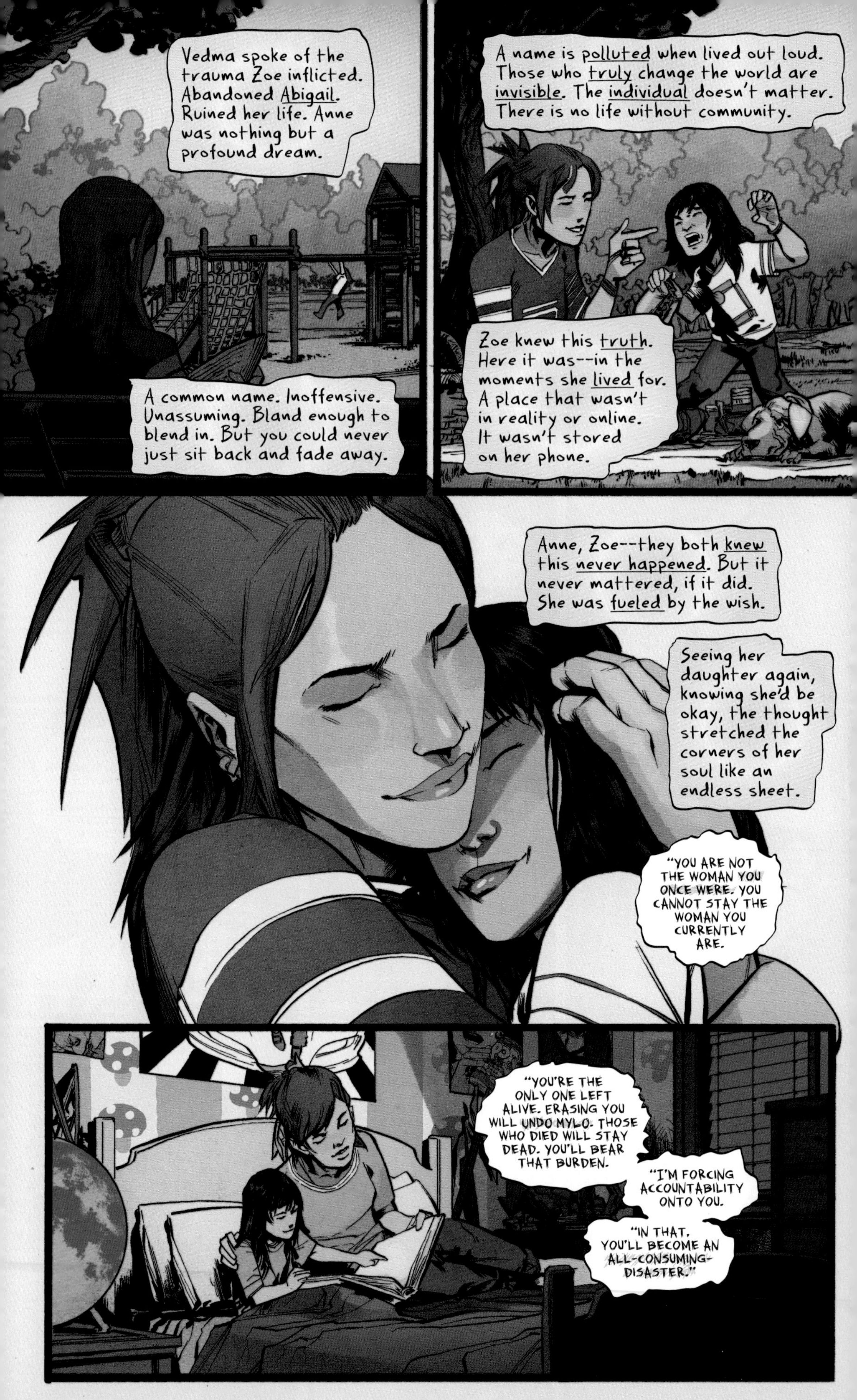

Vedma spoke of the trauma Zoe inflicted. Abandoned Abigail. Ruined her life. Anne was nothing but a profound dream.
A common name. Inoffensive. Unassuming. Bland enough to blend in. But you could never just sit back and fade away.
A name is polluted when lived out loud. Those who truly change the world are invisible. The individual doesn't matter. There is no life without community.
Zoe knew this truth. Here it was--in the moments she lived for. A place that wasn't in reality or online. It wasn't stored on her phone.
Anne, Zoe--they both knew this never happened. But it never mattered, if it did. She was fueled by the wish.
Seeing her daughter again, knowing she'd be okay, the thought stretched the corners of her soul like an endless sheet.
"YOU ARE NOT THE WOMAN YOU ONCE WERE. YOU CANNOT STAY THE WOMAN YOU CURRENTLY ARE.
"YOU'RE THE ONLY ONE LEFT ALIVE. ERASING YOU WILL UNDO MYLO. THOSE WHO DIED WILL STAY DEAD. YOU'LL BEAR THAT BURDEN.
"I'M FORCING ACCOUNTABILITY ONTO YOU.
"IN THAT, YOU'LL BECOME AN ALL-CONSUMING DISASTER."

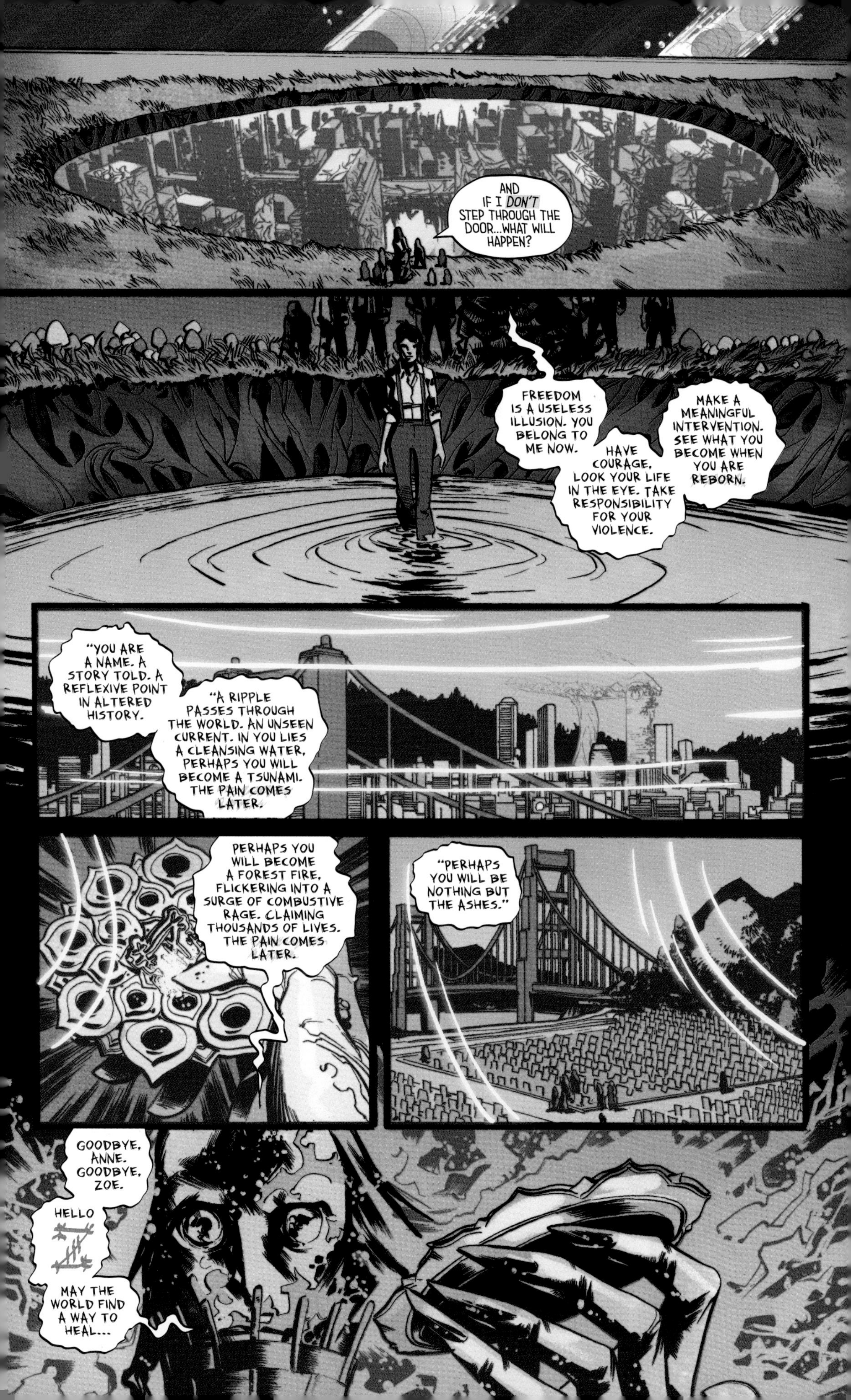
AND IF I DON'T STEP THROUGH THE DOOR...WHAT WILL HAPPEN?
FREEDOM IS A USELESS ILLUSION. YOU BELONG TO ME NOW.
HAVE COURAGE. LOOK YOUR LIFE IN THE EYE. TAKE RESPONSIBILITY FOR YOUR VIOLENCE.
MAKE A MEANINGFUL INTERVENTION. SEE WHAT YOU BECOME WHEN YOU ARE REBORN.
"YOU ARE A NAME. A STORY TOLD. A REFLEXIVE POINT IN ALTERED HISTORY.
"A RIPPLE PASSES THROUGH THE WORLD. AN UNSEEN CURRENT. IN YOU LIES A CLEANSING WATER. PERHAPS YOU WILL BECOME A TSUNAMI. THE PAIN COMES LATER.
PERHAPS YOU WILL BECOME A FOREST FIRE, FLICKERING INTO A SURGE OF COMBUSTIVE RAGE. CLAIMING THOUSANDS OF LIVES. THE PAIN COMES LATER.
"PERHAPS YOU WILL BE NOTHING BUT THE ASHES."
GOODBYE, ANNE. GOODBYE, ZOE.
HELLO
MAY THE WORLD FIND A WAY TO HEAL...

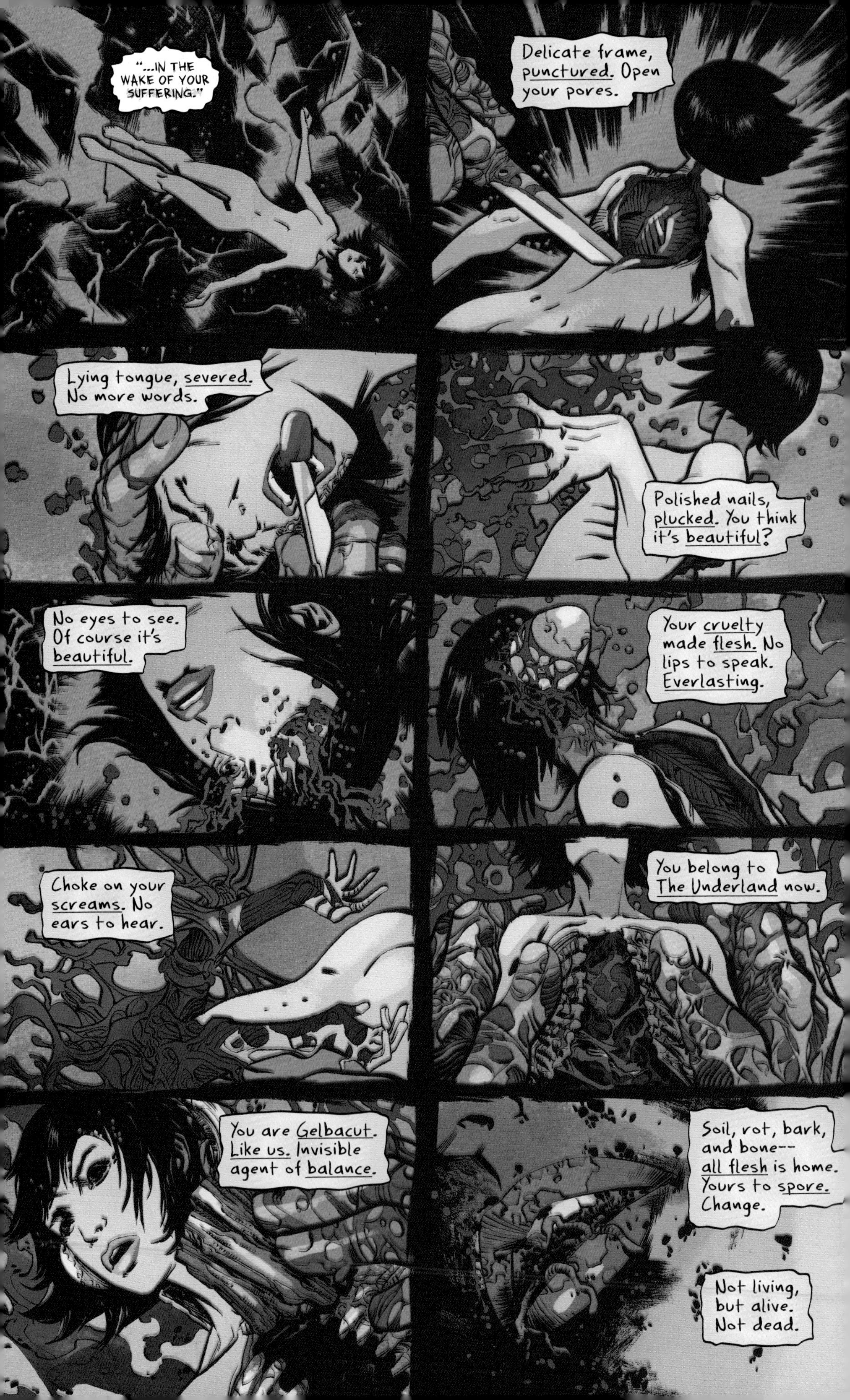
"...IN THE WAKE OF YOUR SUFFERING."
Delicate frame, punctured. Open your pores.
Lying tongue, severed. No more words.
Polished nails, plucked. You think it's beautiful?
No eyes to see. Of course it's beautiful.
Your cruelty made flesh. No lips to speak. Everlasting.
Choke on your screams. No ears to hear.
You belong to The Underland now.
You are Gelbacut. Like us. Invisible agent of balance.
Soil, rot, bark, and bone-- all flesh is home. Yours to spore. Change.
Not living, but alive. Not dead.

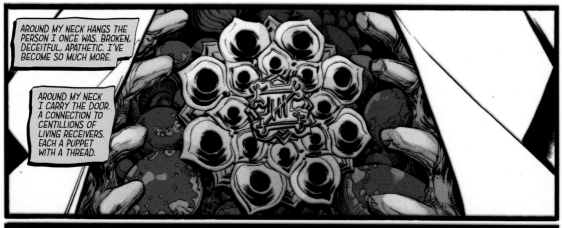

AROUND MY NECK HANGS THE PERSON I ONCE WAS. BROKEN, DECEITFUL, APATHETIC. I'VE BECOME SO MUCH MORE.

AROUND MY NECK I CARRY THE DOOR. A CONNECTION TO CENTILLIONS OF LIVING RECEIVERS. EACH A PUPPET WITH A THREAD.

I WAS MEANT TO HAVE CHILDREN. TO RAISE THEM. WITH PATIENCE AND SELF SACRIFICE. I AM SHE WHO IS NOT--

AS MOTHER, I REWORK THE WORLD BY DESIGN. COMMUNICATING WITH THE LANDSCAPE. WHISPERING TO THE MICROPARASITES CRAWLING ALL OVER YOUR BODY.

I AM COMMUNICATING WITH YOU IN INTIMATE WAYS. UNSEEN BUT MANIPULATING YOUR BEHAVIOR. SUBTLY AT FIRST.

I AM INSIDE YOU NOW. SOAKING UP YOUR LAST PORTION OF JOY. I WON'T DIE QUIETLY.

DID I REMAKE THE WORLD?

DID I BECOME SOMETHING THAT MATTERED?

WHAT WAS I?

DO YOU REMEMBER ME?

DO YOU?

DOES SHE?

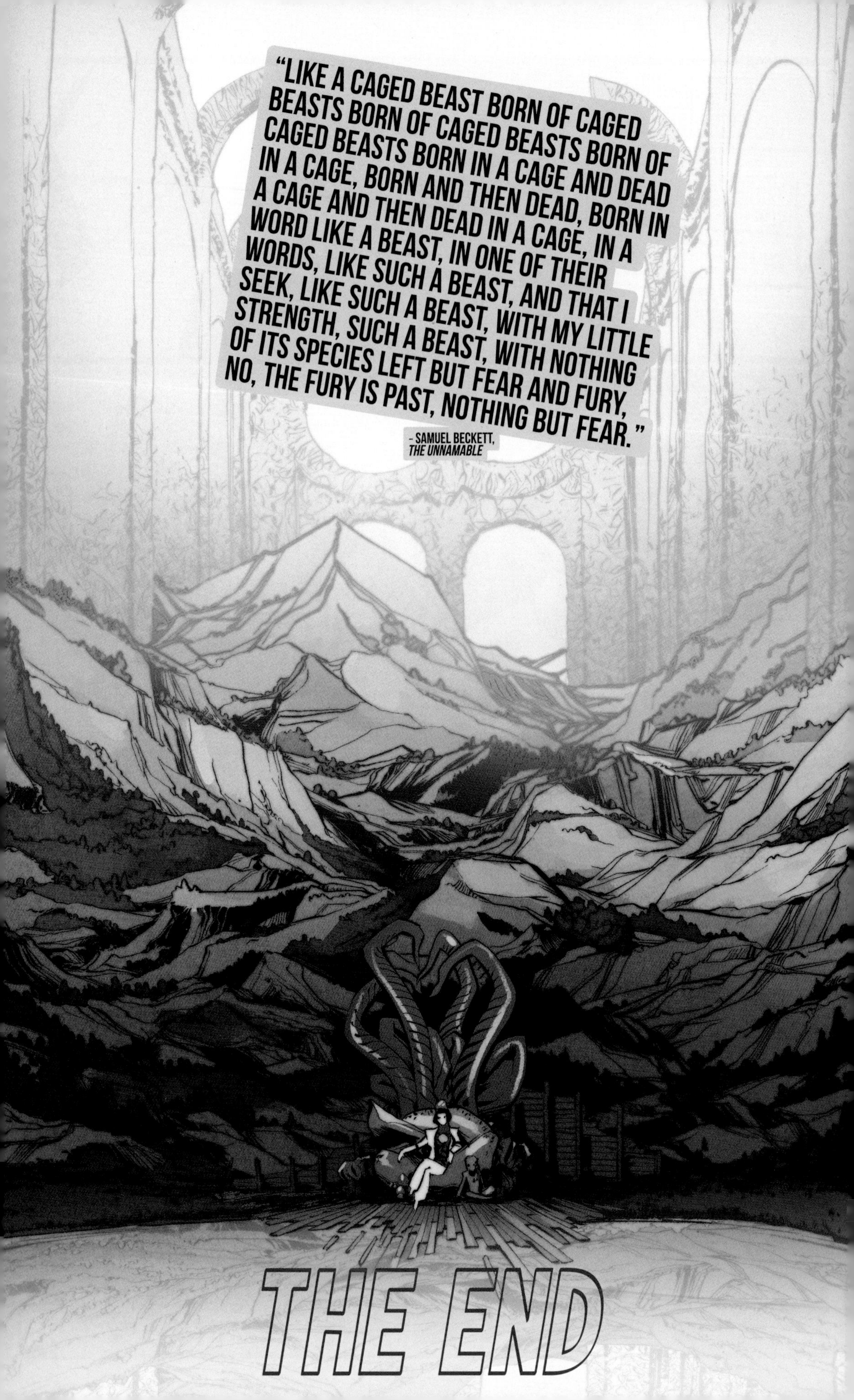
"LIKE A CAGED BEAST BORN OF CAGED BEASTS BORN OF CAGED BEASTS BORN OF CAGED BEASTS BORN IN A CAGE AND DEAD IN A CAGE, BORN AND THEN DEAD, BORN IN A CAGE AND THEN DEAD IN A CAGE, IN A WORD LIKE A BEAST, IN ONE OF THEIR WORDS, LIKE SUCH A BEAST, AND THAT I SEEK, LIKE SUCH A BEAST, WITH MY LITTLE STRENGTH, SUCH A BEAST, WITH NOTHING OF ITS SPECIES LEFT BUT FEAR AND FURY, NO, THE FURY IS PAST, NOTHING BUT FEAR."
- SAMUEL BECKETT, *THE UNNAMABLE*
THE END

I BREATHED A
BODY
™

EXTRAS & COVER GALLERY

How Mylo Caliban

Defied the Rules of Celebrity to Become a

GOD

Among His Followers

From his secret video game project, to
his dream of building a community around his
name, Mylo Caliban explains his unorthodox
route to success and influence.

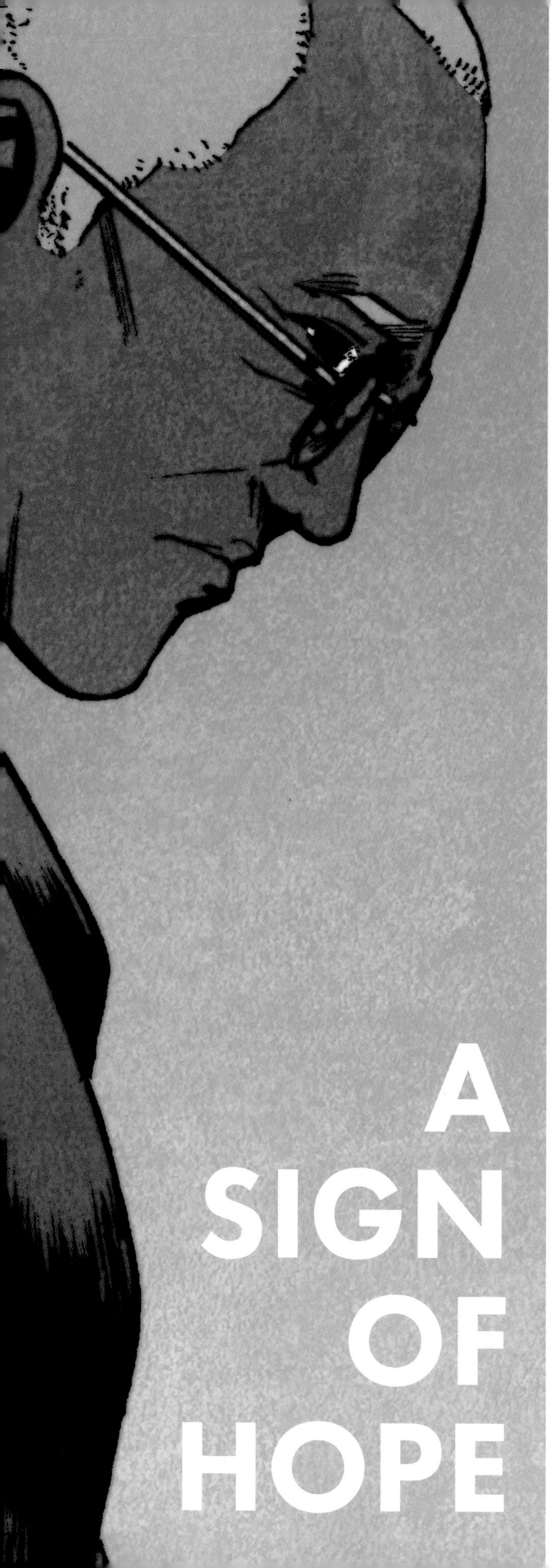

A SIGN OF HOPE

If you really want to know what shaped Mylo Caliban's attitude to success, he'll tell you it was his father (CEO of MyCena Biotechnology, ***Bramwell Caliban***). But if you want to dream up the creation myth that better explains his attitude toward living or why he refuses to be anything but himself, then you need to look at the day he was born. Mylo's father was traveling in Penang, Malaysia during the 2037 tsunami that claimed 302 lives. In fact, Mylo was born in Penang the day after the catastrophe.

If you ask Mylo about that moment, he'll nonchalantly scratch the side of his mullet before boiling it down in simple terms: "I live for everyone else." Perhaps that's what people find so attractive about the influencer sensation, who just this week reached 400 million subscribers, becoming the most followed channel on MyCee. Despite his father owning the social media company that is responsible for his fame, Mylo's growth and fanbase appear organic. One only needs to spend a day in his embrace before you bear witness to his fiercely loyal subscribers and their affection for the prankster.

It wasn't until I first met Mylo that I began to understand the allure. That was six months ago. A hot summer day, I was invited to his home just outside San Francisco—a sprawling mansion with accompanying grounds simply called ***The Estate.***

A conversation with Mylo can feel like watching one of his videos. He's thoughtful and charming and has an incandescent presence that reveals itself in the way he speaks with the entirety of his five-foot-ten frame. His words tend to race out of his mouth in rapid, rhythmic bursts, especially when he's excited. So, it doesn't really surprise me that he doesn't have a routine or a plan for most days.

"I just go," Mylo says. "Keep moving forward."

If you are over the age of 25 and want to understand the appeal of Mylo Caliban—like I did—there's no better place to start than with **DreamEye.** The free massively multiplayer video game which has evolved into its own self-contained universe where hundreds of millions of players spend hours a day on their MyCena phones. In this virtual battleground players talk to their friends while pointing rifles at strangers. Teens and young adults are more intimately familiar with the landscape's nooks, crannies and strategies to kill the infamous **King of Sleep.**

I JUST GO.
KEEP MOVING
FORWARD.

Mylo is one of the few influencers who understands the video game as well as the millions of young people who populate the servers of DreamEye every day (most use their MyCee page to login). Mylo inked a deal to show up *in the game.*

Appearing in 3-D motion capture, running around the game as a literal god—he's a giant shape-shifting deity who remade the battle map to his liking and whose presence altered the game for weeks. His appearance created more chaos than the game had seen in years. 47.7 million people (more than the population of Canada) attended the event. In the wake of his appearance, Mylo's likeness was inserted into DreamEye and his entire live-streaming catalogue became available for in-game watch parties.

The event wasn't one-sided for DreamEye. Mylo exited the deal with a stronger brand than ever. His accompanying Mylo Caliban x DreamEye merch drop quickly sold out. His MyCee follower count rose by over fifty million in twenty-four hours, setting a single day record highest recorded growth on a MyCee page. The deal was orchestrated by Mylo's notoriously camera-shy social media manager, Anne Stewart (who in just 3 years has created an elaborate personality and brand for Mylo that expands far beyond North America).

Mylo is too sly to say it outright, but this is all part of his vision. He's taking people on a tour through the trippy wonderland he's curated in his mind. He's concerned with showing humanity in himself and others. He swears that his pranks (which critics call crude and dangerous) are designed to reflect the joke back onto him. And for his part, he means it earnestly.

His manic, always online presence is undeniably captivating. He's raw and honest. Wildly unpredictable. Seemingly passionate about everything. It's understandable why he's the most potent culture mover of his generation. One minute he'll be leaving a long confessional-style rant on his page, while his next video could have him showing up at a busy food court only to throw pig's blood onto everyone. As annoying as it may seem, it makes a statement for the ethical consumption of meat. (Something his father takes very seriously with his MyCena Meat brands).

After watching hours of crude pranks, bizarre confessionals, highly energetic dance videos, or last-minute trips to third world countries to deliver clean drinking water—Mylo is inscrutable. Perhaps that is why his influence has evolved beyond typical fame. He is uniquely attuned to decoding the frequencies of the moment—existing as a beacon for America's lost generation. The kids who were left behind by the failures of the past and the collapse of the state have found someone who's fluent in the language of manic apathy.

Mylo himself has been trying to figure out how he fits into the big picture of the world. The dream is to build a name for himself, something that lasts long after his death as **"a sign of hope"**. He doesn't have a clear grasp on what that means exactly, and that's okay. The idea of building a community is at the front of his mind.

"I want my fans to have a place to be themselves," he says. "To show them we're safest in this world together."

I WANT MY FANS TO HAVE A PLACE TO BE THEMSELVES.

Issue 1
TREVOR HENDERSON
Incentive Cover

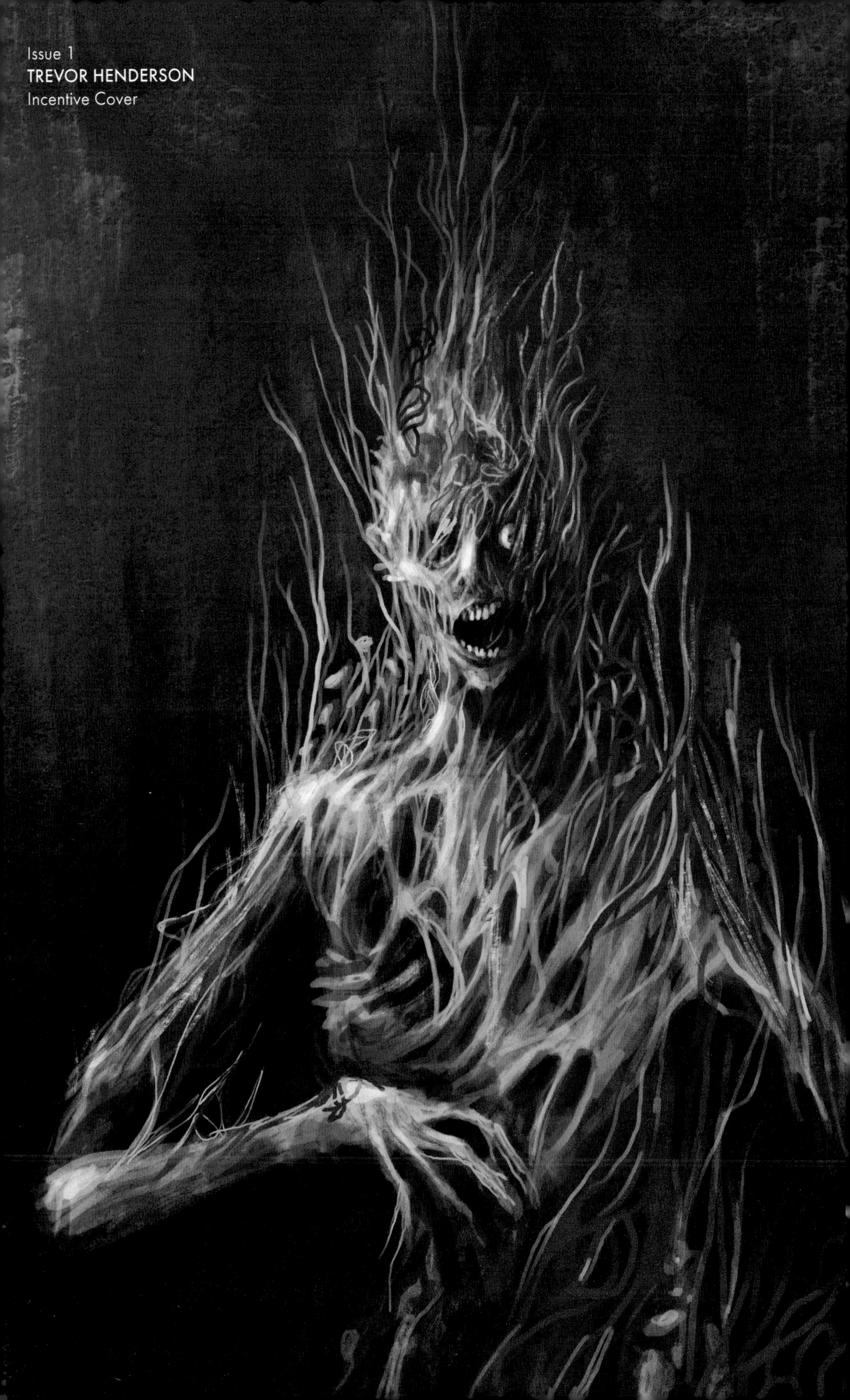

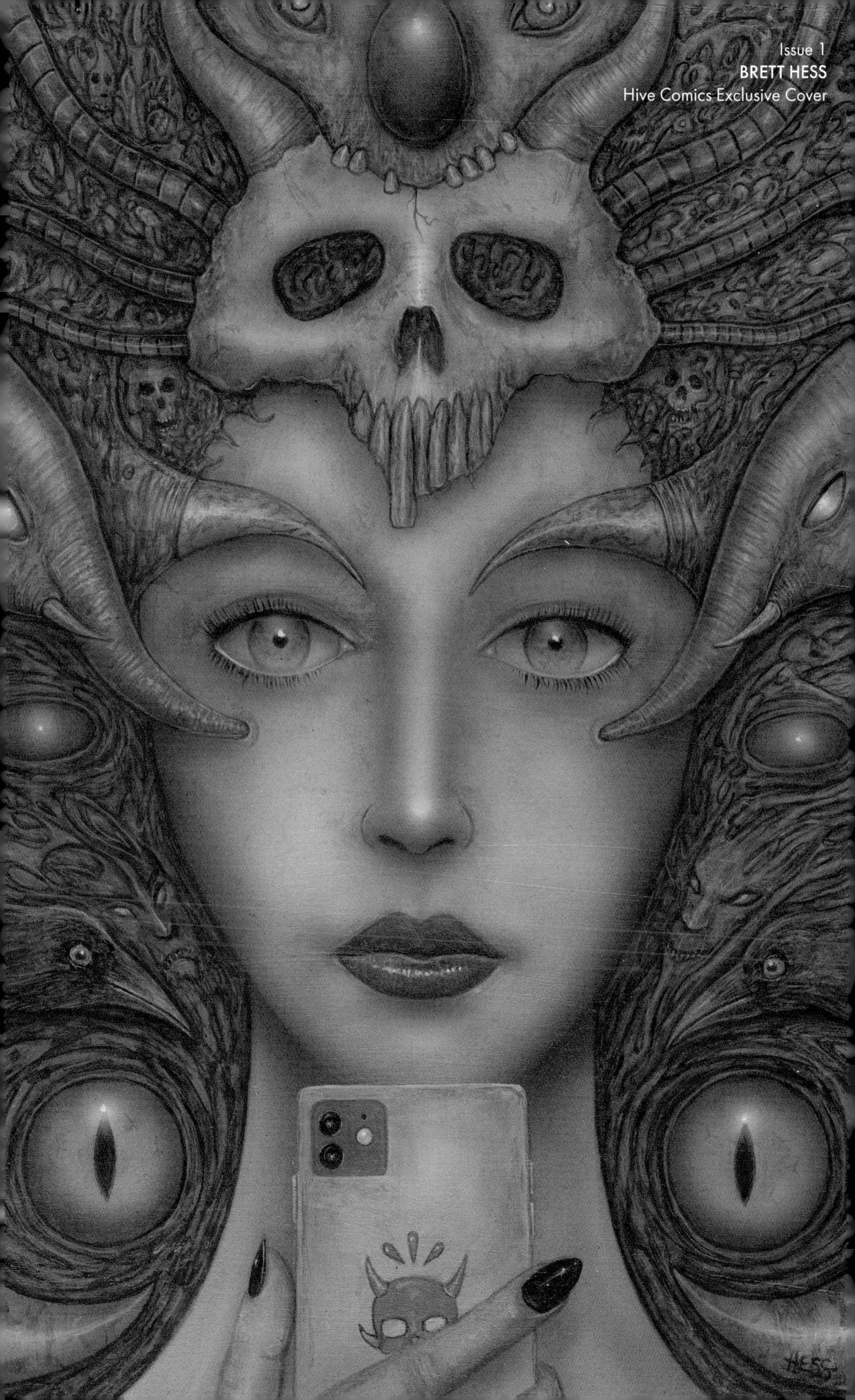
HESS

Issue 1
BRETT HESS
Hive Comics Exclusive Cover

Issue 1
CASEY PARSONS
Gotham Central/El Rey Comics Exclusive Cover

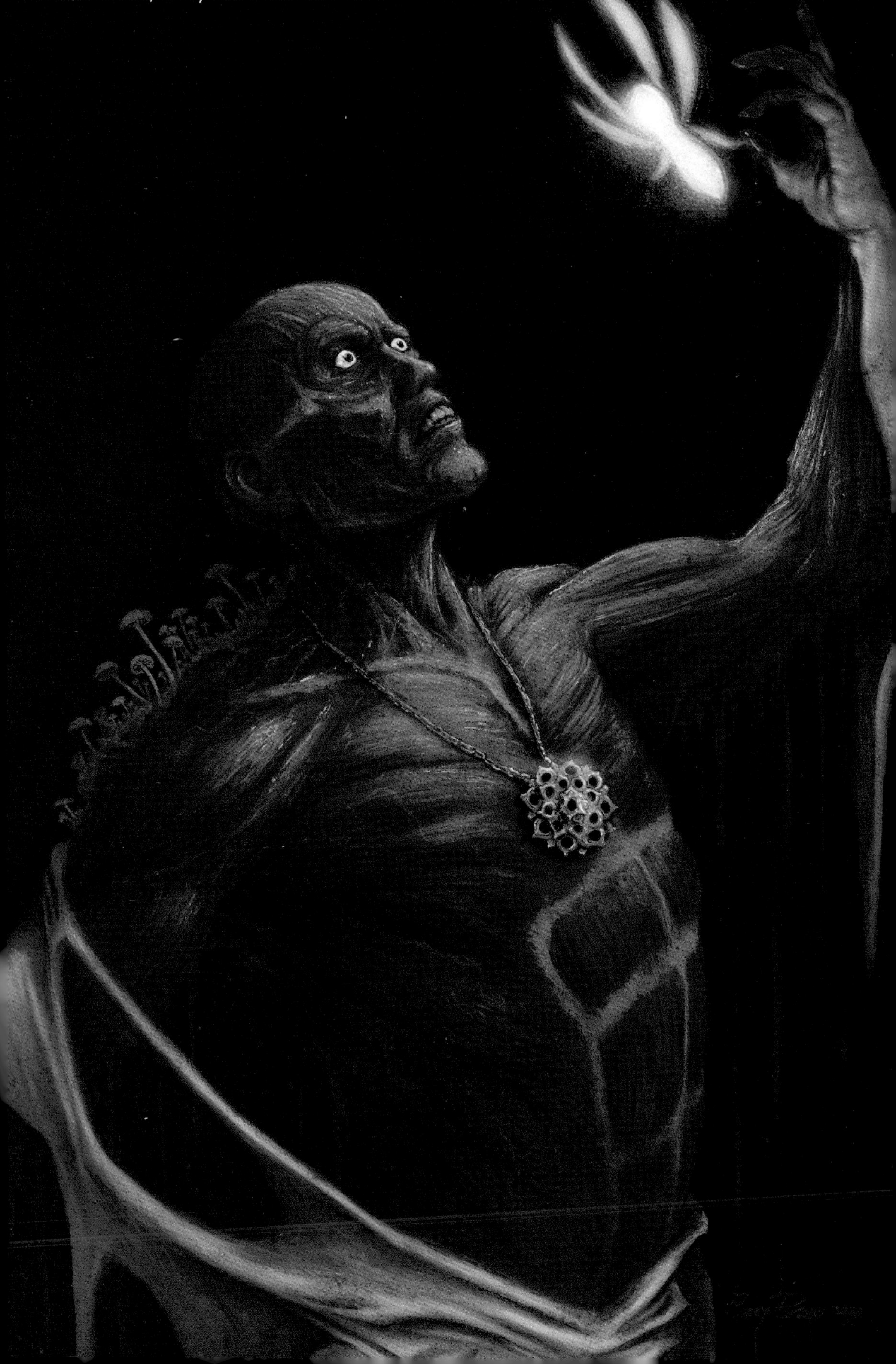

I BREATHED A BODY

Sketchbook

ANDY MacDONALD

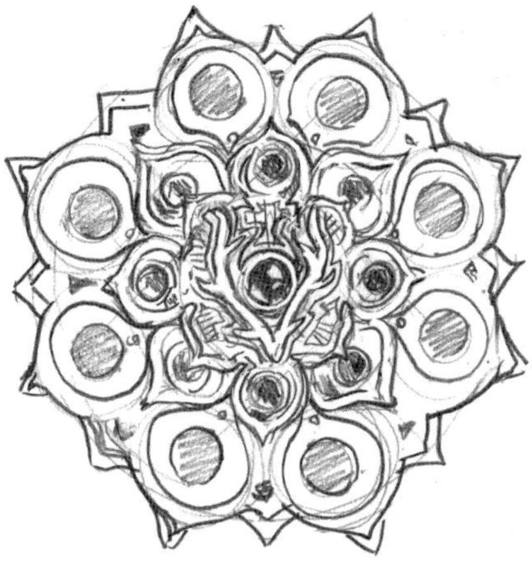

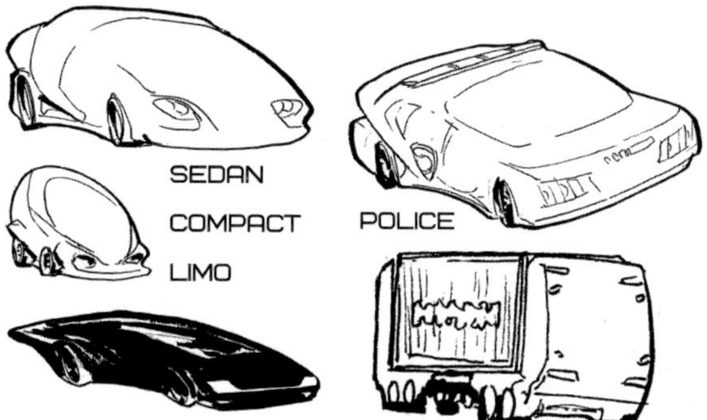
SEDAN
COMPACT
LIMO
POLICE
FREIGHT

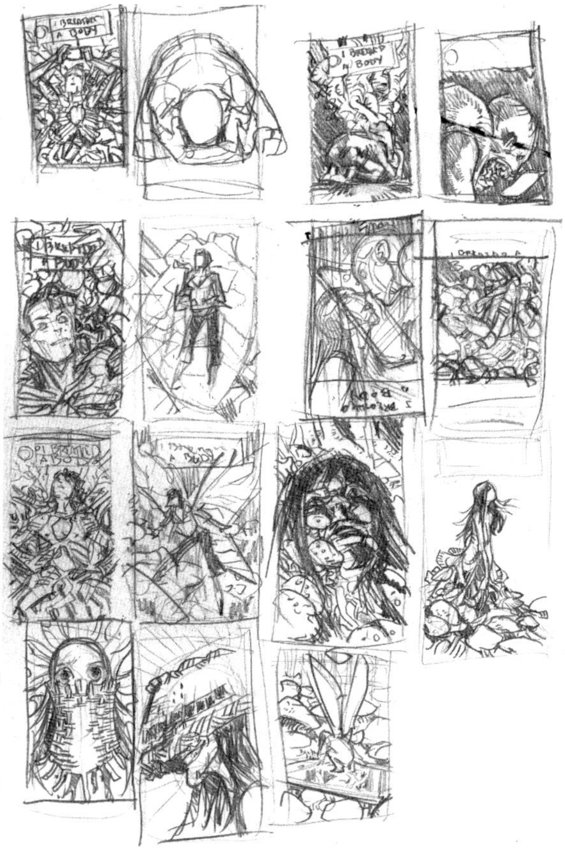

Used & Unused Cover Sketches

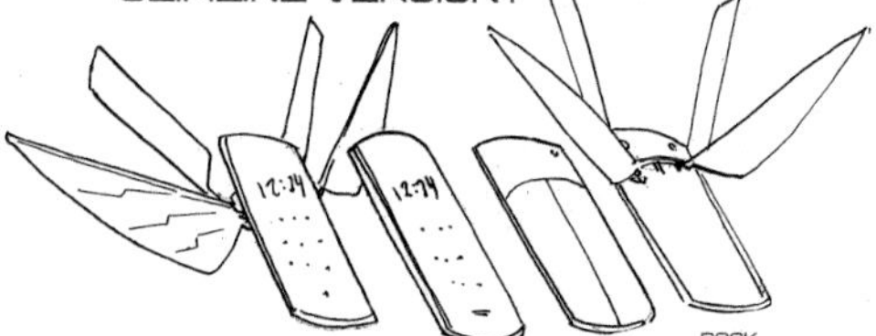
SLIMLINE VERSION?
FACE (OPEN)
FACE (CLOSED)
BACK (CLOSED)
BACK (OPEN)

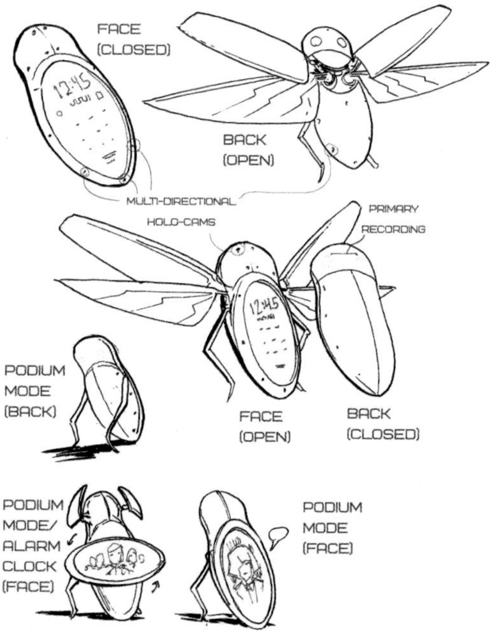
FACE (CLOSED)
BACK (OPEN)
MULTI-DIRECTIONAL HOLO-CAMS
PRIMARY RECORDING
PODIUM MODE (BACK)
FACE (OPEN)
BACK (CLOSED)
PODIUM MODE/ ALARM CLOCK (FACE)
PODIUM MODE (FACE)

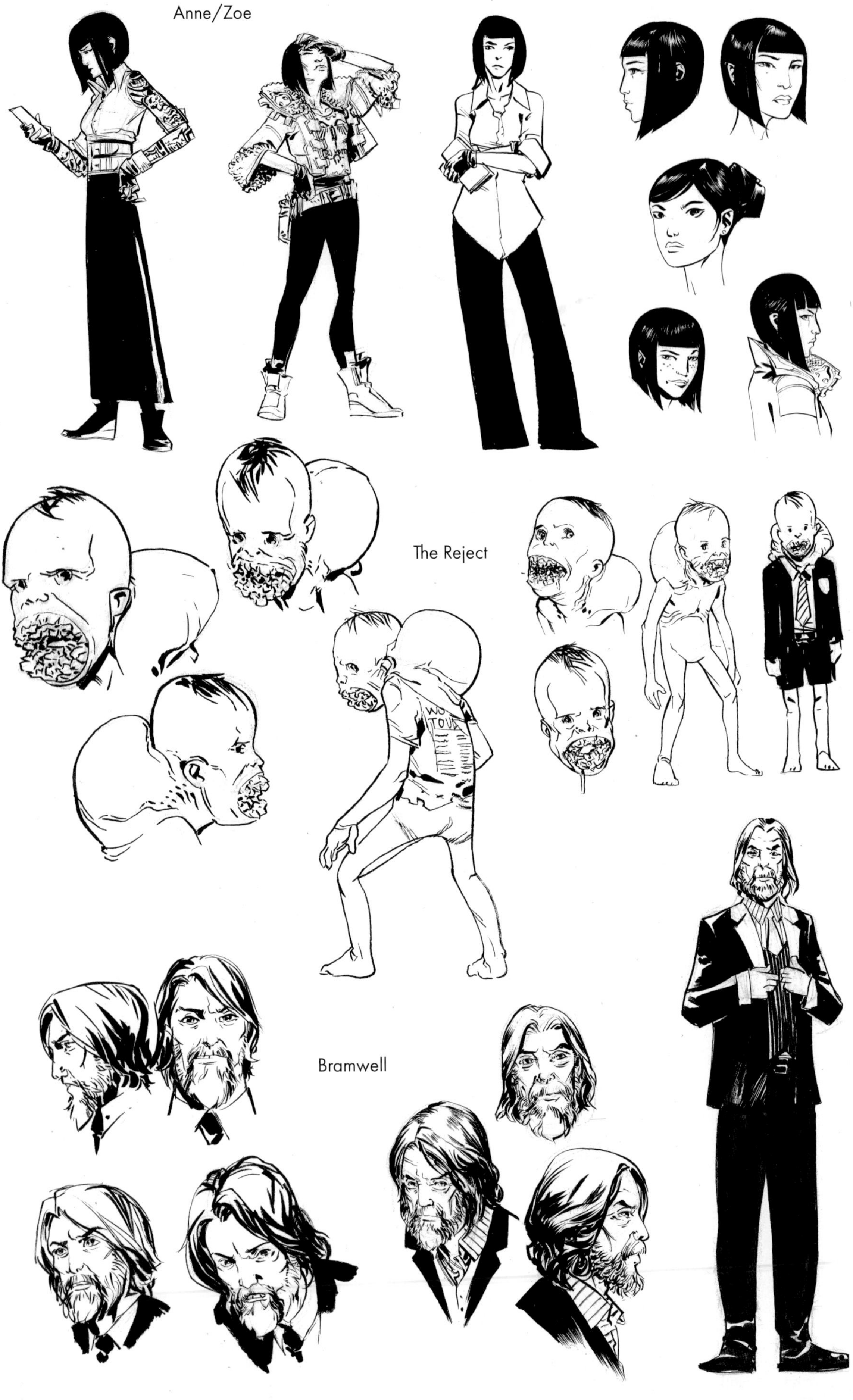
Anne/Zoe
The Reject
Bramwell

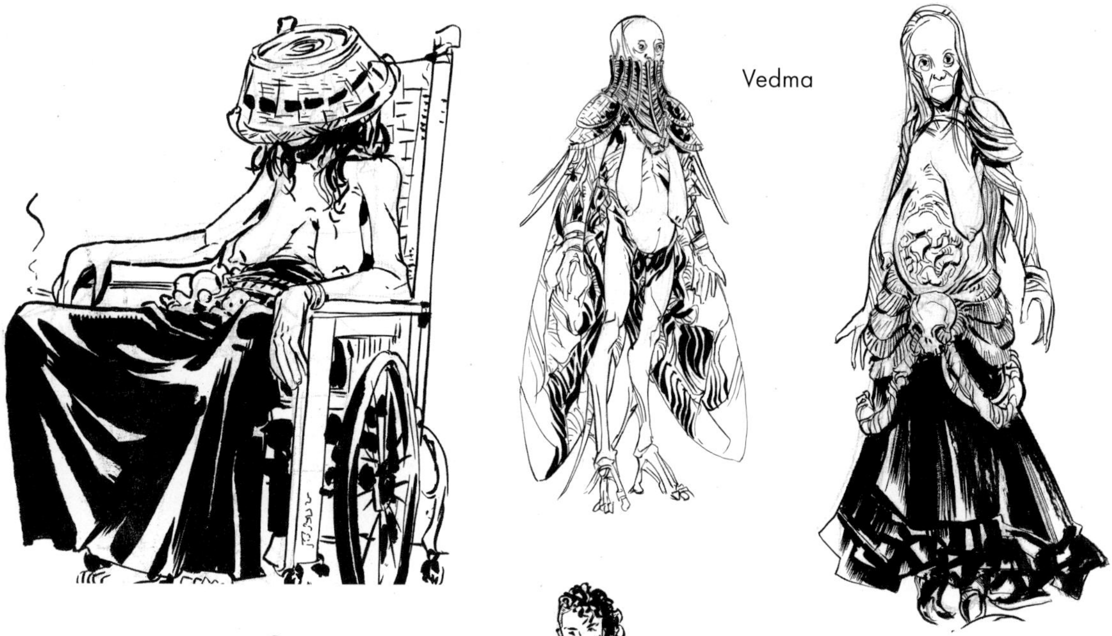
Vedma

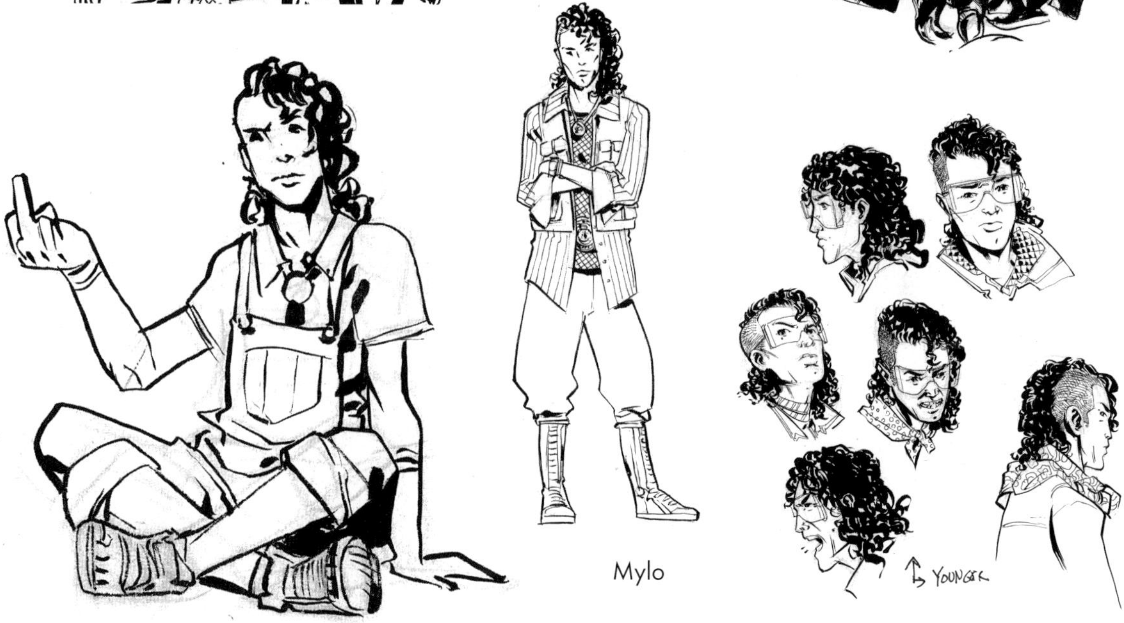
Mylo
YOUNGER

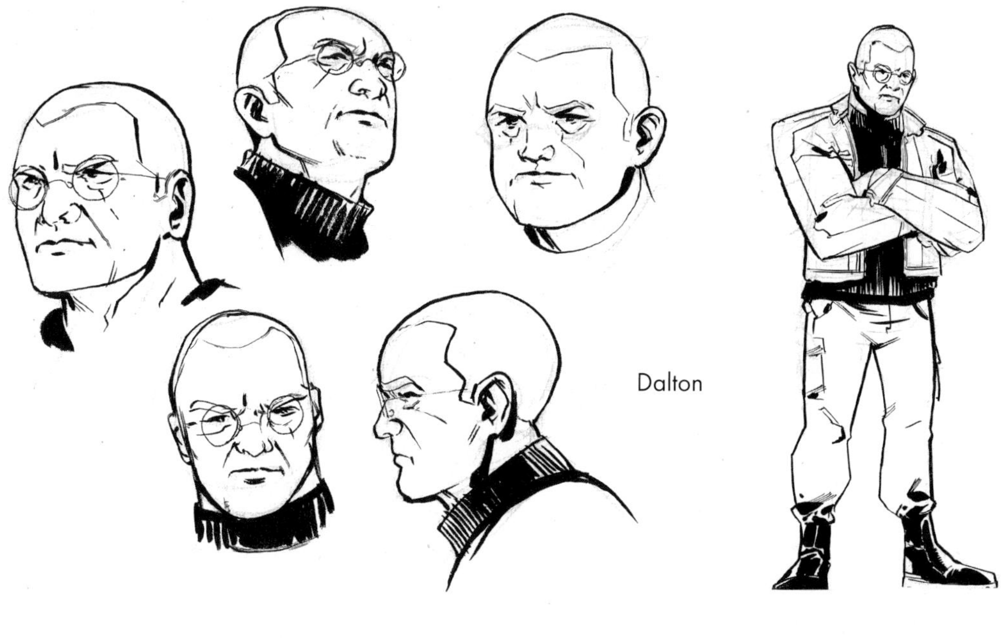
Dalton

I BREATHED A BODY ™

ZAC THOMPSON
🐦 @ZacBeThompson   📷 ZacBeThompson

Zac Thompson is a critically acclaimed writer from Prince Edward Island, Canada. He's written titles like *Marvelous X-Men*, *Cable*, and *Yondu* for Marvel Comics. Along with indie books such as UNDONE BY BLOOD, *No One's Rose*, and *The Dregs*. His original graphic novella, THE REPLACER, was called the best horror comic of 2019 by HorrorDNA. His debut novel, *Weaponized*, was the winner of the 2016 CryptTV horror fiction contest. Zac is an avid cyclist and overly excitable weirdo.

ANDY MacDONALD artist
🐦 @andymacdeez   📷 andymacdeez

Andy MacDonald...wealthy, young, handsome. A man with the brightest of futures. A man with the darkest of pasts. From Africa's deepest recesses, to the rarified peaks of Tibet, heir to his father's legacy and the world's darkest mysteries. Andy MacDonald, master of the secrets that divide man from comic book, comic book from man...

TRIONA FARRELL colorist
🐦 @Treestumped

Triona is an Irish comic book colourist who has worked on titles such as *Crowded*, *Black Widow*, *Spider-Man* and *Terminator*. She currently lives in Dublin with her partner and her cat!

HASSAN OTSMANE-ELHAOU letterer
🐦 @HassanOE

Hassan Otsmane-Elhaou is a writer, editor and letterer. He's lettered comics like *Shanghai Red*, *Peter Cannon*, *Red Sonja*, *Lone Ranger* and more. He's also the editor behind the Eisner-winning publication, *PanelxPanel*, and is the host of the *Strip Panel Naked* YouTube series. You can usually find him explaining that comics are totally a real job to his parents.